The Heart
of Healing

Inspired Ideas, Wisdom
and Comfort from
Today's Leading Voices

edited by
DAWSON CHURCH
www.NewHealer.com

Elite Books
Author's Publishing Cooperative
Santa Rosa, CA 95403
www.EliteBooks.org

Cataloging-in-Publication Data:

Church, Dawson.
    The heart of healing : inspired ideas, wisdom and comfort from
    today's leading voices/edited by Dawson Church. -- 1st ed.
    p. cm.
    Includes bibliographical references.

    1. Medical personnel & patient. 2. Healing—Psychological aspects.
    3. Holistic Medicine.   I. Church, Dawson. edt   II. Title

    2004   610.69

Cover and Interior design by Dawson Church
Typeset in Mona Lisa and Book Antiqua
Printed in USA
First Edition

10 9 8 7 6 5 4 3 2 1

CONTENTS

Dedication

This book is dedicated to every healer
— from the long-forgotten shamans of antiquity
to the most advanced practitioners of today —
whose heart is filled with the passion
of helping his or her fellow human beings become well.

Acknowledgments

Several people helped midwife this book. I edited a similar book with Alan Sher, DC, fifteen years previously, and the idea of a new edition nagged at me for years. At the start of 2003, as I meditated on the best use of my experience and energy in the forthcoming year, the impulse to actualize that vision took shape. I began the one-year process of making the book happen. I would especially like to thank the contributors; their work has inspired me, without exception. As I have had the privilege of meeting them, sharing with them, and being treated by some of them, I have experienced that their work truly represents the living heart of healing today. These are people who practice what they preach.

Thanks also to Geralyn Gendreau, who was the liason with many of the coauthors, in addition to contributing a chapter. Thanks also to the late Bill Bahan, DC, who mentored me on my own healing journey. Thanks to the sales representatives at Midpoint Trade Books, who saw the potential of this book early on and encouraged me.

The royalties for this book go to charities in the fields of health care and social services, and I thank them for their work. Among them are The Family Connection (www.thefamilyconnection.org), which helps families make the transition from shelters to safe and stable long term housing, and the Isla Mujeres rural hospital (no web site. Sometimes no running water or bandages!).

Special thanks to my toddler Alexander. To paraphrase P. G. Wodehouse, without Alexander's help this book would have been completed in half the time.

Part One

Reclaiming the Soul in Healing

BERNIE SIEGEL:

Understand Why

Many years ago my great-grandfather told me of the persecution he experienced in Russia, which led him to come to this country. He said the Cossacks would pursue him at night, when he was out teaching, and slash him with their sabers. One night he was on the hill above his village with his rabbi, the Baal Shem Tov. As they looked down they could see the Cossacks riding down and killing their Jewish brethren. They might have felt the same had they seen their loved ones being taken away to become slaves in a foreign land.

My great grandfather heard the rabbi say, "I wish I were God."

He asked, "Do you want to be God so you can change the bad into the good?"

"No, I wouldn't change anything. I want to be God so I can understand."

Remember, our present problems are not new to humankind. Ninety percent of the natives of South America died when the explorers brought infectious diseases to their continent. Forty percent of Europeans died during plagues in the middle ages. Man-made wars and holocausts have taken millions of lives, and with today's destructive weapons we are more of a threat to each other than are infectious diseases, which we can learn to resist. The question is not, "Will there be difficulties and threats to our existence?" but rather, "How will we deal with them and what can we learn from them?" How can they become blessings to society, as a life-threatening disease is to an individual, by teaching us about the meaning of our life and existence?

Bernie Siegel, MD, is a legendary figure in modern medicine. As a cancer surgeon, in 1978 he originated Exceptional Cancer Patients, a form of group therapy that utilized patients' drawings, dreams, images and feelings to facilitate lifestyle change and personal empowerment. His best-selling book *Love, Medicine and Miracles* (Bantam, 1986) detailed those experiences. He lives with his wife and co-worker Bobbie in Connecticut, surrounded by children, grandchildren (8 at last count), animals and projects, as he continues his goal of humanizing medical education and care. His most recent book is *Prescriptions for Living* (1998). Photograph courtesy of Barry Bittman, MD.

When I was a young boy several of my friends became seriously ill. Another friend was hit by a car while bicycling to my house. When each of them died, I asked my father, "Why did God make a world where terrible things happen? Why didn't God make a world free of diseases, accidents and problems?"

He said, "To learn lessons." I didn't like that answer and asked my rabbi, teacher and others. They said things like, "God knows"; "Why not?"; "Who knows?"; "That's life," or, "To bring you closer to God." Some were honest enough to just say, "I don't know." This didn't leave me feeling satisfied or enlightened. When I told my mother what they said, she answered, "Nature contains the wisdom you seek. Perhaps a walk in the woods would help you to find out why. Go and ask the old lady on the hill that some call a witch. She is wise in the ways of the world."

-§-

The question is not, "Will there be difficulties and threats to our existence?" but rather "How will we deal with them and what can we learn from them?"

-§-

As I walked up the hill I saw a holly tree had fallen onto the path. As I tried to pull it aside, the sharp leaves cut my hands. So I put on gloves, and was able to move it and clear the path. A little further along the path, I heard a noise in the bushes, and saw a duck caught in the plastic from a six-pack. I went over and freed the duck, and watched him fly off. None of this seemed enlightening.

Further up the hill, I saw five boys lying in a tangled heap in the snow. I asked them if they were playing a game, and warned them the cold weather could lead to frostbite if they didn't move. They said they were not playing, but were so tangled they didn't know which part belonged to whom. They were afraid they'd break something if they moved. I removed one of the boy's shoes, took a stick and jabbed it into his foot.

He yelled, "Ow!"

I said, "That's your foot—now move it." I continued to jab until all the boys were separated—but still no enlightenment.

As I reached the top of the hill I saw, in front of the old woman's cabin, a deer sprawled on the ice of a frozen pond. She kept slipping and sliding and couldn't stand up. I went out, calmed her, and then helped her off the ice by holding her up and guiding her to the shore. I expected her to run away, but instead of running away she, and several other deer, followed me to the house. I wasn't sure why they were following me so I ran towards the house. When I reached the porch and felt safe. I turned, and the deer and I looked into each other's eyes. Then I went into the house.

I told the woman why I had come and she said, "I have been watching you walk up the hill and I think you have your answer."

"What answer?" I asked.

"Many things happened on your walk to teach you the lessons you needed to learn. One is that emotional and physical pain is necessary, or we cannot protect ourselves and our bodies. Think of why you put on gloves, and how you helped those boys. Pain helps us to know and define ourselves and respond to our needs and the needs of our loved ones. You did what made sense. You helped those in front of you by doing what they needed when they needed it.

"The deer followed you to thank you for being compassionate in their time of trouble. Their eyes said it all. What you have learned is that we are here to continue God's work. If God had made a perfect world it would be a magic trick, not creation, with no meaning or place for us to learn and create. Creation is work. We are the ones who will have to create the world you are hoping for — a world where evil is to not respond to the person with the disease or pain, whether it be emotional or physical. God has given us work to do. We will still grieve when we experience losses, but we will also use our pain to help us know ourselves, and respond to the needs of others. That is our work as our Creator intended it to be. God wants us to know that life is a series of beginnings, not endings, just as graduations are not terminations but commencements.

-§-
God wants us to know that life is a series of beginnings, not endings, just as graduations are not terminations but commencements.
-§-

"Let me tell you about people who have been my teachers. The first was a teenager sexually abused by his parents who now has AIDS. When he was about to commit suicide by jumping in front of a subway train I asked him why he didn't kill his parents instead. He said, 'I never wanted to be like them.' Love has sustained him and he is alive today.

"Another young man, with a life-threatening illness, said, 'What is evil is not the disease. Many great creative works will come from individual suffering, but what is evil is to not respond with compassion to the person with the illness.'

"I know some parents whose young child died. Now they are dedicated to improving the lives of other children, and raising funds to find a cure for the disease which took their child, so other children will not have to die as their child did.

"How do we turn our afflictions into blessings? How do we use them to help us complete ourselves and our work, and to understand the place for love, tolerance and kindness? How can we learn, as Jacob did, from the experience of wrestling with an angel? Justice and mercy must both be a part of how we treat those who terrorize, because when you understand, you can forgive, and when you can forgive, you do not hate. When you do not hate, you are capable of loving, and love is the most powerful weapon known to humans. It is not an accident that we have sayings like "kill with kindness," "love thine enemies," and "torment with tenderness."

"As Golda Meir said, 'The only way to eliminate war is to love our children more than we hate our enemies.' When we raise a generation of children with compassion; when parents let their children know they are loved, teachers truly educate them and not just inform them, and the clergy let them know they are children of God, we will have a planet made up of the family of humankind. Our differences will be used for recognition and not persecution. Words and experts cannot be our Lord. Our Creator must be who we have faith in, so we can live as Abraham and Jesus did, fearing only separation from their Lord."

> -§-
> When you accept that you are here for a limited amount of time, you will find yourself paying more attention to your heart's wisdom, and what feels good and makes you happy.
> -§-

As I walked down the hill, I reflected upon all that I had learned. I know the feeling of abandonment, and how important it is to feel connected to someone and to a sense of meaning in your life. I believe we are all here to serve and to complete the process of creation. First, we must know ourselves, so that we may be alone but not lonely, and second, to feel a sense of family with all of God's creatures. It is our connections and the responsibility we feel towards them which keeps us alive.

As a surgeon, I know something you may not; that we are all the same color inside, and members of one family. To paraphrase Rabbi Carlebach, let us hope that some day, all the Cains will realize what they have done, and ask forgiveness from the Abels they have killed. In that moment, we will all rise and become one family, accepting that we are here to love and be loved. Until that moment, may you accept and learn from your mortality what is truly important in the time of your life. When you accept that you are here for a limited amount of time, you will find yourself paying more attention to your heart's wisdom, and what feels good and makes you happy, rather than what your head and intellect tell you to do because of what others demand of you. Don't wait for a disaster to awaken you. Start living your chocolate ice cream now and save your life. Let the untrue self die—and give birth to yourself. The difficulties of life can be your labor pains and all be worthwhile.

ANDREW WEIL:

Can Spirituality Heal?

During my travels throughout the world, I've met many healers who believe that the primary causes of health and illness are not physical but spiritual. While I certainly believe that both physical and emotional factors influence health, I also believe that you can't be truly healthy if you're feeling spiritually disconnected. The root meaning of *health* is "wholeness," and health necessarily involves our bodies, minds, and spirits.

Many people consider spirit to be the province of religion, but I make a distinction between spirituality and religion. To my mind, spirituality has to do with the nonphysical, immaterial aspects of reality — our energies, essences, and our conceptions of a higher power. Religion attempts to institutionalize spirituality. While religion can be a person's main avenue for spiritual work, it doesn't have to be. I often encourage my patients to explore activities that can enhance spiritual well-being, including practicing breathwork techniques (in many languages, the words for *spirit* and *breath* are the same), meditating, spending time in nature, reading inspirational books, enjoying music and art, observing a moment of gratitude before meals, doing service work, spending more time with people who raise your spirits, and even keeping fresh flowers in your home.

That being said, most of the research studies to date on spirituality and health have examined religious factors such as church attendance or regularity of individual prayer. This is probably because personal spiritual practices are more difficult to measure, but it's my hope that future studies will consider them as well. Meanwhile, recent studies have linked

An internationally recognized expert on medicinal herbs, mind–body interactions, and integrative medicine, Andrew Weil, MD, is a clinical professor of internal medicine as well as the founder and director of the Program in Integrative Medicine at the University of Arizona's Health Sciences Center in Tucson, where he is training a new generation of physicians. Dr. Weil established the nonprofit Polaris Foundation to advance the cause of integrative medicine through public policy, education, and research. In addition, Dr. Weil is the author of eight books, including the national bestsellers *Spontaneous Healing* (Ballantine, 2000) and *Eating Well for Optimum Health* (Quill, 2001).

religious involvement to lower blood pressure, better immunity, lower rates of depression, higher survival rates following cardiac surgery, and greater longevity. One large study *(American Journal of Public Health,* June 1997) followed more than 5,000 Californians for twenty-eight years: Those who attended religious services at least once a week had a twenty-three percent lower risk of dying during the study period than those who attended less frequently, even after the researchers controlled for lifestyle factors and social support.

-§-

[These studies] challenge the basic materialistic assumptions in science—such as that changes in the physical body must have physical causes.

-§-

Even more intriguing are studies suggesting that praying on behalf of others (so-called intercessory prayer) may help the sick. A randomized trial newly reported in the *Archives of Internal Medicine* (October 25, 1999) examined this effect in nearly 1,000 heart patients admitted to a Kansas City, Missouri, hospital over a twelve month period. Half of the patients were prayed for daily by community volunteers for four weeks, while the other half didn't have anyone assigned to pray for them. None of the patients were aware of the study. After four weeks, the prayed-for patients had suffered eleven percent fewer complications—a small but statistically significant difference. I consider this study and a similar (though less rigorous) 1988 trial conducted in San Francisco to be noteworthy because they challenge the basic materialistic assumptions in science—such as that changes in the physical body must have physical causes.

A New Frontier for Medicine

I'm pleased to see that this growing body of research has captured the attention of the medical community. In the mid-1990s, only three US medical schools taught courses on religious and spiritual issues; today, more than sixty (about half of medical schools) offer such courses. Duke University has its own Center for the Study of Religion, Spirituality and Health, and the University of Minnesota's Center for Spirituality and Healing has recently opened a Mind Body Spirit Clinic.

Here at the University of Arizona's Program in Integrative Medicine, we encourage the physicians in our fellowship program to explore spiritual practices in their own lives and train them to take a spiritual inventory of patients seen at our clinic. An inventory typically begins with an open-ended question such as, "What are the sources of strength in your life?" When patients express strong religious beliefs, we might ask if they would be interested in talking with a clergy member or pastoral counselor about any issues arising from their medical condition. For nonreligious patients, we might ask if they would be open to trying spiritual practices such as breathwork or meditation.

Some physicians may be hesitant to discuss spiritual issues with patients, because of a lack of training or because they consider it inappropriate to their role as a physician. If you feel comfortable broaching the subject with your doctor, you might start with a general question such as, "Do you think that spiritual practice could influence my health?" As more medical schools

-§-
You can't be truly healthy if you're feeling spiritually disconnected.
-§-

cover the topic of spirituality and health, I expect that physicians may become increasingly open to discussing these issues, and that the result will be more satisfying partnerships between patients and doctors.

Sandra Ingerman:
The Once and Future Shaman

For tens of thousands of years people around the world have been practicing shamanism. Although the word "shaman" is a Siberian word referring to a spiritual healer, shamanism has been practiced not just in Siberia but in parts of Asia, parts of Europe, Australia, Africa, and native North and South America.

Shamans have taken on the role of healer, doctor, priest, psychotherapist, mystic and storyteller in tribal communities.

One of the most common ceremonies performed by shamans is the shamanic journey. During a journey a shaman goes into an altered state of consciousness, usually by listening to some form of percussion. This altered state allows the shaman's soul to take flight, journeying outside of time and space into what Carlos Castaneda termed "non-ordinary reality."

Through these journeys the shaman has access to invisible worlds, where there are helping spirits. The spirits typically take the form of guardian animal spirits which some call power animals, and human spiritual teachers who are willing to share information and healing help.

In traditional shamanic cultures, there were one or a few people in a community acting in the role of the shaman and journeying on behalf of the community. Today we are seeing a revival of shamanism, but the form is much different than that of a tribal culture. We see people from all walks of life learning shamanic practices.

Sandra Ingerman is the author of *Soul Retrieval* (Harper, 1991), *Medicine for the Earth* (Three Rivers, 2001), *Welcome Home* (Harper, 1994) and *A Fall to Grace* (Moon Tree Rising, 1997). She teaches workshops in shamanism worldwide, and is a licensed marriage and family therapist and professional mental health counselor. She is recognized for bridging ancient cross-cultural healing methods into modern culture and adapting them to the needs of our times. She has done a series of remarkable experiments showing that environmental pollution can be reversed using spiritual methods. She lives with her husband Woods in Santa Fe, New Mexico.

The shamanic journey is a method of direct revelation. It gives people access to spiritual guidance without the need for an outside authority figure. There is an obvious need for this in our culture today.

One of the basic principles in shamanism is that everything that exists is alive and has a spirit. Shamanism teaches us about the interconnectedness with the earth and all of life. Back in the 1940s and 1950s, quantum physicists discovered that there is a field of energy that connects all life. Shamans and quantum physicists both speak of a web of life.

Living in a technological culture affords us many benefits. In many ways that I am sure you can relate to, technology has cut us off from the web of life, and from experiencing our connection with nature and its cycles and rhythms.

As we moved from a people that honored the spiritual worlds and the cycles of nature, we started to only trust the rational and scientific mind which believes that only what you can see, feel, hear, taste, and smell in our ordinary world exists.

-§-
As children we all knew we received great comfort by communicating with loving and caring beings in the invisible worlds.
-§-

Through the socialization process we were taught to believe that the invisible and spiritual worlds are merely part of our imagination.

At this point a spell was cast upon us, having us believe that the spiritual worlds are in our imagination, that we are separate from each other, other living beings, and nature, and that amassing material wealth is the only way to happiness.

This spell has created physical and emotional illness in our world today. The meaning of life has been lost, creating a deep sense of despair in many people. Antidepressants have taken the place of meaningful and passion-filled lives.

As we no longer connect with the cycles of nature, we are out of harmony and balance with the rhythm of life, we are no longer flowing with the river of life. This has created a stress, which manifests as emotional and physical illness.

The cure for all this is to re-establish our connection with the field of energy that unites us all, and to bring back spiritual practices into our lives.

I started practicing shamanic journeying and healing in 1980. In the practice of shamanism we look at the spiritual aspect of illness. Classically a shaman might diagnose an illness as power loss, soul loss, or a client might have a spiritual intrusion or harmful energy in him or her. Through the guidance of my helping spirits, I learned how to bridge the classic method of soul retrieval into a modern day culture to help people heal from trauma.

From a shamanic point of view whenever we suffer an emotional or physical trauma there is the possibility that a part of our soul or essence leaves our body and goes into non-ordinary reality where it waits to be recovered.

In psychology we talk about this as dissociation; in shamanism we call this soul loss. Soul loss is how we survive pain and shock. The psyche has this brilliant self-protection mechanism; we "go away" while pain is occurring so that we don't have to experience the full impact of the pain. If I were going to be in a head-on car collision, the very last place that I would want to be at the point of impact is in my body.

Today, causes of soul loss might be any kind of emotional or physical abuse, wartime stress, or being in a physical disaster like an earthquake, hurricane, or fire. Another cause might be surgery. I often hear people complain that they have not been the same since being under anesthesia. Other causes might be being in an accident, or experiencing a traumatic separation like divorce, or the death of a loved one. Anything that causes shock could cause soul loss.

Some of the more common symptoms of soul loss include dissociation, post-traumatic stress syndrome, chronic depression, addictions, illness such as immune deficiency problems, and the inability to get over the grief of a divorce or death of a loved one.

Looking at soul loss and addictions is interesting. When, on a conscious or unconscious level we don't feel filled up with our own soul, we often look to the external world to fill us up. Some people use drugs, substances, food, relationships, or work to try to fill up empty feelings. Some of us think that by collecting more material wealth or material objects we will feel filled up.

The drive in the world today to collect and gather material wealth and objects is a clear symptom of soul loss on a mass level. When we look at how political decisions are made, for financial reasons, without honoring their effects on animals, plant life, or our environment, one has to wonder how dissociated we must be to put money over life.

Creating Intentionally

Part of the evolution of the work has to do with how we tell our clients healing stories. Oftentimes we are unaware of how much power the imagination has to heal. A good healer can tell stories that stimulate a person's imagination to heal.

People don't need bad news, or to hear stories that plant seeds of fear. People need stories that plant seeds of hope, inspiration, and love. These are the stories that heal. Learning how to share healing words and stories is what I most emphasize in teaching soul retrieval today. If we can inspire people with what gifts might return to their lives, this creates the possibility for positive change to occur.

When a person goes to a doctor, a psychotherapist, a shamanic practitioner, or another alternative practitioner, they are going for a cure for their problem. Over time, I started to realize that there is a difference between healing and curing.

For a cure to hold, healing must take place. After there is an alleviation of symptoms, it is important for the client to look at what is needed to restore harmony into his or her life. Disharmony causes disease and harmony creates health. This does not mean the client should blame himself for being ill or having a problem. Blame and judgment only adds to more disharmonies.

But it is important to look at how to create change in our lives that supports the benefits we receive through different healing modalities. I call this "life after healing." If we only do the spiritual curing work, we just give a spiritual aspirin without long-term results.

One part of healing is helping people reprioritize their lives. We need to work with all aspects of what is needed to have a healthy life: diet, exercise, aligning oneself with the cycles of rhythms of nature, and looking at our relationships, to name just a few. It is important to add daily spiritual practices such as meditation or shamanic journeying to help alleviate stress, create harmony and balance, and provide a way to receive personal direct guidance.

There is another piece of the puzzle that is not always talked about. When a client is physically ill or emotionally depressed it takes a lot of energy to go about the day. To run errands when you are not feeling well—either emotionally or physically—takes a lot of energy.

When you are "cured" of the illness, this means that you have a lot more energy available to you. Many people today end up taking that energy and unconsciously creating another illness, trauma or drama with it. We are not taught how to use our creative energy in positive ways. In school we were trained to obey rules and fit into society. You may have been taught that there are only select creative people on the planet—and that doesn't include you.

We are completely unaware of how much creative potential we all hold to create a positive present and future for the world and ourselves. To accomplish this we must retrieve our God-given gift of imagination, and be able to dream a new world for ourselves into being.

In my own work with people I try to get them to take small steps into using their creativity. I ask clients, "How do you want to use the creative energy that is returned to you during your soul retrieval, in a positive way?" It might be something as simple as taking a class, or taking more walks out into nature. If people come up with overwhelming goals, they become paralyzed.

If all the mystical traditions are correct, which I think they are, we are a merely a reflection of the creative force of the universe. This means that we have the potential to manifest a positive world, which contains beauty, harmony, love and abundance. It is crucial at this time on the planet for all of us to learn about our creative potential. This takes using our imaginations and the recognition that we are spirits in a body that came to learn to manifest beauty on the planet, as the Creator did in creating our world.

-§-

When you are "cured" of the illness, this means that you have a lot more energy available to you. Many people today end up taking that energy and unconsciously creating another illness, trauma or drama with it.

-§-

We live in a time when people look to medications and outside authority figures to change their lives. The truth is that the only person who can change your life is you. And this is not a burden. This is one of the joys you came here to experience when you chose as a spirit to take a body to learn how to manifest form in the world. We have just forgotten our own soul's purpose.

During the time I was focusing on teaching clients how to use their creative potential, I had an experience working with someone that took the principle of creativity to another level.

On a hot fall day in New Mexico, Mary came to see me. By looking at her one could see that she was obviously quite ill. When we started to talk, she shared with me that she had advanced AIDS.

I told her that I would do what I could to help her. Death, in our culture is often seen as a failure. But death is oftentimes the next step in our healing process. In shamanism, death is not seen as an end, but rather a transition.

Looking at how far Mary was in her illness, I knew that the next step in her healing process could be life and the next step could be death. In bringing back lost soul parts for her I knew I would bring enough of herself "home" so that her soul could choose the next step.

One piece of information that came up in our conversation was that AIDS was the third life-threatening illness that she had experienced in her life.

As I journeyed, I found myself in a surrealistic scene. My helping spirits were obviously exaggerating the scene to make a point. I found myself in a suburban neighborhood that was depicted like a cartoon. The sky was bright blue with a bright yellow sun with eyes and a smile shining down on everything. The cars were very bright colors and they all had faces and smiling. The trees were swaying and singing. The birds were singing loudly. The houses all had smiling faces and were singing and swaying. I was seeing life in all its vibrancy.

There was Mary at about the age of three, on a tricycle, riding down the street—with no expression on her face. There was such a difference in how she looked, compared to the life around her.

This is the message my helping spirit then imparted to me: "Mary's illness is due to apathy and the cure is passion. Her lesson in this lifetime is what happens when another life-form in your body has more passion to live than you do. It thrives—and you do not."

Mary did die about six months later. But I felt as though she left me with an incredible message to share with the world. For I do not see our modern day culture embracing life with passion. Most of us just try and survive and get through the day. Is one of the reasons we are seeing such strong bacterial and viral infections today that these life forms want to live more than we do? It seems that they have a faster learning curve than we do and are learning to thrive no matter what medications we come up with to destroy them. The true antidote is to find what brings meaning into our lives.

Shamanism has been a practice that evolved from hunting and gathering communities. It was important to have a shaman who could divine food sources as well as heal members in the community.

Today I teach people, after a shamanic healing session, to journey for themselves to get personal spiritual guidance on how to make changes in their lives that will support their healing. We all know that plants and trees grow from seeds. The seed gives the plant and tree the information needed to grow and adapt to stay healthy. We all have a seed of light within us that has all the information we need to heal. Shamanic journeying is one way for clients to tap into their knowledge within.

I don't have clients go to their helping spirits and ask what they should do. This would be giving their spiritual authority away and would not honor the client's own inherent wisdom. Rather, I have clients contact their helping spirits to receive guidance that gets the client using his own wisdom and creative energy.

Medicine for the Earth

When we have worked on our own process for a time it is important to learn how we can be of service to all life on the planet.

The timing on this will differ from individual to individual. Some people need more time to heal inner wounds than others do.

Rivers have always reminded me of the magic of life. My love for rivers led me to wonder whether it is possible to reverse river pollution, which led to an interest on a broader level in the reversal of all environmental pollution.

In 1978 I graduated with a bachelor's degree in biology, specializing in Marine Biology, from San Francisco State University. My curiosity about the question of reversing river pollution led me to apply for a master's degree in biology. My thesis proposal was to be on reversing the pollution in our world's rivers.

At that time I realized I did not want to stay in the field of science, and instead enrolled at the California Institute of Integral Studies where I pursued my master's in counseling psychology.

Although my path through the 1980s and 1990s was devoted to teaching shamanism, I personally used shamanism to explore reversing environmental pollution through the use of spiritual methods.

One of the most important messages I was to receive over my twenty years of journeying on this issue was this: It is who we *become* that changes the world and our environment—not what we do. Harmony within will create harmony without. The true work is learning how to change our thoughts, attitudes, and belief systems. A change in our inner environment will be reflected in the outer world.

-§-
Is one of the reasons we are seeing such strong bacterial and viral infections today that these life forms want to live more than we do?
-§-

It is time to bridge science with spirituality to address our environmental problems today. All spiritual traditions teach that everything that manifests on the physical level begins on the spiritual level. As we bring daily spiritual practices into our life, which change our inner environment, the change will be reflected back to us in the outer world.

Besides working with my own shamanic journeys, I started researching miracles. Stories that come from the Bible, the Kabbalah, and from various Taoist, Hindu, yogic, alchemical, Egyptian, and shamanic works, show that miracles were once an everyday occurrence. I researched different spiritual traditions to give me clues as to how miracles were performed by ancient cultures, mystics, and saints. As I read about miracles, a formula of elements that seem to be part of all miracles began to form. The formula that came to me is hologram. The elements cannot be taken separately but combined with each other create transmutation. The definition of transmutation I am using is the ability to change the nature of a substance. The work of effecting environmental change is how to change toxic substances into neutral substances.

The formula I arrived at is intention + union + love + focus + concentration + harmony + imagination = transmutation. These elements all work together.

For all miracles to happen we must hold a strong intention of what we want to see happen. This involves concentration and also the ability to hold a focus on our goals.

All miracles involve union with a divine force. Union is the key element involved in the miracles of healing performed by Jesus or the great Indian gurus Sai Baba and Ammachi, and even the miraculous self healing of the modern day mystic Jack Schwarz, who while being tortured by the Nazis healed his wounds before their eyes. These are just a few examples of people who could perform miraculous healings. All of them teach that they are one with God or the divine while these miracles take place.

-§-
When one creates sacred space that contains the energy of love, healing just happens. The power of love and appreciation has unlimited potential to heal.
-§-

Love is an essential ingredient in all miracles as it is only love that heals. Techniques do not heal and they never have. When one creates sacred space that contains the energy of love, healing just happens. The power of love and appreciation has unlimited potential to heal. Harmony within creates harmony without.

Imagination is another key in performing the miracle of transmutation in that we must be able to envision an environment that is pure and clean and which supports all of life. With our imagination, we have to ability to sculpt the world.

We have to be able to see, feel, hear, smell, and taste the world we are trying to create as if we have already created it.

Tools for Reversing Pollution

There are two levels I work with in teaching people how to reverse environmental pollution.

The first level is the personal work we must do to learn how to transmute and transform the energy of our negative thoughts and feelings paying attention to the energy we are sending into our field. This does not mean we should not have negative thoughts and feelings. To do so would be to deny our humanness. But we can learn how to transform the energy of these feelings.

Words have power. Words are vibration. We can learn from the Hindu, Hebrew, and ancient Egyptian traditions that teach when we say a word a vibration is sent up to the universe manifesting form back down on earth. "Abracadabra," the Aramaic "abraq ad habra," means, "I will create as I speak." We must become conscious of what we are creating for others and ourselves through the words we use. Almost all creation myths, of whatever culture, start with the world being created with a sound or a word.

We need to learn how to honor and be in a place of love and appreciation for nature and all of life. As we honor the earth, air, water, fire, and all the life forms that live in these elements, as well as honoring the cycles of the moon, stars, and seasons, we work in cooperation and collaboration with the spirit that lives in all things and the web of life. Among the Salish people of the Pacific Northwest, the word "skalatitude" is used to describe what life is like when true kinship with nature exists: "When people and nature are in perfect harmony, then magic and beauty are everywhere."

It is important to perceive ourselves as connected to one field of energy, the web of life. There is no us v. them. There is only one.

The second level of the work is to join together as community to perform ceremonies to transmute and transform the environmental pollution that does exist today. The hope is that as we learn how to honor our environment, we will stop polluting the elements that give us life.

In my Medicine for the Earth gatherings, I teach people how to transfigure or shapeshift into their own divinity to be in a place of harmony, and share spiritual light from this place of being. We also add toning as a way to stay in a transfigured state, using sound along with spiritual light to create healing. If one mystic in history could transmute toxins, it means we all have knowledge within us to tap into our divinity to do the same.

-§-
One way shamanism is evolving today is that it is asking practitioners to perceive their power as equal to the spirits and work in collaboration and partnership for healing others and the planet.
-§-

In former times we might have asked the spirits to clean up the pollution for us using the principle of divine intervention. I see this as a childlike approach, like saying, "Mommy, Daddy clean up my mess." Part of the evolution of consciousness today is for us to stand up and take a role of true partnership, working with an abundance of helping spirits to clean up our environment. One way shamanism is evolving today is that it is asking practitioners to perceive their power as equal to the spirits and work in collaboration and partnership for healing others and the planet.

In my trainings we have been doing controlled experiments where we intentionally pollute deionized water (pure water with no minerals in it) with ammonium hydroxide, a common and dangerous pollutant in our environment. As ammonium hydroxide is a strong base it is easy to check its presence with pH strips and pH meters. In all the ceremonies we have performed we have been able to change the pH 1-3 points toward neutral. In all these experiments we used pH strips to test for changes.

In one ceremony we had ammonium hydroxide in water in one beaker and nitric acid in water in another beaker. The pH of the beaker with the nitric acid went up two pH points toward normal while water with ammonium hydroxide went down two pH points toward neutral. Both a physicist and a chemist confirmed these results.

Here is an analogy for pH change. Imagine a 1,000 square foot room with white wall-to-wall carpeting. Now imagine that the carpet has a huge grape juice stain that covers the entire 1,000 square feet. The completely stained carpet corresponds to a pH of 11. If the pH changes from 11 to 10, 900 square feet have been cleaned. If the pH changes from 11 to 9, then 990 square feet of the carpet has been cleaned.

The time for the myth of one hero that saves us is over. I believe our descendants will read new myths of how communities of people gathered together to focus their spiritual energies to change the world.

Earth, air, water, and fire (as the sun) give us life. When you pollute that which gives you life, illness occurs. It's time for us to connect the dots why there are such high levels of cancer and other immune deficiency problems, especially among women and children, today. We have created an environment that no longer supports the feminine and innocent in our world.

Healing the Waters Within

After we began having success with changing the pH level of polluted water, I started inviting people into the middle of the circle along with the water. Since our bodies are mostly water, it only makes sense that the same ceremony used to transmute toxins in the water can transmute illness in the body.

During one ceremony, a woman named Susan was one of the people in the middle. For the previous few years she had been suffering from debilitating lupus. She could barely walk and relied on a service dog in her life at home.

The day after we performed the transmutation ceremony she was hiking. That was a year ago—and she is still hiking away.

One of the reasons that shamanism continues to be practiced tens of thousands of years after it began is the spirits' ability to help evolve the work to address the needs of new cultures and new times.

Today, so much illness is being caused by chemical pollution that we can't keep using the same methods that were used thousands of years ago.

Although I still teach and use some of the classic methods, I have begun offering new trainings teaching the use of spiritual light and sound for healing. Some quantum physicists state that in the future, the use of sound and light will be the main form of healing. I can see the trend moving in this direction.

I have been training practitioners to use their own divinity, as well as the light from the pure vibration and energy of the power of the universe, to share spiritual light and sound to stimulate a client's own healing ability. For you can never truly heal another person. As healers, we can only stimulate that golden seed of light within others that knows how to heal. As healers, we must perceive our clients as pure divine light to help raise their vibration. This is not to take away from the fact that the client perceives himself as suffering. But as a healer, if we perceive the client as divine and perfect, this lifts his own vibration and resonance so that he can heal.

-§-
Techniques don't heal; it is only love that heals.
-§-

I have also collected some extraordinary case studies of students who practice the journey of transfiguration into their own divinity, source, oneness on a regular basis. Health problems, relationship issues, and work issues are clearing up. As people are feeling one with the field of energy, a different resonance and frequency is set up within, getting people back in flow with the river of life.

I am encouraging practitioners to teach clients how to find this light, source, oneness inside of themselves. In this way the client can keep up with raising the vibration, resonance, and sense of spiritual light within that the practitioner stimulated in their work together.

Once again, if one mystic in the world could transmute poisons and toxins, we can all do the same for the planet and ourselves. But we must perceive ourselves and all of life as pure divinity and light, and what we take in as divine and as light.

My next step in the world is to bring the work of honoring the environment and spiritual light to children. I predict this will be an emerging trend. For after all, our children are our future.

In closing, a good healer can heal with pure love. If a practitioner can create sacred space by being fully present, in his or her heart, and in a state of love and honoring the divine in everyone that walks into the office, healing just happens. Techniques don't heal; it is only love that heals.

Lorin Smith:

Journey of a Pomo Indian Medicine Man

Editor's Note: Lorin Smith is a traditional Pomo healer. He lives in Northern California, and teaches in Europe and the U.S. His story about how he became a medicine man, and how he experiences healing, is fascinating. I was introduced to Lorin by Richard Geggie, who schedules sessions with him on an irregular basis whenever Lorin leaves the reservation and his passion, which is teaching the traditional tribal ways to young Pomos and others. Before recounting my interview with Lorin, here's the story, in Richard Geggie's own words, of his healing experience with Lorin:

"In the early 1990s I was in Toronto, Canada. I went to see my doctor because I felt tired and listless. He sent me to have an electrocardiogram. Later that day, when he got the results back, he told me that my heart was at serious risk. He told me to stay calm, not exert myself, keep nitroglycerine pills with me at all times, and to not go outside alone.

"The doctors administered several tests over the course of the following three days, and I failed them all because my arteries were severely clogged. They included a fluoroscope examination, another electrocardiogram, and a treadmill stress test. When I started the bicycle test, the clinic staff didn't even let me finish. They stopped me partway. They were afraid I was going to die on the spot, my arteries were so clogged. As a high risk patient, I was given an immediate appointment for heart bypass surgery.

Lorin Smith is a Native American healer of the Pomo tribe of Northern California. He travels widely, teaching native healing ways. He uses his hands to move energy in the bodies of those he treats, as well as Pomo medicine songs. He also uses herbs in various formulations. While he has focused on healing individual people for many years, his current passion is passing traditional Indian healing knowledge on to a new generation of young people. His healing talents were discerned in his teen years by the elders of his tribe.

"The day before the surgery, I woke up feeling much better. I went to the hospital and I was given an angiogram. This involved shooting dye into my arteries through an injection in my thigh. The surgeons wanted to discover the exact location of the blockages prior to the operation. I was prepared for surgery. My chest was shaved, and the doctors were about to mark my skin where they planned to make the incision. When the new angiograms came back from the lab, the doctor in charge looked at them. He became very upset. He said he had wasted his time. There were no blockages visible at all. He said he wished his own arteries looked as clear. He could not explain why all the other tests had shown such severe problems.

"I later discovered that my friend Lorin Smith in California, upon hearing of my heart trouble, had assembled a group of his students for a healing ceremony the day before the second angiogram. He covered one man with bay leaves and told him that his name was Richard Geggie. For the next hour, Lorin led the group in songs, prayers, and movement. The next day, I was healed.

"I have seen Lorin facilitate other amazing healings. Sometimes he works in a trance, invoking his grandfather, Tom Smith, who was a very famous healer. When he emerges from trance, he's unable to remember what he has said."

Lorin Smith:

"When I was in my 20s, I got tired of the good times: drinking beer, hanging out in places I shouldn't have been, 'Going with the wrong crowd' as my mother used to say. The tribal elders began talking to me. They asked me if I would be interested in becoming a healer. At the time I didn't feel I could do anything like that. I didn't feel strong enough to follow the rules. The elders said, 'We feel you can do this.' That is how it happens in our Pomo Indian tradition. You don't start by yourself. The elders will see something in you that you don't know about yourself. They've been around healers for years and they can tell if someone is right for the work. But they can only ask and tell you about it. Once they ask you to be a healer, you have to make your own choice.

"The Pomo prophecies teach us about clearing ourselves and cleansing the earth. It is our way of helping the planet. So I travel, gather with people in different cities, and help them. The people who come to my gatherings may look very white, but they almost all have Indian blood in them.

"I especially like working with young people. They may not know each other, but when I sing a medicine song, everyone feels welcome.

Some come from Oklahoma, some from New York, some from Germany. Twenty or thirty people start out as strangers, but they all get to know one another, hugging and laughing. I have taught kids from my tribe who were so filled with hatred over all of the things that were done to Indian people by the white men, that these kids had become warmongers, like other races. I've taught young boys and girls who had faced so many difficulties in their tribes and in their families that they felt that they had nothing to live for. They had given up on life itself. Many of them don't even have a home. Young kids with all these bad habits and nothing to do, what can they do to change their neighborhood? It is a healer's job to wake people up, encourage them to help each other. This way, there is a link between ceremonies. So I teach them. They learn medicine songs. They learn how to run a family group. When I leave, they know how to run things themselves. Some of these people from the younger generation that I've taught are now singing their own songs and leading their groups.

"People of the younger generation become interested in healing when they discover what a joy it is to heal others. Once you start doing the work, you gain a sense of what your purpose on this earth is. Young people can see that. Before, they may be having a good time, but they don't have that feeling of purpose. They may have finished their education, but something is missing from their lives. They want to know what they can do for people in the world. That's how it was for me. My life got boring and I wanted to do something for people in the tribe.

-§-

Becoming a healer in the Pomo way means learning the healing songs. The most powerful healing work is in the language itself.

-§-

"Becoming a healer in the Pomo way means learning the healing songs. The most powerful healing work is in the language itself. Pomo is not a written language like English. If I speak in my own language, whether you understand or not, you will feel energy coming to you through the songs and the prayers. I learned to speak Pomo from my mother and my dad. When I talk to non-Indians, they say, 'We feel the energy more than when you speak English.' The healing prayers are in Pomo. The elders say it's important to speak the Pomo language and it doesn't matter if someone doesn't understand. The *feeling* a person gets from the prayers is what's important.

"When I first began to walk this path, people started asking me for healing while I was still learning and gaining experience with the songs. People who came to me were comforted, but I still felt I knew very little about healing. People would knock on the door or call and say they were coming over for healing. That scared me at first, but I learned to call on the ancient healers for help. I'm not talking about somebody you can see. I know that is hard to believe at first, at least it was for me.

"It happened when I wouldn't know what to do with someone who came to me for healing. I would hear a voice say, 'This is what he needs…' For example, I might be working on clearing a blockage in someone's body. I wouldn't know at first how to clear it. I had to learn by listening, letting the elders teach me. Much of what I do now is what I know from my own experience, but if I get confused I can call on the elders and ask them what I need to know. When they tell me, the healing is real simple. It takes not even five minutes to heal the person of what's troubling them.

"Also important is learning the right kind of food to eat, learning about the healing herbs and where to get them. These are things I learned from other healers, most of them women. They knew enough to teach me what to look for. Once you know the basics, you learn by finding various kinds of herbs that feel right and trying them. Certain teas give lots of energy. Other herbs take pain away. I used to wonder, 'How can a root have that kind of energy?' But the plant comes through every time, giving the body energy for healing. For example, if you soak in a eucalyptus bath, it gives you energy and takes away your tiredness. After a lot of years, I know what to suggest for most of the needs people have.

-§-
When I look at the person with my eyes, and when I move my hands over the body, I see different colors going through a person's body.
-§-

"A relative of mine in Southern California got sick with leukemia. The doctors gave her a blood transfusion, but her blood turned poisonous again. Every time they gave her new blood she'd be sick right after. The doctors told her she had three months to live. I suggested eucalyptus. We made tea out of it. That was the first time I thought eucalyptus would work for leukemia, because before I had used eucalyptus only for the flu. I just had a feeling it will work with her. She stopped getting sick. She went back to Southern California, and she took some of the tea with her and kept using it. The doctors wanted to know how come her blood didn't get poisoned anymore. She's still well today, after twenty years. She has kids now. The doctors have no clue as to why she is still alive and how her blood could have got purified with eucalyptus tea.

"When I look at the person with my eyes, and when I move my hands over the body, I see different colors going through a person's body. They look like rainbow colors but smaller, almost like an electric cord. I can see where it's broken; in those areas I see flashes. I might see blue or different colors, especially in the heart area. When I notice that the heart needs some energy, I see a flash, like lightning, only smaller. A blockage looks knotted, tied up like a fist. Sometimes I see the blood flowing very slowly. When I see more than one problem, I try to work with both. I start with hand work. I might use my hands at the bottom of the feet, places that feel safe. When an area of the body receives the healing, the knots stretch out like a rubber band. What I do, and what the healers told me too, is work on the area to soften it, or soften another part so that the first part won't snap from tension.

"Most times disease is caused by blockages. Blockages in the body cause the heart to work overtime and the breathing gets heavy. A person might come to me knowing a fancy name for what ails them. I don't have a clue what the fancy name means, but as I work on their body, I can tell where the blockage is, where it's going and what it's connected to. Maybe it's down in the leg and the person is very tired so I clear all the blockages in the joint area. If it's in the heart, I can help by figuring out where the blockages are in the body and unblock them. Sometimes the blockages in the lower leg are connected to the heart. By clearing the leg, people get clear of their heart problem. Many people carry worries in their stomach so I clear that too. Decisions people make affect different parts of the body. I use my hands and give energy to those parts.

"People ask, 'Where does the energy come from?' I get my energy from the sun. I asked for energy, saying, 'You listen, sun, I am coming out to you,' and walked outside. I put my hand up in the air. A weight hit my hand. My hand got very hot. That's how I learned to use the energy from the sun. I use that energy for bodywork. Sometimes the elders will tell you how to draw energy from nature. When the energy of nature hits you, like the sun hit my hand, that's when you experience the power of nature for real.

-§-
The man didn't know how to tell his doctor because most Western doctors don't believe in native healers like us.
-§-

"When I work on someone, one of my hands goes around the body and takes out the negative energy, while the other hand replaces it with positive energy. Even if I cannot see the weak places with my eyes, my left hand will find them. Then, my hand will pull the negative energy out like a magnet. My right hand will rub the area with good energy. Sometimes, I will work on the area more, but many times just pulling out the negative energy makes weak spots better. The negative energy goes into the air and disappears. Some of it used to go into me, but now I drink special herbs just for that purpose. Healers in the old days drank angelica root for the same reason.

"A man who had cancer in the throat came to a group session in Bodega. He was an opera singer from San Francisco. He came to me crying, saying I've probably only got a couple months to live. He had asked his doctors to operate, but they said he had very little chance of surviving surgery. It was the first time I'd seen him. I looked at him and wondered, 'What am I going to do?' I had him drink some tea. I did some prayers in Pomo. He went back to the city and two months later, returned to his doctor. The doctor said, 'What happened? You had something in your throat. It's not there any more!' The man didn't know how to tell his doctor because most Western doctors don't believe in native healers like us. To this day, many years later, this singer is still alive.

"In another case, a woman came to me with a cyst in the stomach. She had also been told she was going to die. She came to Kashia Ranchero where I live. She was crying. I said, 'I don't know if I can help you, but I'll see what I can do.' She had a cyst the size of a golf ball between her ribs. Her doctors did not know what it was and wanted to open her up to see. I did the same thing with her, made a drink and did prayers in my language. I gave her a strong tea from angelica root and her cyst just dissolved.

"When she went back to the doctor, he wanted to know who had done this to her. She said she didn't have to explain because she knew that what I did to her works even in this generation. I got emotional, wondering, 'Did that herb really work that well?' But it did. One thing a healer must know: You can't doubt yourself. Her cyst was something I didn't really know about but there was no doubt in my mind it was going to disappear, even though I didn't know how. Sometimes people wonder, 'How did that healing happen?' You don't really need to know how; all you need to know is that the person is healed.

-§-
If you find yourself feeling impatient, that is the time to clear your mind, find time to relax and step out of the healer role for a while.
-§-

"You have to talk to the people who come to you, and really listen. This is how you learn what works. You can't just say, 'You're healed now,' and send them away. When they come back to visit you and tell you that what you did felt good, that's when you learn.

"If you are a healer, you must know how to take care of yourself and gain understanding of your role. It is important for a healer to know how to let go, how to find places that help you relax. When people find out you are a healer, they are full of questions: 'Why is my body reacting this way?'; 'Is there something wrong with my heart?' They will even start talking about their relationship with their spouse, or ask why business is so slow. What healers do is mysterious to people. You may find yourself saying the same things over and over and people don't hear. If you find yourself feeling impatient, that is the time to clear your mind, find time to relax and step out of the healer role for a while.

"If I am too tired I will go to the river. In the old days healers used to go to the river or the ocean to bathe and cleanse. One night, I went to Bodega Bay with a lot of people. It was way past midnight and I went into the water all the way up to my neck. I walked into the water backwards, never looking behind me. As a little kid, I had always been afraid of the ocean, so I did this to cleanse my fears. I stood there for a long time in cold water up to my neck.

"People on the beach started getting worried, running around on the beach looking for me. Then I heard a voice tell me to come back to the beach slowly, the way I had gone in. I found myself standing on the shore. Suddenly, my mind was clear and many things made sense that had been confusing before.

"If I were asked to explain, step by step, how a healing happens, I could not answer. Doctors sometimes ask me, 'How did that healing happen? She was sick, she was getting weak, and she could not even eat. There is no way her disease would go away without surgery.' It is very mysterious to me, because I am not a sucking doctor.

"Sucking doctors are usually women, and they are the most powerful healers in our tribe. They can do a lot of things others can't by sucking things out of the body. When I was about sixteen years old, a sucking doctor removed something from my forehead. I was going blind; I couldn't see even a few feet in front of me. I would not surrender to the pain, but deep within my mind I knew someone could help me.

"The sucking took a long time, but the healer took something out of my head. There was no scar, and no skin was broken. I can't do that, and I can't pull disease out of the body with my hands the way some healers can. I use herbs to flush them through, and the herbs crumble the illness somehow. When the person goes to the bathroom, what ails them goes with it. I don't have to know how it works. The critical thing is this: as a healer, you can't doubt yourself. Especially if someone is going to die, because your certainty will give them hope and sometimes that is all they need.

"One lady came from Oklahoma to see me when I was in New Mexico. She told me she couldn't breathe. I listened to her story. She had tried everything to get well and I was her last hope. It is always frightening when people tell me I am the last hope. I helped her breathe better, gave her eucalyptus tea, and a lot of bodywork. I took out the negative weak spots. Her husband and son were in tears when she said she could breathe again. To this day I don't really know what happened to her. All I know is that it worked. They believe in me, I'm the last hope, so it works. Many would say it's a miracle. It was just a feeling I had and most of the time my feelings are right."

Carol Banyas:

The Higher Self as Ultimate Physician

Susan is a thirty-six-year-old executive career woman. When she first came to me for psychiatric help, she was severely depressed. She was on antidepressant medication. She was not sleeping, and had thoughts of suicide. She had just broken up with a boyfriend, and her medical history included a previous bout with breast cancer.

I used several energy healing modalities with Susan. They uncovered a whole series of traumas. Her brother had died, and she felt guilty over his death. Together we discovered many masked selves, which manifested in perfectionism and a need for continued validation.

She began to connect with her higher self more and more deeply, and shed many energy blockages. When the blocks were removed, she began to feel her emotions deeply for the first time in years. Her depression began to lift. She found the process painful and difficult, yet her tears were made easier because she knew she was on her way out of a state she called "darkness invisible with no way out."

As she developed tools to help her stay in touch with her higher self, she was able to reduce the amount of medication required, and eventually live entirely without it. Her depression ended, and she regained a vitality that allowed her to look forward to her life with anticipation.

True healing recaptures these displaced aspects of self, and reintegrates them back to the higher self. Disease is often a pathway for that to occur. Disease, in essence, is often power displaced from the higher self.

Carol Banyas, MD, Ph.D., is a charismatic physician who envisions the integration of energy medicine and spirituality within the practice of psychiatry. She has many years of training in both traditional Western medicine and alternative healing techniques, and has authored many articles. Her posts include Medical Director of Geriatric Services at California Pacific Medical Center in San Francisco, a fellowship in Geriatric Psychiatry at the Neuropsychiatric Institute in Los Angeles, and the co-creation of the Research Program at the School for Advanced Healing Research, where she currently teaches. Her web site is www.integratepsych.com.

Where We Began—And Where We're Going

Every human society has had a fascination with healing the sick. Early tribal societies believed the cause of illness to be the projection of an evil force or object, unseen but felt, brought about by magic or sorcery. Healing involved driving out the evil spirits and perhaps bringing back a lost soul. Hippocrates, the father of modern medicine, proposed more rational explanations, that disease existed in the physical body, and that the mind and emotions were separate and located in the brain.

The field of psychiatry has seen dramatic advances, spanning history such as the incarceration of patients in asylums in the nineteenth century, to the revolution of Sigmund Freud and Carl Jung, with their concepts of the unconscious mind and psychological conflict. Today, the explosion of research into the neurochemistry and structure of the brain, the effects of different medications, and a vast array of psychotherapeutic modalities all encourage a comprehensive understanding of disease, and the mind-body implications for physical disorders.

-§-
Disease, in essence, is often power displaced from the higher self.
-§-

In order to make the next shift, into psychiatry for the twenty-first century, we need to expand on the postulate of the unconscious mind, updating it with information about the unseen, but highly profound, energetic fields of the human body. We are multidimensional beings; just has emotional wounds can contribute to physical disease, true healing goes far beyond the physical recovery of the body. Illness can be a doorway for spiritual transformation to occur.

The Language of Energy

Everything is made of energy. Every living organism, plant, animal and material substance has its own unique signature pattern of vibration and movement that can be perceived and felt. In the living body, each electron, atom, chemical bond, molecule, cell, tissue and organ has its own vibration, or rate of speed, organized into fields that permeate the entire structure. These energy fields or vibrational levels are organized, not random. They have the capacity to react, interact, and transact—they can respond to, and unite with, other fields.

It is their "energy signature" that draws us to some people and withdraws us from others. Our thoughts and emotions also have a vibratory rate; on certain levels of the energy field they can be perceived as having shape and form. Likewise, every disease has its unique consciousness level or energy pattern that can be perceived in the energy field of the body, as well as outside of the body.

When molecules move faster than the speed of light, they disappear from our sight. This does not mean that they do not exist, rather we are unable to *perceive* them because they have crossed the boundary into another level or dimension. These higher levels—where our souls reside—are what ultimately guides us in our healing process. These vibrational frequencies interpenetrate the same space as us, and are a part of our being that we can access.

This energy field holds the highest level of memory. It contains information about the physical body, about thoughts and emotional states, and about present and past life experiences. Barbara Brennan and Helen Hunt are two pioneers who have transformed the healing profession's understanding of healing and the energy field. They have found that all events occur first in the energy field—before a physical event takes place. Illness will first show in the energy field before it enters the physical. Therefore healing needs to be accomplished in the energy system before filtering

-§-
It is their "energy signature" that draws us to some people and withdraws us from others.
-§-

into the physical. The speed of the atoms and electrons are slower and more dense in a physical body, thus a healed energetic pattern takes time to configure or align with the physical body vibration.

The energy field also holds all the emotional and psychological experiences that have occurred in this life and even other lives. In the journey back to wholeness, a person can often re-experience and release traumatic emotional events that are not in their present conscious awareness.

How We Heal

When we view a person's energy field with higher sense perceptions, we can perceive energy blocks. We can perceive them in various ways. Some people see them symbolically, or literally; others see colors. Some have an intuitive or gut feeling, while others have a kinesthetic or feeling sense. Some have an "inner knowing" of things and are unable to explain where it comes from. We each develop an individual style that we draw from a vast array of present and past life experiences.

These energy blocks are often perceived in a level of the field called the astral (the level of the emotions and the bridge between the spiritual and physical), but can be found on other levels. They can be released in a variety of ways. But first it is important to understand the nature of these blocks. These can be thought forms, traumas, or life experiences that have a particular energetic pattern or shape. For example, some thought forms from this lifetime can create the same energetic pattern in the field as a past life trauma. Because of the like pattern, healing one can heal the other. These blocks can be found anywhere in the field, but when they filter down into the physical, the lowest and densest frequency, they can manifest as disease. Certain configurations of patterns in the auric field can be the precursor to physical disease. The physical disease is the manifested form of that pattern.

Rochelle was forty-three years old when she walked into my office. She complained of pelvic inflammatory disease and fibroids. Despite many attempts, she was unable to become pregnant. She was acutely aware of her childlessness because she worked with children professionally. She was aware of healings because her mother was a well-known healer living in South America.

Rochelle and I initially discussed her physical complaints. But soon she began to talk about some of her feelings. She was guilty that she had not visited her mother recently, who was recovering from a leg amputation. Rochelle had been referred to me because of her depression. She had been raped at an early age, in fact this was her first sexual encounter. She became pregnant as a result of the rape, and had a therapeutic abortion.

She began to identify an energy in her third chakra area (solar plexus). I used a technique called "energetic dialog." Here the patient identifies a particular energy or feeling; often it's a blocked trauma or an aspect of the self that became dissociated at a younger age. A dialog is established with that particular energy or consciousness that allows a release of the painful experience and also the experience of safety, which was often lacking when the trauma occurred. Often a dialogue is needed between the inner child of the patient, and their adult self. This "inner child rescue" is a powerful tool. It can provide a ground for the young child and adult to meet in present time, and re-experience the trauma in an atmosphere of safety and healing.

Rochelle began to process the anger she felt about the rape, and toward the man who did it. In subsequent sessions with me, Rochelle revealed that she had become pregnant again, more than once, and had other abortions. She was haunted by what she felt were the spirits of her unborn children. She felt responsible for their deaths, and was filled with guilt and shame. She continued to have colitis and other intestinal problems.

Throughout our sessions, my attention was continually drawn to her heart chakra. I sensed that it was the key to unlocking all of the blocked energy that I felt throughout her abdomen. I sensed a fear that she had about her own death. When I expressed this sensing to Rochelle, this turned out to be her core issue. She indeed did have a profound fear of dying herself, and in turn a fear that she would never see her parents again. This opened up a fear that if she did have her own child, she would die at an early age. So she had manifested the physical disorder of being unable to conceive.

She then began to recall intuitive powers that she possessed as a child. Early in her life, she had been able to foresee death and illness. When she discovered how disruptive this knowledge could be, she suppressed her abilities.

During another session, while attempting to remove blocked energy in her lower abdomen, she experienced a past life in which she did indeed have two children and died early from a tumor in her stomach. This insight was a turning point in her healing journey back to completeness. She understood that she was recreating similar experiences in this lifetime order to heal.

-§-

A person will often re-create similar life experiences as the soul seeks to bring the dark aspects of the past to light.

-§-

As we go through painful experiences in our lives, we naturally try not to feel the pain. This begins in childhood. We cut off the pain by withdrawing our consciousness from that particular area of the body. We cut off emotional pain by repressing it into the unconscious. However, the energy that contains the physical and emotional pain also contains other, positive, aspects. Thus, by stopping the pain and anguish, we also stop the positive experiences. We then become unaware of the deeper aspects of our present experiences, and stop the creative process.

Each time in the past that we stopped the flow of energy during a painful event, the event becomes frozen in that time, creating an energy block. This block is termed *frozen energy* or *frozen consciousness.* That part of the psyche associated with the event is arrested in its development, and does not mature as the body ages. It continues to remain locked at the age the event occurred until it is healed by getting energy into that block to begin the maturation process.

Like attracts like. These frozen energies often have a similar pattern of energetic makeup in different people. Often they are centered on a particular theme. In Rochelle's case, fear of death, abandonment of responsibility for herself, and abandonment of family were clearly repeated in experiences throughout this lifetime. These themes are unconsciously held in the individual's belief system and in their energy field. A person will often re-create similar life experiences as the soul seeks to bring the dark aspects of the past to light.

The energy field does not exist in a linear time/space continuum. Unresolved issues from past lives are held frozen in time in the energy field. They're then attracted to similar patterns reflected in this lifetime, causing present-day psychological and physical pain.

During healing, as the traumas from this life are cleared, the frozen aspects from other times are released. In such releases, a person may experience the entire life-stage during which the old trauma occurred as if it were happening in present time. Also, when traumas from this life are cleared, related past life traumas may reveal themselves for the purpose of healing, especially if they have the same energetic resonance pattern. The individual is then able to clear similar current life circumstances that other types of traditional therapy cannot touch. This type of work is extremely effective in thoroughly transforming an individual's life.

There are various methods of energy healing. One of the most ancient is hands-on healing, also called the laying-on of hands. This is a method by which the healer clears and charges the patient's energy field by running energy through each chakra, from feet to head. This allows the healer to clear blockages, access the patient's astral realm, and remove trauma from the field. The healer often works with guides from other realms, including medical guides that work with specific diseases. When this occurs, the healer's hands are guided by these other forces. The change first occurs in the energy field; it then may take days or weeks before the new pattern is transferred to the dense vibration of the physical body. The patient's higher self and healing guides may have their own agendas; many patients report healings in parts of the body that were not intended, but obviously needed. Healing energy is transmitted through the healer's energy field as well as through the guides that work through them.

-§-
The patient's higher self and healing guides may have their own agendas; many patients report healings in parts of the body that were not intended, but obviously needed.
-§-

Unwinding is an energetic technique used with patients who are unable to, or have difficulty with, moving into the conscious experience of a traumatic event. When unwinding begins, the body begins to move spontaneously as it releases blockages stored in the energy field. The body knows what do to, guided by the higher self. Sometimes, once a patient identifies a particular energy that needs to be released, the body begins to unwind spontaneously.

Radiatory healing is an energetic technique in which the practitioner focuses his or her awareness on a particular energy block, stagnation, or distortion within the patient's energy field. This focused awareness allows the block to begin to move, open and release. The practitioner uses his or her energy field to radiate a healthy energy pattern to the patient.

John was ninety-two years old. He was dying from cancer. He was also suffering from depression, and I was the psychiatrist he had been referred to, as part of his outpatient day treatment program. One day John came into the clinic looking even worse than usual. He was in a great deal of physical pain. Uncharacteristically, he required a wheelchair and oxygen. His doctor believed that he had only a few days or weeks of life left.

Even though his case looked hopeless, my instincts told me to try energetic healing on him rather than traditional psychiatry. I placed my hands on him. I felt a dense, tight energy stream, the result of a lifetime of unprocessed traumas. I felt an incredible amount of sadness gathered in his field. The vitality of his energy field was low.

As I cleared his energy field, I felt a tremendous amount of energetic discharge. His legs began to shake as they unwound ancient, stored traumas. Debris fell off his field, and I cleared and charged his chakras.

What followed was almost miraculous. He got out of the wheelchair and stood up straight. He dropped his oxygen feed. He felt lighter, and walked around unassisted. He told me his pain had decreased greatly. He had the twinkle of vitality in his eye. I was amazed at the dramatic change in John; it reminded me that we can never predict what will happen when we invoke the power of healing from a spiritual level.

Role of The Higher Self in Healing

Healing is not complete without including the higher self. This is the part of our being that holds the template or energetic pattern of our true divine essence. It guides us through our incarnations and soul progression and holds the infinite wisdom of the universe. It is not separate from us; it is a part of us as we are part of the whole.

In order to create change on any level of the energy field and thus the physical body, the healer needs to first perceive the higher self of the patient. When patients present themselves for healing, they are in dis-harmony, cut off from their true essence self. The healer needs, first and foremost, to perceive these qualities, which hold the key to the patient's healing.

Disease is the body's way of telling us, "Look here! This is the place where I am sick or blocked." Disease points out an imbalance between the essence qualities of the higher self and what is being reflected. By holding the reality of the essence qualities of the patient and bringing focused awareness to them, the healer allows them to unfold in the body. As the healer finds his or her higher self, and connects with the patient's higher self, a safety net is formed for template of health to begin to emerge in physical form.

One can then enter into the healing process. From a soul or energetic perspective, full power is having 100 percent of your energy available to you. That is vitality. When there is less, that portion of the energy has been *displaced*. These are the energies that are cut off from the higher self.

Displaced energies seek to validate themselves. They take on a life of their own and are attracted to other energies of similar patterns on other energy levels, and can be perceived as traumas. Then, disconnected from our higher selves, we develop defenses that allow us to function in the world. This is sometimes called the masked self. Our disconnected selves don't feel authentic, and we may be afraid of being found out. We then create circumstances in our lives that recreate the original wound.

The higher self holds the wisdom to heal our energy fields and thus our physical bodies. Templates are patterns that are manifested in form through the soul. They are powerful and can impact the level of change and consciousness rapidly.

In healing, it is of utmost importance to connect up with our own higher selves as well as the higher self of the individual being healed. Through healing techniques like the ones I've described, patterns from the higher self are transmitted through the healer. I have seen this work with healing physical as well as emotional problems.

Much work has been accomplished in treating life-threatening illness such as cancer through these techniques. Tumor markers decrease, scans show tumor shrinkage, recovery time after surgery is shorter, and the side effects of toxic medications are ameliorated. All organs in the body have an energetic template of perfection. In a beautifully symbiotic relationship between the healer, the individual needing healing, guides and higher selves, new energetic patterns can be placed in a person's energy field. These patterns of health and wholeness often come directly from the person in need of healing, are transmitted through the healer and through higher self connections, and are then brought through to the lower levels of the energy field.

-§-
Our disconnected selves don't feel authentic, and we may be afraid of being found out.
-§-

These templates of perfection also exist for the emotional body. Here it is essential that a bridge be built between the person and their own higher self. The healer can often transmit a pattern of safety and well-being to the patient if they have never had a secure experience.

And so we have come full circle. We have gone back to the roots of healing and reawakened ancient practices to encompass the full spectrum of healing.

LARRY DOSSEY:

Embracing the Trickster

Problem solving is one of the great joys of the practice of medicine, particularly when the solution enriches the life of a sick person in the process. During my medical training the surgery trainees used to call us internal medicine residents "swamis" and "crystal ball gazers." These gentle jibes about our method of solving problems suggested we were hopelessly given to thinking as opposed to doing, which was their turf. There was wisdom in their observation. Most physicians are trained to be thinkers, analysts, logicians. When we encounter clinical problems such as cancer, heart disease, or AIDS, our search for solutions begins with the assumption that we need more facts and information, which form the substrate upon which reason can operate. Only an approach anchored in analysis and reason, we say, stands a chance of working.

In contrast, many cultures have recognized that an intellectual approach to life's problems can be carried to excess. They have accorded great respect to irrationality and foolishness in its many forms—play, humor, nonsense, lightheartedness. One of the most universal expressions of this point of view is the trickster figure, which has appeared in the mythology and folklore of perhaps every culture on earth.

In modern psychology *trickster* is often used to refer to a universal force or pattern within the mind—what psychologist C. G. Jung called an archetype that represents the irrational, chaotic, and unpredictable side of human thought and behavior. This aspect of the mind is contrasted with the logical, analytical, and intellectual side that values order, precision, and control. According to the tenets of depth psychology, a balance

Larry Dossey, MD, is a physician of internal medicine. He was a battalion surgeon in Vietnam, and chief of staff at Medical City Dallas Hospital. He has lectured all over the world, including the Mayo Clinic, Harvard, Johns Hopkins, Cornell, and numerous major universities. Among his many books are *Space, Time & Medicine,* (Shambhala, 1982) and *Prayer Is Good Medicine* (Harper, 1997). He executive editor of the journal *Alternative Therapies in Health and Medicine.* This chapter is reprinted from *Healing Beyond the Body* © 2001 by Larry Dossey. Reprinted by arrangement with Shambhala Publications, Inc., Boston, www.shambhala.com. Photo by Athi Mara Magadi.

between these two vectors of the psyche is required for optimal mental health. When either the rational or the irrational side dominates, self-correcting forces come into play to restore some semblance of harmony between the two. The countless trickster tales describe how this process plays itself out in everyday life.

We pride ourselves on order and reason in practically every area of modem life. The messy, unlovely, and foolish aspects of human nature are accorded secondary status or rejected outright. Ignoring these traits—which everyone possesses to some degree—does not dissolve them but shunts them into the unconscious part of the mind, often called the shadow. The trickster operates, therefore, largely outside conscious awareness but always from within the human mind, not from without. We *are* the trickster, and when we describe trickster phenomena we are always describing aspects of ourselves. Thus the trickster has been called a *speculum mentis:* a mirror into the mind.

-§-
"The one-sided get blind-sided."
—Jeremiah Abrams
The Shadow in America
-§-

The Trickster in Native North America

Trickster lore flowered in the mythology of native North America as well as in traditional cultures throughout the world. Not only does the trickster exhibit trickery, buffoonery, and crude behavior in indigenous tales, he also appears as a creator, culture hero, and teacher. He is partly divine, partly human, and partly animal and is an amoral and comic troublemaker. Although he appears most frequently as the coyote in the cultures of the Southwest, the Great Basin, California, and the Great Plains, many other creatures are also represented, including the raven, crow, blue jay, mink, rabbit, spider, raccoon, mud hen, opossum, and bear, according to Sam Gill and Irene Sullivan's *Dictionary of Native American Mythology.* Trickster figures also abound outside native cultures, such as in ancient Greece, where they appeared as Prometheus, Epimetheus, and Hermes. In the European Middle Ages, the court jester or fool served the trickster function. In our time clowns, comedians, movie actors, and cartoon characters often fulfill the role.

According to Gill and Irene Sullivan, *trickster* was probably first used in 1878, by Father Albert Lacombe in his *Dictionaire de la Langue des Cris,* in which he wrote that the name of the Cree figure Wisakketjak means "the trickster, the deceiver." *Trickster* was picked up by Daniel Brinton in his 1885 article "The Hero-God of the Algonkins as a Cheat and Liar," in which he cites Lacombe's use of the word. Soon afterward *trickster* was widely embraced as a character type broadly applicable in Native American mythology.

However, *trickster* is not a term or category used by any Native American culture; it is an academic invention intended to make more comprehensible various Native American figures who share common traits. Peculiarly, once invented, the term came to have a seductive power and has taken on more reality—at least for academics—than the various figures such as Coyote and Raven who are classified as tricksters. In other words, the trickster is generally referred to as though it were a person rather than a category invented to facilitate study. A list of the scholars who have written about the trickster reads like a *Who's Who* in the social sciences, humanities, and psychology.

The Trickster and Modern Medicine

The goal of modern medicine is to be scientific, which has naturally led to an overwhelming reliance on reason. The trickster principle suggests that intrinsic balancing forces come into play in the psyche when reason—or any other quality—gets the upper hand. Do trickster phenomena exist in modern medicine?

Probably everyone involved in health care sooner or later confronts the fact that all medical therapies, for all their power and popularity, can be frustratingly capricious and sometimes harmful. This is true not only for drugs and surgical procedures but also for the alternative/complementary and consciousness-based methods that are becoming increasingly popular. All therapies work only some of the time; they work sensationally for some people and not for others; they sometimes kill as well as cure. One can never predict with certainty in a given case whether any therapy will work; one can only provide a statistical probability that it will do so. Moreover, scientific studies demonstrating efficacy often give conflicting results. They sometimes show that a therapy that was previously thought to be helpful is actually harmful, and vice versa.

-§-
The trickster principle suggests that intrinsic balancing forces come into play in the psyche when reason gets the upper hand.
-§-

The trickster perspective suggests that some of these problems and paradoxes may result from too much, not too little, reliance on logic, analysis, and reason—the very bedrocks of modern science. Is the trickster afoot in medicine? Evidence for trickster effects is subjective; we have no detection devices to get a direct readout of the trickster's presence. In spite of this limitation, we can look at some specific areas in contemporary medicine where the trickster may be leaving his tracks, areas where confusion and chaos arise in frustrating degrees. We will notice that the confusion often takes the form of paradox.

• In a study reported by T. E. Strandberg in the *Journal of the American Medical Association,* 3,490 Swedish business executives were given maximum attention to reduction of risk factors for cardiovascular disease. After five years of intervention and a total of eleven years of follow-up, even though they succeeded in reducing their risk factors by 46 percent, they had a higher mortality rate than control subjects.

• In the highly publicized "Mr. Fit" (Multiple Risk Factor Intervention Trial) study, researchers at twenty-two medical research centers in the United States studied almost thirteen thousand men. Half of them received an all-out push by physicians to reduce their risk factors for heart disease. But at the end of seven years, even though they were successful in lowering their risk factors, their death rate was higher than that of the control group, for reasons that are still being debated.

• In spite of the fact that exercise is known to have many beneficial effects on the heart and circulation, "there-still is no clinical trial to demonstrate that increasing physical activity in a group of sedentary people reduces the rate of disease vs. sedentary controls," according to a 1991 study published in the *Journal of the American Medical Association.*

• A study reported in the *Archives of Internal Medicine* points out that "there is considerable interobserver variability in the roentgenographic diagnosis of pneumonia" — in other words, that pneumonia diagnoses from chest X-rays depend very much on who's looking at them. "This variability does not improve with increasing experience."

• *Science News* reports on a study on calcium: "Because most kidney stones are made of calcium, physicians often recommend that patients who have already suffered from stones reduce their calcium intake.... A research team from the Harvard School of Public Health reports that men who ate a diet rich in calcium faced a 34 percent lower risk of developing kidney stones than did men who consumed a restricted calcium diet. 'This goes against everything we had been taught,' says kidney specialist Gary C. Curhan, who led the calcium investigation."

• "Although the periodic health examination was introduced over 80 years ago, it remains a controversy in internal medicine. There have been few data from controlled studies to document the examination's efficacy for adults; nevertheless, its popularity has become a multimillion-dollar industry in the United States," states H. C. Mitchell in *Annals of Internal Medicine.*

• "A new study suggests that physicians and nurses should offer this seemingly paradoxical advice to patients awaiting surgery: Don't relax, be worried." Although relaxation training before surgery helps people feel less tense, researchers investigating anxiety before surgery found that the greatest postsurgical increases in adrenaline and cortisol, two hormones associated with the body's reaction to stress and danger, were significantly higher among patients given relaxation training prior to their surgical procedure, compared with control subjects.

• A study on men with low cholesterol published in *Science News:* "Sometimes you can't win for losing. Case in point: New evidence indicates that elderly men boasting low cholesterol levels also suffer markedly more symptoms of depression than peers with moderate or high cholesterol levels…. Several cholesterol-reduction trials have found unexpected jumps in suicide and other violent deaths…. Neither weight loss (which often lowers cholesterol) nor the presence of various medical problems accounted for the link between cholesterol and depression."

• "The current coronary heart disease risk factors explain only about 50% of new events," says R. S. Eliot in the *Journal of the American Medical Association.*

• Professional working women enjoy lower blood pressure than women who stay at home, concludes a study reported in *Science News.* "Basically, the theory that job stress will make women as susceptible as men [to high blood pressure] doesn't bear out."

• Data on infant health presented in the *Journal of the American Medical Association* challenge the widely held assumption that United States women, who usually enjoy higher levels of education, employment, and income, have healthier infants than immigrants. According to statistics from San Diego County from 1978 to 1985, the lowest infant mortality rates were seen in Southeast Asian and Hispanic women, most of whom were foreign-born; highest rates were seen in white and African-American women, most of whom were United States-born. The United States, which prides itself on having the most advanced health-care system in the world, is number twenty-two in infant mortality when compared with other developed countries, according to a report published in The Sciences. In 1992 corporate health-care expenditures exceeded corporate profits. Yet we offer fewer services and have a shorter life expectancy at birth than many other industrialized countries.

• According to data published in the *Journal of the American Medical Association,* each year 225,000 people die in hospitals in the United States as a result of medical errors and the side effects of drugs. This makes hospital care the third leading cause of death in the United States, behind heart disease and cancer.

Our usual approach to paradoxes such as these is to design more and better studies to clear up the ambiguities. The problems, we say, are not a failure of reason but a lack of sufficient information to which reason can apply itself. Can we eradicate all the confusion with good studies? It would be foolish not to employ our intellect as skillfully as possible. But how fully can reason serve us without becoming susceptible to the self-correcting, intrapsychic forces of irrationality and unpredictability?

It is not popular to propose limits to reason in medicine. To do so sounds defeatist. But the trickster perspective suggests not that the problems we face are intractable or that reason is somehow "wrong" but that the problems may not be penetrable by logic alone. We may not be able to bludgeon our way to solutions solely with reason, as we habitually try to do. The path toward clarity may lie, paradoxically, with unreason.

Alternative Medicine and the Trickster

All schools of healing conform to some sort of mythology. Modern medicine largely follows the hero myth, which is based not only on reason but also on effort, will, and courage. Alternative/complementary medicine also generally follows a rational, causal framework: if you do X, Y will follow—whether X means taking vitamins or herbs, using a homeopathic remedy, or praying, imaging, or meditating. In alternative circles, as in orthodox medicine, heroic vigor and assertiveness are also routinely emphasized, epitomized by the frequent advice that patients "take charge," "assume responsibility," and "fight" their illness.

-§-
The trickster sows confusion *wherever* hyperintellectuality is manifested.
-§-

As complementary medicine attempts to match the intellectual rigor of orthodox medicine, there is a risk that it, too, may ignore the trickster forces in the psyche. If so, it may find itself susceptible to the unpredictability and confusion that so often plague conventional medicine. The field of complementary medicine is not off-limits to trickster effects; it enjoys no privileged status. The trickster sows confusion *wherever* hyperintellectuality is manifested.

Many researchers and clinicians in alternative medicine realize that it may be impossible to subject some healing methods to the rational strategies favored in contemporary biomedical research such as double-blind methodology. Consider, for example, studies involving the effect of prayer among patients who are seriously ill. How can one establish a control group that, by definition, should receive no prayer? People facing serious illness routinely pray for themselves, whether or not they belong to a control group. Even if they did not, their loved ones pray for them. No one has yet devised a way of annulling the "problem of extraneous prayer." An alternative research approach has been to study the effects of prayer not on humans but on nonhumans—assessing, for example, the effects of prayerful intentionality on growth rates of bacteria or fungi or on the healing rates of surgical wounds in rats or mice. Presumably the bacteria or mice in the control group do not pray for themselves, nor are they being prayed for by their fellow creatures.

In spite of these difficulties, we should not abandon the customary forms of investigation that are based on reason in favor of an "anything goes" policy, for this approach would lead to the opposite excess in which too little, not too much, reason is employed. We should push the limits of reason as far as possible in our research strategies, recognizing in advance that the limits are real. We should also be willing to search for creative alternatives when we encounter paradoxes we cannot penetrate.

The Trickster and the Creative Process

The trickster, therefore, suggests *not* that we abandon our rational faculties altogether but that reason must be complemented by unreason if it is to achieve full flowering. Nowhere is this lesson clearer than in the creative process of great scientists.

When Jonas Salk was researching the polio vaccine that would bear his name, he decided to distance himself from his work for a short period by going to the monastery of Assisi in Italy. Salk had a keen interest in architecture, and his encounter with the shapes and spaces, light, materials, and colors of this monastery, and its history, had a profound impact on his mind and spirit. Salk became highly energized. "Under that influence," he later recalled, "I intuitively designed the research that I felt would result in the desired vaccine. I returned to my laboratory in Pittsburgh to validate my concepts and found that they were indeed correct!"

Salk's experience is not unique. Throughout history researchers have often achieved success only when they allowed play and other distractions to mingle with the intellect—in other words, when they invited the trickster to come out to play.

Arthur Koestler observes in *The Act of Creation:* "The creative act, in so far as it depends on unconscious resources, presupposes a relaxing of the controls and a regression to modes of ideation which are indifferent to the rules of verbal logic, unperturbed by contradiction, untouched by the dogmas and taboos of so-called common sense. At the decisive stage of discovery the codes of disciplined reasoning are suspended—as they are in the dream, the reverie, the manic flight of thought, when the stream of ideation is free to drift, by its own emotional gravity, as it were, in an apparently 'lawless' fashion."

The paradoxes involved in the creative process are vividly exemplified in the life of England's Michael Faraday (1791-1867), one of the greatest physicists in history. Perhaps the most remarkable fact about Faraday is that he lacked any mathematical education or gift, and was "ignorant of all but the merest elements of arithmetic," according to Koestler. Faraday was a visionary in the literal sense. He was able to see stress lines around magnets and electric currents as curves in space, for which he coined the term lines of force. For him these patterns were as real as if they were made of solid matter. These images "rose up before him like things," says Koestler, and proved incredibly fertile, leading to the birth of the dynamo and electric motor, and the postulate that light was electromagnetic radiation.

In the 1940s the mathematician Jacques Hadamard performed systematic research into the psychology of highly creative mathematicians, whose work generally is considered the purest example of reason and logic. In his book *The Psychology of Invention in the Mathematical Field,* he reports that "among the mathematicians born or resident in America…practically all of them…avoid not only the use of mental words but also…the mental use of algebraic or any other precise signs;…they use vague images. The mental pictures…are most frequently visual, but they may also be of another kind, for instance, kinetic. There can also be auditive ones, but even these…quite generally keep their vague character."

-§-
There is a trickster-ish, uncontrollable, unpredictable side of creativity in which reason is flouted.
-§-

Einstein was one of the individuals in Hadamard's survey. He described his creative process thus: "The words or the language…do not seem to play any role in my mechanism of thought. The…elements in thought are certain signs and more or less clear images…. This combinatory play seems to be the essential feature in productive thought—before there is any connection with logical construction in words or other kinds of signs which can be communicated to others."

Such reports contradict the stereotypical view that creative research is only a dogged exercise of the rational mind. There is a tricksterish, uncontrollable, unpredictable side of creativity in which reason is flouted. This implies that "creativity on demand," the kind often taught in weekend workshops, is an oxymoron.

Writing in the 1950s in *Scientific American,* Frank Barron, an expert on the psychology of imagination, captured the essentially unharnessable nature of the creative process:

"Creative individuals are more at home with complexity and apparent disorder than other people are…. The creative individual in his generalized preference for apparent disorder, turns to the dimly realized life of the unconscious, and is likely to have more than the usual amount of respect for the forces of the irrational in himself and in others…. The creative individual not only respects the irrational in himself, but courts it as the most promising source of novelty in his own thought. He rejects the demand of society that he should shun in himself the primitive, the uncultured, the naive, the magical, the nonsensical…. When an individual thinks in ways which are customarily tabooed, his fellows may regard him as mentally unbalanced.... This kind of imbalance is more likely to be healthy than unhealthy. The truly creative individual stands ready to abandon old classifications and to acknowledge that life, particularly his own unique life, is rich with new possibilities. To him, disorder offers the potentiality of order."

Barron's statement might well serve as a kind of Trickster Manifesto, emphasizing as it does the central role of the irrational, chaotic elements of the psyche in the creative process.

In my practice of internal medicine, one of my colleagues was concerned with how we might nourish the creative impulse in the physicians in our group. A tireless traveler himself, he knew it was important to set the stage for creative insights — by journeying to unfamiliar surroundings, for example, just as Salk did in the aforementioned instance. He therefore proposed that each physician be encouraged to go periodically on an extended sabbatical outside the city, investigate a topic of personal interest, and formally report his findings back to the group. This would not only challenge the individual physician but would stimulate the other doctors as well. As an enticement, the physician would be paid for doing so. The proposal was resoundingly rejected. This example shows that we physicians, as well as practically anyone else, will go to great lengths to remain locked into familiar routines, which can have a deadening effect on our creative potential.

In Greek mythology the classic trickster figure is Hermes, the fleet-footed messenger of the gods and the deity of speech, communication, and writing, whose first act as a baby was to steal cattle from Apollo. Thus we see in Hermes the qualities of thievery, trickery, and deceit combined with the skill of communication.

This may appear to be an odd combination of traits, but if we look closely we can see that the pairing of deception and communication makes sense. Because trickster happenings are paradoxical, confusing, and chaotic, they take us off guard mentally and jolt us into seeing unexpected patterns and new meanings. G. K. Chesterton, the English writer, emphasized this "breakthrough" potential by defining paradox as Truth standing upside down to attract attention. In the wake of paradox, we see connections and patterns to which we were previously blind. It is as if our normal modes of perception have been tricked. The logical mind, accustomed to following old paths of reason previously laid down, is momentarily sidetracked into a different mode of perception. A new communication channel with the universe suddenly opens and grand patterns are revealed — creativity and discovery as a prank played on the habits of reason.

"Messing Up the Mind"

Similar processes happen in healing.

Myrin Borysenko was a prominent researcher in immunology at Tufts University School of Medicine. He was intrigued by the work of Harvard's David McClelland on the impact of belief in healing. On one occasion Borysenko asked McClelland how a particular healer in the Boston area healed people. "Oh, he messes up your mind," McClelland replied.

One morning while at his laboratory Borysenko began to come down with symptoms of flu—fever, aches, cough, and congestion. By noon he felt miserable. Unable to function, he decided to leave work and go home to bed. On his way home he suddenly thought of the psychic healer he had discussed with McClelland. Why not give the healer a try? Besides, he told himself, no one will ever know.

He found the healer in a dilapidated part of the city. As he climbed the rickety stairs he began to have second thoughts. "What if my colleagues could see me now?" he worried. The door to the healer's apartment was open as if Borysenko were expected. He entered to find an enormously fat, unkempt man sprawled on a sofa watching a soap opera on TV and drinking wine from a gallon jug. Summoning his courage, Borysenko said, "I hear you can cure people. Can you cure my flu?" Without taking his eyes off the TV the healer reached for a small bottle of purple liquid on the floor. "Go into the bathroom, fill the tub half full of water, pour this stuff in, and sit in it for thirty minutes. Then you will be cured."

-§-
A new communication channel with the universe suddenly opens and grand patterns are revealed.
-§-

Borysenko did as he was told. As he sat in the tub, up to his waist in the densely purple water, he was struck by the sheer absurdity of what he was doing. He felt so silly he began to laugh uncontrollably. He was still laughing when he realized his half-hour was over. He dressed and walked to the living room to find the healer still engrossed in the soap opera. He simply said, "Now you are healed." Then he pointed to the door, indicating he was free to go.

Driving home, Borysenko gradually realized he felt different. He sensed no symptoms whatever. He felt well—so well that he decided to return to work. He worked late. As he recited his adventure that night to his wife while undressing for bed, she suddenly burst into laughter. Looking into the mirror, he knew why. He was purple from the waist down.

Borysenko's healer was a first-rate trickster—one who upsets expectations, creates confusion, and jumbles the normal categories of thought.

Borysenko was enticed to abandon everything he believed about how healing worked, put his intellect on hold, and simply "let it happen."

It is perfectly natural to try to find approaches to healing that are completely objective and that can be successfully applied to all individuals who have the same illness. One might try, for example, to reduce Borysenko's experience to an algorithm whereby every patient with a diagnosis of the flu is advised to add a specific amount of the purple liquid to his bath water. But when used in a repetitive, formulaic way, these approaches rarely work as dramatically as for Borysenko, perhaps because they do not "mess up the mind," as McClelland put it. This is perhaps one reason behind the adage, "One should use a new medication as often as possible, while it still has the power to work."

Arrogance and the Trickster

Author Richard Smoley captured the essence of the trickster in *Gnosis* magazine:

"As long as we lie to ourselves, the Trickster will be with us. He'll show up just when we least want him, to embarrass us on a first date, to prove us fools in front of the learned company we're trying to impress, to make us miss a power breakfast with that all-important business contact. Yes, he'll leave at our bidding, but he always comes back with a vengeance. The only way to get rid of him is to listen to his message—and to admit the truth about ourselves in all its beauty and ugliness."

-§-

The trickster warns us of the dangers of arrogance and hubris.

-§-

The trickster not only deceives others; he is always himself being duped, often by pranks that backfire. Trickster tales show that humiliation is never far away; thus the trickster warns us of the dangers of arrogance and hubris.

In 1994 I had been preparing an important address for several days. The night before Halloween I had a trickster-type dream that was an important lesson about the pitfalls of pride:

I am waiting to give a speech at a prestigious gathering. The setting is imperial—an outdoor, semicircular structure of marble Corinthian columns with a podium in the center. I am to be introduced by Albert Einstein. As Einstein rises from his seat and walks to the podium, I realize that something about him is different. He is feisty and animated, not the avuncular, shy, saintly figure I expected. I suspect something unusual may be about to happen. Einstein introduces me with a flourish, and I walk to the podium to deliver my sensationally important address. I hear murmurs from the dignified scientists seated with Einstein, who have come from around the world to hear my speech. I suddenly realize the cause of the whispers: I am naked except for a pair of shorts, which are black and white. For some reason, I am not fazed. I realize that a grievous complication has arisen, with which I must contend. I excuse myself, walk to the left of the stage, and discover that a men's room is handy. I step inside, close the door, and see that a complete set of clothes is hanging on the wall, just waiting for me—a tuxedo and shirt, black and white, matching my shorts, precisely my size. I realize this delay is only temporary and will not be fatal to my talk. I dress, reenter the stage, assume the podium, and proceed with great care.

In medicine we often find ourselves symbolically without clothes. Arrogance and recklessness often set the stage for these humiliating situations. When we make rash assurances to patients that "everything will be fine," that our favored therapy is sure to work, or that we can find the problem when a string of prior diagnosticians have failed, we are setting ourselves up to be tricked. "You can think as much as you like," a Russian proverb warns, "but you will invent nothing better than bread and salt."

What if modern medicine were to become all-powerful? What if healers one day were able to cure all illnesses and make people live forever? A Winnebago trickster story contains a warning about the hubris that often accompanies such fantasies:

-§-
The more aggressively the rational mind tries to tame the trickster, the more ferociously it resists.
-§-

"Hare decides to help out the human beings and makes all the animals defenseless against them. 'Now the people will live peacefully and forever,' he thinks. But his wise Grandmother disagrees. 'Grandson, your talk makes me sad. How can you make the people live forever, as you do? Earthmaker did not make them thus. All things have to have an end.' Grandmother's body begins to undergo destruction before Hare's eyes. 'If all the people live forever,' she continues, 'they would soon fill up the earth. There would then be more suffering than there is now, for some people would always be in want of food if they multiplied greatly. That is why everything has an end.' Hare is disconsolate. His motives were so admirable!"

In Herrymon Maurer's *The Way of the Ways,* we find a similar warning about the incessant attempts of reason to fix things from Lao-tzu, the reputed founder of Taoism in China around the sixth century B.C.E.: "It is ominous to improve on life, Injurious to control breathing by the mind."

These warnings are often criticized as antiquated recommendations for a retreat into passivity, but their lessons lie deeper. Light does not come without darkness, they seem to be telling us, nor life without trouble. All opposites interpenetrate and sustain each other, as the trickster element of the psyche reminds us. We cannot have it one way. When we forget these eternal polarities, a price will be paid.

Is the Trickster Dangerous?

One of the most common ways of dealing with the trickster patterns of the psyche is to intellectualize them. According to this point of view, if we read enough books about trickster lore we can eventually decipher the meaning of the trickster tales and escape the pitfalls about which they warn. Such a project is impossible in principle, for two reasons. First, the trickster element lies so deeply in the unconscious that it is essentially beyond the reach of reason. It belongs to what has been called the really unconscious. Second, something of the trickster refuses to be analyzed. The more aggressively the rational mind tries to tame the trickster, the more ferociously it resists.

Anthropologist Barre Toelken describes his forty-year experience doing fieldwork with the Navajos in southeastern Utah, during which he investigated their Coyote trickster stories. At one point his Navajo informant asked, "Are you ready to lose someone in your family?" Toelken did not understand. "Well," the man said, "when you take up witchcraft, you know; you have to pay for it with the life of someone in your family." The Navajo storyteller saw that Toelken was approaching the Coyote tales intellectually, dismembering them analytically, discussing the parts and motifs separately in a typically academic way. When the tales are disrupted this way, Navajos believe, the various elements of the stories can be used by witches to promote disharmony and thwart healing. Thus the Navajos were concerned that Toelken, against his knowledge, was flirting with witchcraft. "My advice to you," his Navajo informant told him, "is: don't go deeper into this subject unless you're going to join the witches."

After the Navajo storyteller narrated the Navajo Coyote tales to Toelken, a series of disasters befell the informant and his family. The man developed a problem with his legs; he later died from a heart attack as he emerged from a sweat lodge. An auto accident killed his granddaughter and was nearly fatal to his daughter. A son developed schizophrenia. A brother died in a rock fall. The family became scattered and largely estranged from one another. Toelken's own Navajo foster son committed suicide. Toelken raises the chilling question of whether these incidents were coincidences or retribution for divulging the Coyote tales. His answer: From the standpoint of reason, they are coincidences; from the Navajo perspective, they are punishment for misuse of the stories.

Toelken eventually decided that although a particular area of scholarly inquiry might be "interesting" and "important," these reasons do not always justify continuing a research project. "Just as a moment of enlightenment may lead a scholar to pursue a subject further," he decided, "it may also clarify the need to call a halt." Thus he chose to abandon this area of fieldwork after deciding that it "stood a strong chance of being dangerous to the informants as well as to myself and my family." Toelken does not advise others to avoid the study of trickster phenomena. He does imply, however, that if one chooses to investigate these matters, there may be a high price for doing so.

-§-
We can never banish the trickster. To do so would be to amputate a vital part of ourselves, including our need to create, to frolic, to love.
-§-

Many psychologists who have plumbed the depths of the unconscious have come away with a reverence for this aspect of the mind. Typical was C. G. Jung, who wrote of the folly in trying to compel the unconscious to reveal its secrets. Jung wrote of the need to wait patiently, to see what the unconscious chose to deliver of its own accord. Can we imagine a future in which experiments are selected with reverence—as if research were an exploration of sacred space—and only after due reflection on what the consequences of the intellectual foray might be?

Be Aware or Beware

Why can we not function as rationally as a computer? Why does the psyche revolt when we become too logical and analytical? Why do we require a balance between reason and unreason, spontaneity and control? Why do we need irrational experiences such as laughter, play, and love?

We don't choose to be foolish, irrational, and playful; the need is innate. Foolishness is required for our psychological health; we can develop a shortage of foolishness just as we can acquire deficiencies of a vitamin.

The need for balance between the irrational and rational forces in the psyche is often rejected by "hard" thinkers who believe there are no limits on how rational we should strive to be. People of this persuasion often say that we do not have the courage to follow the intellect, and they describe the fall into irrationality as a lack of nerve. This point of view is perhaps more heroic than wise, because it ignores the stubborn facts of human experience and the findings of modern psychology on the role of the unconscious in our mental life. Transpersonal psychologist Ken Wilber wisely wrote, "After all, you will own [your opposites], or they will own you—the Shadow always has its say…. We may wisely *be aware* of our opposites, or we will be forced to *beware* of them."

Infatuated as we have become with the achievements of reason, there is always the temptation to reject everything that is irrational in favor of order and control. But we can never banish the trickster. To do so would be to amputate a vital part of ourselves, including our need to create, to frolic, to love—to be, in a word, human.

PART TWO

Sexual Healing

Allan Hardman:

The Impotent Hero

Romantic relationship has been both a blessing and nightmare for many people in this new millennium. In the past, the rules of relationship were relatively structured and well enforced by families and cultures. Many relationships were based on the need for security and financial well-being in an uncertain world. Often, mates were chosen based on others' expectations, class, race, or religious backgrounds.

Now, with financial independence being available to most, and ethic and cultural distinctions blurring, men and women are left more to their own discernment and integrity for choosing mates and establishing the rules and expectations of relationship. Along with this freedom has come increasing confusion and uncertainty in relationships of romance and marriage.

One consistent factor that I have observed in my work with singles and couples is their caution or outright fear of each other. They are not able to be present in their relationships with the truth of who they are and what they are feeling. I invite you to consider the following suggestions about what causes much of this difficulty.

I am writing this as a man, using heterosexual relationships as the model. Please understand that the dynamics I describe are not limited to those relationships. Wherever I have written "man" or "woman," please substitute "masculine" or "feminine" if it better serves your understanding. Know that the masculine and feminine can be dominant in any gender and interact in any relationship form. It is my hope that these

Allan Hardman is a gifted spiritual counselor and Toltec Master personally trained by don Miguel Ruiz, author of *The Four Agreements* (Amber–Allen, 1997). Allan is a born teacher, whose piercing insight and compassionate humor create a loving environment that supports growth on the path to personal freedom. His healing guidance in relationship counseling has helped many people establish healthy communication. Allan created the Toltec Apprentice Community, a thriving Internet resource. He travels throughout the United States conducting workshops and leads "Journeys of the Spirit" to Peru and Mexico. Allan's extensive web site is www.joydancer.com.

observations will serve you, no matter what form of relationship you choose.

Who Taught You What it Means to Be a Man?

After asking this question of countless men, I have learned that the answer is often not what one might expect. The first responses are usually "I learned to be a man from my Dad," or "my Uncle" or a respected mentor. Then a deeper truth emerges: "My dad wasn't around much," or "Dad left when I was six," or "My dad was an alcoholic." With deeper exploration, most men are surprised to discover that it was not their fathers who taught them what it means to be a man, but their mothers.

-§-
Most men are surprised to discover that it was not their fathers who taught them what it means to be a man, but their mothers.
-§-

They are often even more surprised to realize that the message that they received from their mothers was, "Don't be like your Dad." The message may have been received quite subtly. A boy might observe or imagine that his mother is unhappy, and think it is his Dad's fault. Perhaps Mom has sacrificed too much of her self for the marriage, and feels lost or unfulfilled, and the boy senses her unhappiness.

The message might also have been delivered very overtly, when Mother was home at night and Dad was out drinking. She felt alone, abandoned, afraid. She turned to her young son and said: "I hope you don't grow up to be like your father. He is not home, he is not taking care of us, and I am left to do everything."

Whether subtle or overt, the young boy feels this hurt in his mother, and looks for the cause. He does not have to look far to identify his father as the perpetrator of the abuse his mother is suffering. He knows Mother is hurt, and that Dad is hurting her.

I believe that males are genetically programmed to be Heroes, and to protect and rescue Damsels in Distress. When a young boy sees his mother hurt, lonely, angry, or depressed, he wants to rescue her. It is his nature. To be a good Hero, there must be a Villain—and the boy has learned that the Villain is Dad. If the boy stands up to his Dad and tries to stop him from hurting his mother, he will quickly learn that how impotent he is to protect and rescue her.

And here the boy encounters the conundrum that may be with him for the rest of his life: The Villain is not only Dad, it is "maleness," and the boy has identified himself with that same maleness all of his short life. He is both the Hero wanting to rescue, and the Villain causing the pain.

The young boy becomes the Impotent Hero, trying to protect and rescue his Damsel in Distress from himself, which he cannot do. He takes on the guilt of the Villain, and the guilt of his failure as the Hero. That conundrum has shaped the life and relationships of many of the men that have answered my question about learning to be a man. They go into the world feeling guilty for being male. They know they are a man, and they know that men hurt women. They know their job is to rescue women in distress, and that they cannot. They are both guilty and impotent. Rarely is a man conscious of this drama being played out in his inner world.

The Impotent Hero as the Inner Judge

Another way that a boy learns that his Hero is impotent is when it becomes embodied as his Inner Judge. In a perfect world, everyone would be born into a family that says: "We are so happy that you are here. We will take care of you, and keep you safe. There is nothing you need to do to earn our love—we love you just the way you are." In a perfect world, children would feel safe to be themselves, and mature into healthy, empowered adults.

Since this is not a perfect world, there is unavoidable hurt and wounding that happens to children. Probably the most damaging wound is when the Inner Hero as the Protector, is distorted into an Inner Judge under pressure to conform to the family's system of beliefs.

Imagine that a young boy or girl has a feeling part of the self, and a protective part. For purposes of illustration, I will call the feelings the "feminine" and the rescuer and protector the "masculine." Children express themselves through their feeling side. They experience exuberance and delight, tears and fears. In the not so perfect world, many of these expressions are unacceptable to their parents or other caregivers. The feelings and the behaviors that naturally arise in the child are judged, and the child feels hurt by this rejection. Children are "domesticated" into the prevailing beliefs systems about how to be good, and how to earn and deserve love. They learn to seek out the reward of acceptance, and to avoid the punishment of rejection.

When the child is punished, his or her feelings are hurt. The "feminine" aspect of the self is the Damsel in Distress, and the "masculine" is the Hero that rushes in to protect and rescue. Perhaps that Hero yells out to a parent in a difficult moment: "I hate you, you are mean. Leave me alone!" I think we can imagine (or remember) the response of most parents to this outburst.

If the child is punished for this attempt by his or her inner Hero to stop the abuse against the feeling side, this inner Protector realizes that he cannot stop the outside perpetrators. He is impotent to protect and rescue the feminine, so he must create a new strategy. He must protect the feeling side by getting "her" to stop the emotional behaviors that are causing the rejection and abuse. He learns to make the feeling self wrong for what she feels. The Inner Hero becomes the Inner Judge, a small masculine self, impotent in the outside world, but increasingly powerful in the inner world.

-§-
The Rescuer and Damsel stay bonded in their relationship and unable to change or grow, in fear of losing the love and comfort that their mutually compatible wounds have brought them.
-§-

This new Inner Judge internalizes the criticism and rejection of parents and culture. He recognizes that it is far less painful to his damsel, the feminine feeling side, to be judged and shamed inside by him than from the outside. The Hero turns to his feminine Damsel and says: "Don't cry. That is childish. Don't let them see you like that! Nobody likes a crybaby!" And, "You should never try to tell a story. Nobody cares about what you have to say."

The Impotent Protector becomes the Inner Judge, in both little boys and little girls. He is the masculine, wounded by his domestication, and fighting to protect the inner feminine the best way he knows how. Together they are in a battle for their emotional survival.

Relationship Strategies of the Impotent Hero

When a man enters a romantic relationship, if he does so as the guilty Impotent Hero, it is impossible for him to say to a woman: "I am a man, and want you!" He is afraid that she will criticize him and reject him. He believes his Inner Judge's criticisms, and assumes that his beloved will discover his powerlessness and unworthiness. He needs strategies for maintaining the relationship in the face of his fear of not deserving it.

Probably the four most compelling ways that men enter romantic relationship carrying this feeling of guilt and impotence are as the *Rescuer,* the *Romantic,* the *Rebel,* or masquerading as the *Feminine.*

The *Rescuer* creates relationship by offering a woman relief from the hurt and fear that she feels from living with her Inner Judge. Of course, this means that the Rescuer must find Damsels in Distress to rescue. The Hero makes a promise that he cannot keep: "If you are with me, you will not have to feel afraid or hurt or powerless any more."

He cannot keep that promise for at least two good reasons. First, her distress is not being caused by a deficiency of the Rescuer in her life. Her hurt and fear are the result of experiences from her past, her domestication, and criticism from her own Inner Judge. Second, if he truly rescues her and heals her pain, she will no longer be a Damsel in Distress, and will not need the Rescuer. To stay needed, he must sabotage her healing, and keep her in the Victim role. She knows that to keep the love of her Rescuer she must stay in that role and not claim her personal power. The Rescuer and Damsel stay bonded in their relationship and unable to change or grow, in fear of losing the love and comfort that their mutually compatible wounds have brought them.

The *Romantic* creates beautiful dreams of candlelight and rose bouquets. He is the magician, keeping his beloved's eyes on his tricks, and away from his impotence. Since it is difficult for the Romantic to maintain his diversions in a close and intimate relationship, he must keep his distance. He gallops into the damsel's life, sweeps her off of her feet, and takes her to his castle—but only for the night! If she tries to get too close, he gallops off to find the next moonstruck soul.

-§-
The Feminine Man is the eunuch who dresses up in women's clothing to hide in the harem.
-§-

The *Rebel* is very independent. He doesn't need anyone, especially women that might see through his facades to discover the Impotent Hero within. The Rebel is oddly attractive to women. There is a safety they see in his emotional distance. After many years of exploring why women often accuse men of being "emotionally unavailable" in relationships, I have figured out who is attracted to those men: emotionally unavailable women! This is a safe place for everyone involved. There is no danger of the intimacy that will threaten the facades and reveal the self-judgments and fears behind them.

The *Feminine Man* creates safety in his relationships with women by becoming like them. Some boys, in an effort to rescue their mothers, bond with them emotionally. As adults, they learn feminine ways of relating to feelings, and prefer the company of women. They do not assert themselves in their relationships—they believe in "equality." The Feminine Man is the eunuch who dresses up in women's clothing to hide in the harem. He dresses in women's emotions, to avoid being recognized as a man and revealing his guilt and impotence.

Many romantic relationships are based on this foundation of guilt that the man feels for being a man. He must hide his fear of discovery and self-judgment from his partner, and she must agree not to notice.

The Woman's Role

But what about the woman's role? Remember that girls are raised in the same system as the boys. They have the same Inner Judge, the same insecurities, and the same fear that the Judge is right about their defects. They are often taught that to survive financially they need a man. They, too, observe that Mom is hurt, angry, or lonely. They understand that maleness is guilty of causing the pain, and that they can use that guilt to meet their own needs in life. Perhaps Mom says: "Your father is never home, I have to do everything myself, I am so tired—but he is good to us and provides us with our home and food, so we should be grateful." The message? "The man is guilty of hurting us, but we need what he gives us, so we will use his guilt and impotence to keep him providing for us."

Perhaps the Mother tells or shows her daughters that the real control in the family resides in the females. With their underlying disrespect for their man, they secretly or overtly use their power to manage the family, leaving the man in the role of outside provider—a veritable stranger in his home.

The Unspoken Agreements

If women are afraid of losing their man, and men are afraid of being exposed as Impotent Heroes, then romantic relationship between them will be difficult, at best. They will need many unspoken agreements to manage the dangerous truths that lie beneath the surface.

Many of these silent agreements are brought into the relationship from the distant past, some are from the relationship itself: "I am not really worthy of love, so I am lucky to have found someone who loves me. I will do whatever it takes to hold on to this marriage"; "A good wife is always willing to follow her husband's lead"; "What is important in relationship is the long haul. If I demand too much, it will cause problems"; "She threatens to leave me every time I bring up our problems. It is better to work these things out myself, rather than saying anything."

-§-
Men and women became equals. From this balancing came a new dilemma, however: No one wanted to surrender to anybody else, and nobody needed anyone!
-§-

Every society has its beliefs and agreements about how things "should" be. That society could be a family, a group of friends, a university, a religion, an ethnic group, a political party, or a country. When we are born, we arrive into a family that has already agreed on their system of beliefs. It is their "dream," and they are sticking to it! Since we are born into that dream, we accept it as the truth, learn the intricacies of it, and even teach newer arrivals what we have learned: "Don't cry, mommy will get mad at you!"

As we grow older, we enter more societies with more beliefs and agreements that govern the behavior of the members. Everything a man has learned about how he "should be," in order to be a good boyfriend or husband, a good father, son, employee, boss, or lover become the hidden agreements in his mind. A man absorbs agreements from his religious faith, his business school, his prison buddies, the corporate ladder, and all of the women in his life. His sexual drive, combined with his guilt about being a man, creates eternal confusion and contradictions.

Each of these dreams of being a man contains its unique models of behavior, expectations, and the markers of success and failure.

In relationship, all of a man's beliefs and agreements come together with a partner who has accumulated her own set of agreements about what it means to be a girlfriend, a wife, a mother, a daughter, a boss or employee, a lover, and a member of a community. Since most people are not aware of these agreements in a conscious way, they simply react according to what they "know" to be true.

From the unspoken agreements brought to the relationship by a man and a woman, a new domestication occurs. Each partner learns the agreements required to avoid revealing the insecurities they feel about themselves and each other. The Impotent Hero is safe.

It has been suggested, that men and women are from different planets, and thus talk different languages and have different needs. It is my experience and belief that all of us, men and women, are from the same Earth and have the same desire: To know and love ourselves, to be authentically ourselves in relationship, and to do so without fear of rejection and abandonment.

It is very possible to have that which we desire. To do so, we must become conscious of our many inner voices and the unconscious agreements that they insist we honor. That awareness, in turn, gives us the power to choose which of our beliefs and agreements serve us, and which we wish to discard. In creating our own set of beliefs as adults, we "re-domesticate" ourselves into a new way of life. Our new agreements nurture our freedom to live our lives in love, grace and happiness.

The World's Greatest Lover

Imagine how we might all relate in romantic relationships if men were proud and powerful in their masculine nature, and women trusted themselves and their man. How might a man show up with his woman if he were not afraid of her? And how might that woman receive that man, if she trusted his masculine?

One of my favorite movies is "Don Juan de Marco," with Marlon Brando and Johnny Depp. Don Juan is "The World's Greatest Lover," and in the movie he says: "Women sense that I search out the beauty that dwells within them, until it overwhelms everything else. And then they cannot avoid their desire to release that beauty, and envelop me in it."

That is a great lover: A man who searches out the beauty in the feminine with such authority and love that she cannot help but surrender herself to his love. He has no doubt. He is saying, "I want you." This is a magnificently masculine way of penetrating a woman's heart.

In the past, women needed to make themselves smaller than their man to surrender to him. Then, awakening to their collective dissatisfaction, they fought for their independence, and their right to assert their masculine power in the world. Women became well-balanced in their masculine and feminine energies.

-§-
That is a great lover:
A man who searches out the beauty in the feminine with such authority and love that she cannot help but surrender herself to his love.
-§-

Sensing the change, men set out to connect with their disowned feminine natures. They learned to express their feelings, and to listen to the women in their lives. Many began to say that they preferred the company of women to that of overly masculine men.

Men and women became equals, and this shift in awareness has been very healing. From this balancing came a new dilemma, however: No one wanted to surrender to anybody else, and nobody needed anyone! In this equality many people seem to lack any passion for relationship outside of convenience and sexual pleasure. I would like to suggest that something vital and alive is missing. There is a spiritual healing and purpose to relationship that is available when our Impotent Hero becomes The World's Greatest Lover.

Qualities of the World's Greatest Lover

For a man to be The World's Greatest Lover, he must learn a new way of loving and accepting himself, and his beloved. He must learn that his critical Inner Judge is not telling the truth. He awakens to discover that he was programmed to believe his guilt and impotence, and the program is a lie! The World's Greatest Lover comes to understand that his nature is love, not the fear and doubt that he has lived with all his life.

He comes to this powerful experience when he is no longer judging himself. When our Hero accepts himself exactly as he is, without pride or deprecation, he is prepared to love and accept others just as they are.

The World's Greatest Lover sees the perfection in the universe unfolding exactly as it is. He is no longer victimized by anyone or anything. His power comes from knowing this divine order in life, in trusting it, and keeping his heart open to the wonders of creation. He is in love with life. He knows himself as life, and knows that all of life is that same divine perfection.

Knowing his own perfection, The World's Greatest Lover is neither afraid to feel what he feels, nor to think what he thinks. He is not afraid to want what he wants. He is free to come to the feminine with, "I want you!" He is not afraid of rejection, because he has ceased to reject himself. Of course, this voice is alive in the masculine of both genders. When a man speaks it, and the woman sees that she can trust his authority in it, she has the opportunity to surrender to his wanting. I have not met many women who would refuse to surrender to a man who knows what he wants, through the expression of his divinity. In a woman's surrender to this lover, there is the call to her greatness. She knows she will not be asked to be small, because she feels embraced by the expansiveness of his divine love.

As she surrenders to him, and he possesses her, he experiences the greatest surrender of all. The World's Greatest Lover surrenders to the feminine through his absolute certainty of wanting her.

In larger spiritual terms, we can see that the Lover is opening the feminine to the beauty that he sees. Using the authority of his inner divine, he acts as a mirror for that divinity in her. The feminine, as the mate of The World's Greatest Lover, or as any aspect of creation, sees her reflection in him. All of creation is thus penetrated and enlightened by The World's Greatest Lover.

The Impotent Hero, destined always to rescue, now comes to his Beloved and all of creation as the Lover, to release her from her illusion that she is not divine. He celebrates the highest expression of living as a man: He lives the truth of being The World's Greatest Lover, knowing the truth of his divinity, and reflecting that divinity back to his Beloved. In that reflection, she joins with him in knowing their highest truth as one.

ANODEA JUDITH:
The Body Is the Unconscious Mind

When Ellen walked into my office, the pain in her body was palpable, yet she was unaware of it. She walked stiffly and nervously, her eyes darting about frantically, hypervigilant for her own safety. She spoke rapidly as if with great fear, and the urgency of her words revealed a deep suffering that in forty-six years had never been relieved. Her body was constricted, her limbs thin and wiry. As she told her story, she revealed a number of self-destructive tendencies, including anorexic starvation in an attempt to annihilate her body and live entirely in her mind. She was now developing numbness in her extremities. Her hands, cut off from the waters of her soul, flitted nervously of their own accord, like fish on a line. She could not tell if she was hungry or sleepy, warm or cold. Disconnected from her body, it was no surprise that she felt disconnected from life itself.

This woman was clearly an individual, yet her suffering had common roots with many clients I have seen over the years. She had tried psychotherapists who served the ideals of "mental health" and looked only at her mind. She had seen a variety of doctors who probed and tested her body, prescribing various medications. She had approached her church but felt like an outcast. None could touch the severe separation of mind and body from which she suffered.

Her plight is common to many, in varying degrees of severity. Disconnected from our bodies, we are separated from our aliveness, from the experience of the natural world and the truth of how we live. This tragic division creates a dissociative state. Ruled by the intellectual over-

Anodea Judith, Ph.D., is a somatic therapist. She is regarded as one of the foremost experts on the combination of chakras and therapeutic issues and on the interpretation of the chakra system for the Western lifestyle. She is best known for the classic, *Wheels of Life* (Llewellyn, 1987). She has also released a stunning visual DVD journey through the chakras (2003), available at www.sacredcenters.com, and is the author of *Eastern Body, Western Mind* (Celestial Arts, 1997). She is a dynamic speaker and visionary. She conducted a private practice in mind–body therapy for 20 years, and now travels internationally conducting trainings in her work.

ride of our body's messages, we unwittingly harm ourselves with annihilating jobs and routines, toxic substances, and a disembodied lifestyle.

Disconnection from the body is a cultural epidemic. Of all the losses rupturing the human soul today, this alienation may be the most alarming because it separates us from the very roots of existence. We lose the joy that arises from the dynamic connection with the only living presence we are guaranteed to have for the whole of our lives: our body. Out of touch with the body, we become out of touch with the earth as well, and this epidemic is seeping into every aspect of our civilization.

The alienated relationship between mind and body has its roots in the archetypal divorce between spirit and matter. This wound separates culture and planet, for it devalues the body and any-

-§-
Disconnection from the body is a cultural epidemic.
-§-

thing physical, giving greater power to the mind. As a result, the shadow aspect of the physical world — materialism — looms its rapacious head. Only by recovering the body can we begin to heal the world itself, for as mind is to body, so culture is to planet. Healing the mind-body split is a necessary step in the healing of us all. It heals our home, our foundation, and the base upon which all else is built.

Many are the clients who come to me from years of traditional therapy and say, "I've done all this work on myself and learned all about how my problems are connected with this and that from my childhood — *but it still hasn't changed.*" This is because traumatic experiences are often stored within the tissues of the body as chronic holding patterns, unconscious ways of defending against life and its possibility of hurt or disappointment. Known as *body armor*, these patterns keep us from feeling fully present, vital, and at peace with ourselves. Unless we address the "issues in our tissues," the unconscious responses stored in the body habitually recreate patterns that the conscious mind desperately wants to avoid.

Traditional psychotherapy can be helpful in understanding the source of these issues, but may do little to change health problems or dissolve chronic tension held in the musculature. Bodywork therapies, on the other hand, may relieve tension, restructure one's alignment, or make contact with deeper issues, but if this material is not processed into consciousness, the mind cannot implement the deep changes needed to make this healing permanent. Thus we return each week to our bodyworker with the same sore shoulders or aching back, for another temporary reprieve from our painful patterns.

Mind-body therapies work both sides of the equation at the same time — uniting the physical and the spiritual as an integrated whole. They link our psychological problems to the experience of the body and link our physical problems to the experience of the psyche. This gives us an embodied experience of being whole in the world—fully present, active, and aware.

There are many systems for working the interface between mind and body, loosely associated under the heading of "Somatic Therapy." The art of moving energy through the body and dissolving body armor originated when Wilhelm Reich broke away from Freud. It then expanded to the US through Alexander Lowen, who called it *Bioenergetics,* and John Peirrakos, who called his work *Core Energetics.* Techniques involve using movement or standing postures, some massage, and focus more on the breath.

The ancient practice of yoga, specifically *hatha yoga,* or physical postures has become so popular today that new therapies are arising using yoga postures to access and release hidden emotional issues. Known as yoga therapy, the client merely enters into any of a number of postures or asanas, and observes what arises within the tension that forms their "edge" in the posture. Arising from within the yoga system, the *chakras* (energy centers in the body) are also points where the mind/body interface takes place.

The chakras, as organizational centers for the life force energy, help to distribute energy through the body, and awaken the corresponding consciousness within. The chakras can be accessed through movement, yoga, meditation, sounding or any number of techniques to reveal and heal the deep core issues that help or hinder our life journey. Together, the seven chakras, form a systematic link between the earthly orientation of physical survival, through the egoic realms of interpersonal relationships, and into the spiritual realms of transcendent consciousness—seeing them all as integrated steps along a continuum. To work through the chakras is to systematically work through the various levels in which mind and body connect.

-§-
Unless we address the "issues in our tissues," [we] habitually recreate patterns that the conscious mind desperately wants to avoid.
-§-

Dance, movement, various forms of massage, and martial arts, are also forms of somatic therapy in that they often address body and mind simultaneously. All can be used as healing modalities to enrich our experience in the world and help us to "get out of our heads," and more in tune with the body. All provide a simultaneous spiritual experience—but one that is grounded in the body rather than intellectual abstractions

Body Armor: The Costly Defense Budget

The body is the unconscious mind. Filled with nerve endings that are the sensory receptors for that central processing unit called the brain, the body records everything that happens to us, and then speaks to us in its primal, cellular language. Diseases are ways of telling us what the unconscious mind remembers, but that our waking state has ignored. When these messages come to awareness, the body can be released from having to hold that message. If we heed the messages and change our behavior accordingly, *as well as address the physical symptoms*, tension or disease can be free to dissolve. The emphasis here is on treating the whole person in body, mind, and spirit.

Body armor is the physical component of our psychological defense mechanisms. Defenses cut two ways — while they protect, they also deny. While defenses may minimize the impact of a painful experience, they also create separation, numbness, isolation, distortion, and rigidity. The vital core energy within the psyche is removed from the many sources of energy that surround us, such as love, beauty, communication, information, human touch and consciousness itself. Defense mechanisms literally restrict the life force energy from its free flow of reception and expression.

-§-
Diseases are ways of telling us what the unconscious mind remembers, but that our waking state has ignored.
-§-

Sensations are repressed, both from within and without, limiting the amount of information coming into the system, as well as the passion of life. When the body armor is excessive, we lose our sense of reality and the inner core becomes energetically imbalanced.

Body armor is a costly defense budget that robs us of our life force, similar to the way our national military defense budget diverts funds from other programs that may be more socially beneficial. The result is a kind of "energy crisis" that manifests physical and psychological symptoms of varying degrees of severity. Is it merely coincidence that a social system that supports, and at times even requires, the denial of the body creates a culture with such a massive military budget?

Solving the Energy Crisis

The interface between mind and body is *energy*. One way to view this energy is to think of the body as hardware, as in a computer, and the mind as the software that is "installed" in the body's hardware, consisting of the beliefs and programming that we have collected throughout life. In a computer, the hardware and software are absolutely useless unless there is electricity running through the system. If there's a power failure, nothing works at all. If the current is not flowing smoothly — if the voltage is too high or too low — the programs will not run correctly, and the hardware itself may even become damaged.

So too with a human being. It is the *life force energy* that forms the interface between mind and body. The body runs that energy through its cells and muscles, and converts it into action. The mind, both consciously and unconsciously, holds the programs that tell the body *how* to channel that energy—when to hold it in, when to let it out, which muscles to move in order to accomplish a task, and how to behave in a given situation. The programs we hold in our minds—such as feeling unworthy, unsafe, or compelled to perform heroically—all run energy through the body in particular ways, creating varying combinations of success, failure, repression or exhaustion. In order to balance the energy economy, we must understand the root of the programs running our lives, and simultaneously retrain the deeper structures within the tissues that have become hardwired for these programs. These deeper structures are the chronic holding patterns of the body armor, bound by the energy used to maintain our defenses.

This life force energy has been described by many disciplines and cultures. In yoga philosophy it is called *prana*; to the Chinese it is *Chi*, the Japanese, *ki*. Wilhelm Reich called it *orgone energy*, and Luke Skywalker of *Star Wars* called it *the force*. I like to simply call it *charge*, as that is something we can all relate to. We feel *charged* when we are excited about something or when we are sexually aroused. We feel a *charge* around certain issues that make us angry or upset. If we are afraid, we notice that our fear has a great deal of *charge* that runs through the body. *Charge* can make us alive and happy, or it can make us tense and anxious—depending on whether that charge flows freely or gets locked up in body armor. If we don't have enough charge, we can feel lethargic, depressed, or hopeless.

> -§-
> The programs we hold in our minds—such as feeling unworthy, unsafe, or compelled to perform heroically—all run energy through the body.
> -§-

Ideally, a person charges and discharges throughout the day in relative balance. We take in energy from around us—whether as nourishment, stimulation, or stress—and we discharge this energy through activity and emotions. Food, breath, touch, conversations, noises, or entertainment generally tend to increase charge. Crying, getting angry, dancing, working out, or just plain working hard all tend to discharge.

Body armor develops through repeated difficulties as a way to maintain an *economy of charge*. As in a bank account, you make both deposits and withdrawals, but try to maintain a balance that allows you a feeling of security—a balance that is higher for some people than for others. In the same way, a given person has a customary level of charge in which they feel most comfortable—too much and they feel anxious, too little and they feel depressed.

Just as someone might freeze their assets when times get tough or uncertain, body armor binds the energy in the musculature of the body to keep the level of charge within an individual's comfort range. It shields the core from adverse energy coming into the system and prevents core energy from moving out of the system. Binding the internal energy creates

79

repression of the life force. Armoring against the outer world creates isolation and depletion. Both can lead to imbalances.

Because of body armor—and the stressful circumstances of the modern environment—human energy systems can become chronically overcharged or undercharged. If someone is typically overcharged, they tend toward stress, hypertension, and organ dysfunction, your typical high-strung, type-A personality. If someone is undercharged, they experience, depression, passivity, fatigue and lowered immune response.

Forging a New Relationship

The beauty of working the mind-body connection is that the therapist can enter the client's inner domain from either the physical or mental end of the spectrum. For instance, during psychotherapy, as a client talks about an important issue, there is inevitably a response in the body of heightened charge: perhaps sweaty palms, fidgeting, tension in the face, or change in the breath. By weaving a thread of awareness between the "issue and the tissues," the body can appropriately soften or discharge. Once the message from the body is received by consciousness, the body is free to quiet its cellular communication and can relax. Old patterns are released and both the body and the consciousness within are more able to enter wholly into the present, rather than remain compromised by the past.

-§-
The beauty of working the mind-body connection is that the therapist can enter the client's inner domain from either the physical or mental end of the spectrum.
-§-

Mind-body healing can also be worked from the physical side of things. A client may be unaware of their psychological "issues," yet have a physical complaint or a symptom, such as a chronic pain or illness. ("Symptom" comes from a Latin root that means "to fall together.") By directing awareness to focus on the *experience* of the symptom, one can often recover awareness of the issue to which it is related. This occurs best through a technique called "focus and exaggerate," in which one pretends to worsen their symptom by taking it to its logical conclusion. This might be exaggerating a contraction or an impulse, such rolling up in a ball on the floor, expressing the need to hit or cry, or overcoming the inhibition to reach out for someone.

Ellen, for example, found that she had long inhibited her inner sensations and impulses due to an intense shame about having discovered at a young age that she was gay. Because she had grown up at a time when there was no support or understanding from her family or her peers for her sexual orientation, she had felt that everything within her was inherently wrong or bad. By the time she came to see me, thirty years later, much of the world had evolved its understanding of gay issues to embrace more tolerance and she had been comfortably out of the closet for some time. In her *conscious* mind, she no longer held a negative view of her sexual orientation, as she had found social environments that accepted and supported her. Yet the habits of repressing her most basic urges so long ago and for so many years had worn a deep groove in her psyche and these habits were still acting upon her body.

As we began to bring attention to the subtlest of impulses in her body, such as the unconscious flitting of her arms, allowing them to be magnified enough to be recognized, we uncovered a deep urge to reach out to others. This urge had been so repressed it had rendered her arms nearly numb and lifeless. As her arms came back to life, her breathing deepened and her initially pale color grew more rosy. As we worked toward drawing forth the repressed communication in her throat from decades of hiding and secrecy, her neck pain dissipated. In her life, she began speaking out for gay rights and in so doing found her creativity in writing. As she continued to reclaim lost parts of herself, she became increasingly more alive.

-§-

When buried unfinished impulses are allowed to complete, the energy caught up in inhibiting these impulses is literally freed from the past and made accessible for the present and future.

-§-

The body doesn't lie. It records everything that happens to us. When awareness is brought to the body's innate wisdom, insights can be direct and profound. When buried unfinished impulses are allowed to complete, the energy caught up in inhibiting these impulses is literally freed from the past and made accessible for the present and future. The heart of this healing lies in the experience, a felt sense of waking up to truths that cannot be denied.

The relationship between one's mind and body is the primary relationship in each of our lives. It is the one that occurs within and precedes all others. Like any relationship, it is ultimately brought into harmony through love. And like any relationship, this love is enhanced through communication, compassion, acceptance, and understanding. Since this relationship is the only one that is guaranteed to last for our entire lives, it is the path underlying wholeness.

Rudolph Ballentine:

Peace Plan for the Gender Wars

avid said he was burnt out. He worked eighty hours a week. Though he worked as a healer, he looked not unlike the average 50-year-old man—red-faced, potbellied—angry enough to stay just this side of depression. A psychic had told him that if he continued the way he was going, in a few years he would have "the opportunity to pass over." That got his attention, and he decided that he'd rather make some sort of change so he could stay on the planet. He still had work he wanted to do.

As I worked with him, homeopathic remedies emerged as good bets, and patterns of relating took shape. He had left his wife because she was crazy (he said). But from my tantric perspective—from the point of view of gender work (as I was beginning to term it)—he was clearly identified with an inner masculine that was at war with his own inner feminine. She was, he seemed to feel, unreliable, not nurturing, and liable to irrational fits of pique. He wanted no part of Her.

From a tantric point of view the feminine includes embodiment. My body is my piece of Gaia—my participation in the living matter of the Earth. But being in a body is a messy business: Smelly fluids and constant neediness—food, water, rest, and, most humiliating of all, touch from others. She (the feminine aspect in each of us) demands all this incessantly, and seems resistant to reason. She refuses to be put off (at least not for long), and is openly scornful of His (our masculine part's) logic and businesslike agenda. David wrote Her off. She was impossible. She was, he confided, insane. Though this was said in reference to his ex-wife, it soon became clear that it applied to most women he knew. And it was, I sur-

Rudy Ballentine, MD, is a psychiatrist and holistic physician. He was president of the Himalayan Institute of Yoga Science and Philosophy for 12 years and authored or co-authored books on nutrition, meditation, breath, yoga and psychotherapy, as well as the recent *Radical Healing: Integrating the World's Great Therapeutic Traditions to Create a New Transformative Medicine* (Three Rivers, 2000). He studied for 20 years with a tantric master and leads cutting edge workshops on tantra, gender, and sexuality. He has four children and lives in New York City. He can be reached through his web site, www.RadicalHealing.com. Photo courtesy of Kai Ehrhardt.

mised, how he saw his own feminine—which he didn't own, but projected on whichever female form came near him.

Though David's mother had, according to his account, been unusually distant and his birth especially difficult, he is, as far as I can tell, only a slight exaggeration of what can be seen in most of us—women as well as men. Inside each of us the relationship between our masculine and feminine selves is tense and troubled. Unfortunately, in an effort to accommodate the institutions and pressures of the world we live in, most of us, women and men, identify predominantly with the sort of workaholic masculine that ruled David.

And, like David, this leads us to neglect our bodies. We treat them as irrational pests that are best ignored. What follows, of course, is a multiplicity of diseases, the details of which we obsess about—while we don't notice our fundamental estrangement from our embodiment.

Medicine, meanwhile, stays busy chasing its tail: contriving endless treatments (many of them toxic and destructive) to address the deterioration of the body, without addressing the roots of its demise—our uneasy relationship to it.

This arrogant disregard of our bodies is one of a number of phenomena that have struck me over the course of practicing holistic medicine for thirty-five years that recall principles I learned during my training in the traditions of yoga and Tantra. Some relate to internal conflict between the masculine and feminine, others to the relationship of healing (both personal and planetary) to the spiritual path.

For example, as I detail in my book *Radical Healing*, all healing might be seen as a process of making more whole. The words *heal*, *whole*, and *health* all come from a common root. When we heal, we reconnect with parts of ourselves that were cut off—repressed, for example. The result of repeated healings, or integrations of lost parts of the self, is the eventual emergence of a more whole being—whole in the sense of more fully conscious. From the perspective of the great spiritual traditions this moves us toward oneness with the universal, the divine. Life on this planet, seen from this angle, is a constant process of healings of this sort, leading us bit by bit toward the full realization of ourselves as cosmic beings. A major roadblock along this path is our reluctance to honor our bodies—a sort of alienation of our goal-oriented busy-ness from the pulsing earthiness of our physicality.

-§-
The result of repeated healings, or integrations of lost parts of the self, is the eventual emergence of a more whole being.
-§-

Tantric teachers view this disconnect as a rift between Shiva and Shakti. The body, with its creative potential, is a manifestation of the feminine principle, Shakti. Consciousness, with its source in the cosmos, is a manifestation of Shiva. Only when Shiva and Shakti come together in mutual love and respect is consciousness brought to the body, and energy and power made available to the mind. Such a happy marriage is not common.

Lewis was a case in point. He had no time for pampering his body. He ate whatever was at hand, and sat at his desk where books and papers were piled precariously all around. Though he was an advanced and dedicated student of Tantric Buddhism, his progress was limited by the breakdowns in his body. While his Lama exemplified radiant health, Lewis tried to emulate him through rigid schedules and long hours of poring over his books. Instead of radiant health, the result was tachycardia, atrial fibrillation, asthma, hypertension, sleep apnea, esophageal reflux, Hashimoto's syndrome, Ménière's disease, degenerative disk disease, partial deafness, and a score of allergies. He was on an even dozen strong pharmaceutical medications, not to mention lists of herbs and supplements.

Most of his symptoms were worse on the left side of his body. "Why does my left side suffer?" he asked. When I explained that the left side is the feminine, that he was neglecting Her, he smiled. When that began to make sense to him, I encouraged him to take time, relax, be with his body and ask it—ask "Her"—what She wants, then give Her (his feminine—in this case Her physical, corporeal aspect) that. "She's going to be hard to convince, She's been put off so much in the past," I warned him.

"And note: you still expected Her to be there to pump your blood, feed your brain, and draw your breath. You may not have had time for Her, but She had better be there, keeping the house, when you decided to show up."

At our next session, Lewis was beginning to see how his relationship to his body was like that of an absent, workaholic husband. "The unnoticed feminine is really pissed," he remarked. She was in a rage, he realized, having reached the point of beginning to "wreck the house!" Suddenly his physical collapse was making sense to him.

Of course, Lewis is not unique. Nor is this problem limited to men. Women suffer similarly, if not as severely. Their masculine reflects the same planetary pattern. And this disconnect with the body reverberates holographically throughout life on the planet—showing up in distorted masculine political and economic forces of competition, and exploitation that similarly ignore, neglect and abuse the body of Gaia.

Bringing the War Home

Lest all this become too abstract, it is wise to ground it in the immediacy of bodily experience. "She" resides, according to tantric teachings, in the left side of the body (and therefore the right brain, we would say today). On the other hand, the left half of my body (and my right brain) is activated when I breathe through my left nostril. This is not merely a quaint folk belief. Research confirms it. But more importantly, it's a palpable, verifiable experience. If I pay close attention, I will discover that I am a different person when my breath flows primarily through the left nostril than the person I am when it flows through the right. "She" comes to life when I breathe through the left nostril, "He" when it's the right.

Unfortunately, we don't often take note of this difference, nor the shift from one to the other (nostril flow switches sides every couple of hours). Our lack of awareness of something so immediate and important is an indication of the degree to which these two aspects of ourselves are not integrated, but function in a sort of schizoid, disconnected fashion.

They need not remain so. If this is a central "linchpin" in personal and planetary illness (and I believe it is), then healing it is of utmost importance. There are clues to how to do this in the traditional teachings of tantric yoga. They focus awareness on this alternating breath, and invite us to look for the point of integration (where both nostrils flow equally). This latter is termed *sushumna* and the confluence that leads to it is associated with the opening of the "third eye," or sixth chakra. The consciousness that then emerges brings a unified perspective—to replace the two separate ones with their continual shifting back and forth.

However, this is not a realm where our mechanistic laws of cause and effect operate neatly. So it's not quite so simple as "making the breath equal in order to open the sixth chakra." That's only more macho arrogance. A more gentle, less forced approach is needed. One might imagine a sort of marriage counseling between the inner Him and the inner Her. If they can cease hostilities and come together in joy, then presto! Their union yields an integrated and more profound awareness: the wisdom associated with the third eye.

A good place to start the process is with a sort of inner dialogue. Allow a time at the beginning of meditation to invite this conversation. Start with the side where the nostril is most open. Let Her (if your left breath is the predominant flow) have Her say. The masculine should just listen. Then He gets a chance to talk.

Don't expect it to be all sweetness and light. If you are typical, your feminine, like Lewis's, may well have been ignored for a long time. And she might not be very happy about that.

In one of my workshops, I led an experiential wedding ceremony between the internal masculine and feminine. A participant came to me at the break. "In a nutshell," he blurted, "She said to me, 'You're talking about marriage and we're not even engaged!!'" I chuckled and suggested we have lunch together to discuss this situation. But by midday, he felt less panicky. "I talked with Katy" (one of the staff members), he explained, "and she said, 'Just send Her flowers.'" "Perfect," I agreed.

It was, in fact, a great first step. The feminine in most of us (men and women) has been taken for granted and abused for many years. A little (or even a lot) of remedial attention is usually in order. But my workshop participant was still not fully into the process. *He* was talking to *Her*. When you do this inner work, it's important that you not identify with either your masculine or your feminine. Because most of us are so tightly gender bound, that's easier said than done. At least it was for me. I had to learn the hard way.

I took part in a seminar in a rural area. My small group decided to do a full moon ritual. We invented this as we went—almost all of the six men were spiritual teachers of some sort. Though we allowed time for each of us to address the moon in our own individual ways during the experience, the common theme was an honoring of the Goddess, and an invitation for Her to be more present in our lives. I was unaware of the power of such a rite until I sat the next day in an open meadow on a hillside nearby for a private meditation. A feminine voice—one with impressive presence and considerable *Shakti*—showed up forcefully in my inner space.

-§-
The feminine in most of us (men and women) has been taken for granted and abused for many years.
-§-

At first I was delighted. We began to talk. But the inner conversation was suddenly interrupted when She asked, "Why do you keep addressing me as 'you'?" "Why wouldn't I?" I asked, surprised. "Because I am *you*," She replied. "Now wait a minute!" I shot back, feeling this was getting uncomfortably out of hand. "I acknowledge you are a part of my inner world, but you are *you*—and I am *me* !" "Wrong," She said calmly and clearly. "I am you." Her voice carried an authority and clarity that mine lacked.

I gradually accepted that She was indeed me. But it was awhile before I realized that "He" was also me—in the same way. Then I was able to put Her and Him on an equal footing as two fundamental components of myself. And that perspective was only possible from a higher vantage point.

In other words, the whole problem got solved when I was bumped up to the "third *I*." That may seem like a shameless pun, but the consciousness that begins to take shape at the sixth chakra—the third eye—really is a third I, since it steps us up from identifying with either our masculine or our feminine selves.

Positioning your awareness at the third eye (or I) is essential if you want to function as an effective mediator for this inner dialogue between the masculine and the feminine. But that day, on the hill in the meadow, I was not thinking of how to teach others to conduct an inner dialogue. I had my hands full trying to make room inside myself for this newly discovered, very outspoken, and clearly powerful woman/goddess.

Certainly there is the soft, nurturing—*yin*, if you will—aspect of the goddess, the Lakshmi or Saraswati. But there is also this other aspect of the feminine that can step forward with frightening power, especially when she's been put off for too long. This is the Kali or Durga face of the Goddess, the *yang* aspect of the feminine, and it is connected in Tantra with power or *Shakti*.

She is forceful. She is, in fact, according to tantric lore, the very personification of *power*. The tantric teachings are quite explicit on this point. Shakti is power. She is the *only* power. The masculine does not, in terms of ability to manifest in the world, possess *any* power whatsoever. All creative energy springs from Her. He can only provide the consciousness that guides this power as it creates form.

It is important to reiterate here that we are not talking about men and women. We are talking about the masculine and the feminine. Both are present in each of us, whatever our anatomy. This is important because in order to access our genuine power, our true creativity, we must have access to our feminine. Unfortunately, as is reflected even in the secret teachings of European alchemy, this is a point that has escaped Western civilization.

And it is Western civilization—along with its institutions and values—that has come to dominate the political and economic landscape of the planet. Its conviction that power is an attribute of the masculine may go a long way toward explaining its arrogant negligence of Gaia, her ecology, and its casual exploitation of most of the feminine aspects of life on Earth. If the Western mind appreciated the feminine as the source of all the power it depended on, surely a more reverent attitude to all Her manifestations would automatically result—as it does in many of the traditional Asian, African or Native American worldviews.

According to tantric thought, it is the creative urge—the spontaneous impulse that emerges from free (not habit bound) life—that powers all manifestations on the earth. This is Shakti. On the level of the physical body, it is a careful tending to the urges and ebullient impulses of embodiment that creates health. A parallel attention to Gaia is needed for the health of the planet.

But because it disdains the feminine (the source of all power), our patriarchal, hypermasculine, Western created world order is actually bereft of power, despite its pretenses to the contrary. However much it may strut and boast, divorced from its own inner Shakti, its yang feminine, it is left *impotent*. Angered by the humiliation of the situation, it resorts to a sort of *pseudo* power: coercion by brute force. It rules by the Viagra of military might. It imposes, seizes. Jealous of the power it lacks, it rapes and pillages the Earth in impotent rage.

Gaia is sick because, like Lewis's body in our earlier story, She has been abused and exploited. She has been forced to provide what a twisted masculine demands for his violent campaigns—campaigns he hopes will reinstate his flagging potency. She is rarely listened to, rarely provided the simplest basics to support Her survival. The collapse of each person's individual health is merely a microcosmic reflection of this planetary malady.

The correction of this, the rediscovery of the undistorted masculine and feminine essences deep within each of us, and the healing of the breach between Her and Him that then becomes possible, brings a powerful healing effect to the planetary field. It begins, in fact, to reshape that field.

Violence and Planetary Healing

Meanwhile, the violence being done to our bodies, to each other, and to the planet, is so ubiquitous as to pass nearly unnoticed. Because it arises from an inner alienation between Him and Her, it is woven into the very fabric of our being. The habitual words we speak, the forms of social interaction we favor, the practices of child rearing we perpetuate, the social institutions we construct, all fail to honor the spontaneity from which spring genuine life and creativity. They are designed instead to subtly coerce, to force conformity, to shame diversity, and to penalize uniqueness.

-§-

The collapse of each person's individual health is merely a microcosmic reflection of this planetary malady.

-§-

As a result they are all suffused with a subtle, pervasive violence. Much of what a mother says to her children, what a teacher requires of her class, what a husband whispers in his wife's ear—if it serves to squelch the expression of the true self—is inherently, if inconspicuously, violent. In our current planetary culture, as in our customary attitudes toward our body and health, violence has been defined into normalcy.

I would like to distinguish between destruction (i.e., deconstruction) and violence. The pure yang feminine—the wildest rampage of Kali—is not violent in the sense that oil-hungry military invasions and child-starving embargoes are. She never destroys out of cruelty, greed, or indifference. The destruction of Kali is in the service of birth. The uterus is ripped apart in order to give life. Tearing apart the old to make way for the new is destructive to the established order, terrifying to the ego, but not violent in the way that the impotent rage of the masculine pseudo power is.

Nor is the masculine in its pure manifestation violent. The penetrating intention of phallic energy is not inherently violent. At His unadulterated best He penetrates with consciousness. He looks deeply into the mysteries and sees far into the nether realms of the inner world. Shiva is often depicted seated in meditation with an erection. It dramatizes His penetrating awareness that can support and guide the power of Shakti through Her process of manifesting. Without this help from Him, Her creative power is liable to scatter and dissipate.

These tantric ideals of how masculine and feminine can function, stand in stark contrast to how we have constructed gender and how we have come to suppress true power and resort to violence in our current world. With the masculine wild from wounds to his fragile ego, caught up in a life-threatening tantrum of global proportions, He cannot offer the searching, penetrating consciousness needed to gently and reverently guide Shakti into the creation of the new forms that a planet gone mad so desperately needs.

Caught up in this planetary morphic field, the hierarchical, patriarchal corporation hauls off cartloads of profits extracted by bleeding dry the body of Gaia and undermining its own survival. The husband beats his wife as her precious Shakti is wasted in emotional retaliation, fear, and struggles for her own and her children's survival. The individual pushes his or her body to do more, deal with more toxic chemicals, digest more devitalized food, work longer hours for the money to buy more useless possessions that must be housed and protected from theft. So the abused, exploited body, like the abused, exploited wife, and the abused exploited planet, begins to collapse. What remains of creative energy, Shakti, dissipates in baffled emotion and an increasingly hopeless battle to merely stay alive. It sinks progressively into immune system failure, cancer, chronic fatigue, and other degenerative diseases.

-§-
In our current planetary culture, as in our customary attitudes toward our body and health, violence has been defined into normalcy.
-§-

Such results of control by force are very different from the spontaneous creations that emerge from the arising of Shakti. Her creations are a natural birthing of new life, pushed into existence from the womb of the Goddess, brought to life with the unerring sense of timing and appropriateness. Anything created in this way will tend to supply or support exactly what is needed by all life forms, i.e., what is needed to ensure an intact, complex (and evolving) network of living beings on the planet.

But Shakti does not always rise unfettered simply because violent suppression of it stops. A long history of violence and fear has yielded a whole host of habitual efforts to shore up our sense of safety and security, and myriad consolations—rote indulgences—unconsciously designed to pacify the soul's hunger for freedom and spontaneity. Long channeled thus, Shakti has been, and still is, drained away.

These addictions keep Shakti in a diminished state—drunk, besotted and lying in the gutter between the first and second chakra (coiled, in some versions), asleep. Until these habits are cut, and she is freed from her enslavement, she will be unable to rise and manifest her radiant beauty.

Jason, a lawyer I was guiding through the application of tantric principles in his life, told me what happened when he tackled such a habit. A brilliant man, he had long used casual sex as a way to "let off steam" — actually to drop the level of energy that he felt. That energy (or Shakti), which we often label "anxiety," had built to a higher level as he worked with Tantra. Now it was getting pretty intense. He knew that if he let it build, it could activate major changes. Up until now, he had found that prospect unsettling enough to avoid. Now, he was getting tired of the predictability of the habit and the energy downshift that it reliably produced. So he decided to apply the tantric technique of *tapas* — in other words to defuse the habit.

When he felt apprehension building and the habitual urge rising, he sat down and relaxed. He smoothed his breathing, watched the impulse to go to his old haunts grow in urgency...and did nothing. The windows were open and the wind blew through his office. "The howling wind helped loosen the knot of energy in my lower body," he observed. "I began to feel really big, expansive, serene — instead of tight and angry..."

Here is where the real masculine comes into play. First its phallic penetrating consciousness must identify, one by one, such crippling habits and choose those which are "ripe" for elimination. Then the gentle patience of a different aspect of the masculine principle — the more yin aspect — must break them. (In her remarkable book, *Uniting Sex, Self, and Spirit*, Genia Pauli Haddon terms this yin aspect of the masculine the "testicular," pointing out that the word comes from the Latin, *testa*, clay pot, that which holds, conserves, protects. Though the anatomy illustrates graphically these capacities, that does not mean they are unavailable to members of the opposite sex.)

This yin masculine, in contrast to the active phallic, does by not doing. It uses a sort of Ghandian passive resistance to simply refuse to be moved by the habit. It thereby conserves the energy that would be drained, allowing it to gather, build and ultimately rise, finding new and more genuinely creative routes of expression. This is the crucial role of tapas.

The tantric peace plan for the gender war stipulates that the phallic no longer be (mis)used in an effort to dominate or to create forcibly. Instead, it is used to bring a penetrating consciousness to bear. This consciousness can identify habitual patterns that drain Shakti, and select those ready to break, so that the yin masculine, through tapas, can effortlessly defuse them. In this way, they are in service to Her, and she can then ascend to show her power of creation. As a result, the body is renewed, recreated. The home is suffused with joy and liveliness. The planet becomes a garden where endless diversity blossoms, and each soul's truest expression is welcomed and cherished.

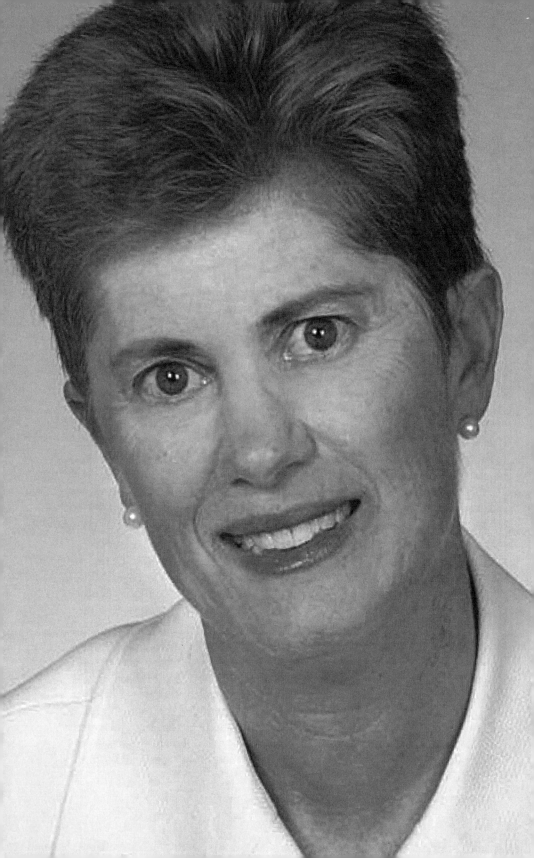

Deborah King:
Prescription: Truth

Sylvia is an accountant and the mother of two small children. At age thirty-nine, she discovered a lump in her breast. Tests revealed that she had breast cancer; it had metastasized to her lungs and bones. Breast surgery was performed and when she came to my office over two years ago, she had just completed a third course of chemotherapy. The chemo had pushed her cancer markers down, but they jumped back up to an all-time high shortly after the treatments stopped. Sylvia felt quite ill and her prognosis was not good. Her emotional state careened between angry rages, feelings of being quite frozen, crying fits, and numbing depression.

Sylvia responded well to our first few sessions. Energy Healing helped her eat and sleep much better, and reduced her fear level. Overall, she felt more stable and better able to manage her emotions. Even her bone pain was less acute. I encouraged Sylvia to nurture her spirit and take time out for herself. I suggested a little reading, recommending books by Deepak Chopra and Carolyn Myss, and urged her to record her thoughts and feelings in a healing journal. Shortly thereafter, she picked up the guitar and began playing for the first time since college.

Then one day, Sylvia confided in me, saying that she had been sexually abused by her father when she was a child. She did not tell anyone about the abuse when it happened, nor had she spoken about it since. "I just stored it away," she said. I encouraged her to tell me what she could remember of what had happened. As she shared her memories and relived the experiences in the safety of my office, I focused on blockages in her

Deborah King, Ph.D., is a former real estate attorney with a doctorate in Healing Science. She practices Energy Medicine, treating clients facing emotional, medical and spiritual issues in her private practice in Santa Barbara, California. She is currently engaged in a long-term study of the efficacy of energy medicine on cancer. Her in-depth study of early life trauma and subsequent disease is the subject of her upcoming book, *Truth Heals*. Deborah lives with her husband and horses on a ranch outside Santa Barbara, California. Her work is featured on her popular website, www.DeborahKingInstitute.com.

energy field, causing them to disperse. I also repaired a tear in her heart chakra and then balanced and recharged it. This change in her field revitalized and nourished her physical body with energy, allowing the physical system to rebalance itself, and in effect, self-heal.

At our next meeting, she said her whole body felt different. She could not remember ever feeling so free and at home in her own skin. Sylvia began another course of chemotherapy and within a month, her cancer markers showed a significant drop. This time, when she finished chemo, the markers stayed low and continued to diminish. We continued to meet regularly, clearing, charging and balancing her field—a technique Energy Medicine practitioners term "chelation." Chelation has many benefits. Among them, it supports the positive side of chemo while ameliorating many unwanted side-effects. Sylvia and I also worked with a number of other energetic modalities during this period and she continued to improve. A year and a half later, follow-up scans showed her cancer in complete remission. Today, Sylvia is cancer-free.

-§-

Whatever I have said about my deeds and words in this trial, I let it stand and wish to reaffirm it. Even if I should see the fire lit, the faggots blazing, and the hangman ready to begin the burning, and even if I were in the pyre, I could not say anything different.
—Joan of Arc, 1431

-§-

Sylvia's story shows how a traumatic experience can be stored in the body like a time bomb, ticking away, eventually setting off a disease process. In cases of sexual abuse, most victims repress the memory and either do not remember the event at all or have only a very hazy recollection of it.

Just over one in three—or thirty-eight percent—of all women in the United States admit to at least one experience of childhood sexual abuse.[1] The National Advisory Board on Child Abuse and Neglect described the situation in child protection as a "national emergency."[2] A UNICEF report in 1997 concluded that violence against women and girls is the most pervasive form of human rights abuse in the world.[3]

Today, in the United States, the subject of incest is no longer hidden from view. Over the past two decades, incest has been brought to our attention by popular films, such as *The Color Purple* and *A Thousand Acres*. The needs of survivors have been discussed in a number of books. *The Courage to Heal* and *The Secret Trauma* are two popular titles. *Capturing the Friedmans*, an important documentary dealing with sexual abuse, was well received when it came out in 2003. In the current climate, we even find celebrities, most notably Oprah Winfrey, openly identifying themselves as victims of sexual abuse. The incest taboo is no longer a hush-hush issue, banished from public discussion. Nonetheless, even today, most cases of incest are never reported. The number of incidents that do get reported belies the true prevalence, representing less than 10% of actual occurrences.[4] Why? Because children instinctively comply with the family demand for silence. Those who do tell rarely speak up until they are much, much older.

In my own life, the sexual abuse I suffered as a child was always very clear in my memory, but only to a specific part of me. I called that part of me "Cindy" and this sub-personality encapsulated and stored all the experiences of incest. Several times a week, for as long as I can remember, I would "talk to" Cindy and she would "tell me" of her experiences. When we were three and four and five, the memories were warm and fuzzy. But Cindy always knew something was not quite right; why else would Daddy make her promise not to tell? At six and seven and eight, when things got out of hand, Cindy was certain it was her fault. Worried that someone might find out, she became a very secretive child. At nine, the situation was far from warm and fuzzy; Cindy was caught up in a cycle of violence, perversion and pain. But she kept everything inside. Cindy's secret had to be set apart, kept separate from the rest of me. This was essential. How else could I love my father so much? An otherwise good and kindly parent, he gave me all his attention and love; he was the center of my universe.

-§-
A traumatic experience can be stored in the body like a time bomb, ticking away, eventually setting off a disease process.
-§-

Before I entered high school, the abuse abruptly stopped. But Cindy persevered, sharing her secret with me as I grew into adulthood, continuing to keep this part of me connected to the rest. Every once in a while, Cindy would periodically "drop in" with her memories. But the violent memories receded, leaving only the warm and fuzzy ones. The older I got, the more distance I put between myself and Cindy—and yet, on a regular basis, I continued to relive those early experiences. I never spoke of this to anyone, not even my husband or therapist. In the back of my mind, I knew what had happened was incest, but it was just too shameful to dwell on.

As a young adult, I wanted to live by the moral code taught by my family and society, but Cindy had other ideas. I was a serious young attorney, intent on furthering my career and being loyal to the husband I loved. But Cindy was promiscuous, and had a tendency to drink too much. Young adulthood found me riding a roller coaster between two extremes in my personality. As time went on, it became more and more difficult to keep myself together. I battled with major depression throughout my twenties. Yet I never considered the split in my personality to have something to do with it. I cited my high-stress career and troubled marriage as the sole cause of my alcoholism and promiscuous escapades—or, should I say, Cindy's.

Chapter Ten

One day, it dawned on me that I had reversed cause and effect. I sought help through Alcoholics Anonymous. It was my first step toward anything spiritual in decades. I removed all addiction from my life and began meditating. I was prepared to clean house, but had no intention of addressing Cindy—those were secrets she and I would take to the grave. And I am fairly sure we would have—had I not developed a life-threatening disease.

In retrospect, my body gave numerous warnings that something was awry. I ignored them all. Later, I learned that the ability to deny pain and other bodily messages is a hallmark of abused children. Then, one day, my symptoms became too severe to ignore, and I sought medical treatment.

-§-
The ability to deny pain and other bodily messages is a hallmark of abused children.
-§-

The doctor took a series of tests and the results were ominous. I took a day off from work and walked around aimlessly, trying to come up with a plan. A sign that read, "massage therapy" caught my eye, and I walked in to the office. As the masseuse began to work on my back and neck, she asked if I was open to energy work. I had never heard the term, but was willing to give it a try. At the end of the session, she said, "You have a lot of safety issues," and I wondered what that meant. We continued to meet twice a week for about six months. In each session, I delved deeper into myself, looking for answers. One day, she gave me a slip of paper with the name of a more advanced healer she believed might be of further help.

I sought out that healer and began having regular sessions. A few months later, while lying on her table one afternoon, all the memories I had stored away in Cindy came rushing back. Behind my closed eyes, my childhood played before me, in vivid Technicolor. But not just the familiar, pleasant memories I relived regularly. All the terrifying, shameful and violent ones resurfaced as well. When the movie was over, I opened my eyes. The healer was standing quietly at my side. When I asked if she too had seen the movie, she simply nodded. I left her office feeling as if I had been in an earthquake. I felt intensely liberated but, at the same time, it was as if the ground beneath me had been swept away. And indeed it had been; like most incest victims, I had been consumed by the predator—we had merged.

From an energetic standpoint, when sexual abuse occurs, the adult often takes over the child's third chakra. If the abuse is ongoing, this can occur to such an extent the child is unable to develop a powerful, central sense of self. The child is unable to distinguish him- or herself from the adult and, later in life, the survivor often has a great deal of trouble establishing boundaries with others. Individuation becomes difficult. In my case, to see evil in my father meant seeing evil in myself, and since that was intolerable, walls of denial were built. I simply *had* to keep my adored father on his pedestal. I could not hold an objective view of him, nor of his behavior.

Pulling down the walls of denial and building my own separate identity took time. I had to develop a dispassionate eye in order to see my father in the clear light of day: as both caring and destructive, both loving and vicious, both strong and very weak. This was liberating, but at the same time quite unsettling. He had been my strength and foundation through the whole of my life. By the time I reached high school, I had effectively eliminated his dark side from my day-to-day awareness.

Reintegrating that aspect of him into full consciousness had enormous benefits. The improvement in my health was immediate and dramatic. I felt the difference within hours of walking out of the healer's office that day. I returned to my doctor, and asked for follow-up tests. The tests came back negative, as I knew they would. Other benefits soon followed: I felt a tremendous sense of freedom for the first time in my life. A host of allergies, weaknesses and special sensitivities began to decline. I had more energy and simply felt more "me" —I was no longer siphoning off an extraordinary amount of energy to keep my big secret.

-§-
Over 50% of patients in psychiatric hospitals and over 40% of patients in private psychotherapy were sexually abused in childhood.
-§-

This amazing physical transformation compelled me to return to school to study Energy Medicine in depth. Ultimately, I jumped ship and left the legal profession, striking out on a new career path. Since then, I have witnessed many remarkable healings of the physical, emotional and spiritual wounds that result from sexual abuse. Over fifty percent of patients in psychiatric hospitals and over forty percent of patients in private psychotherapy were sexually abused in childhood, although many somehow manage without medical or psychiatric assistance.[5] If nothing else, abuse teaches people resilience. But even for those who manage to keep it together and look normal on the surface, the psychological and emotional effects fester like an ugly boil which may not erupt for many years. Research also shows that victims of sexual abuse are far more inclined than the rest of the population to experience depression, mood disorders, substance abuse, troubled relationships and eating disorders.

The link between sexual abuse in childhood and later physical disorders has been established in many studies; survivors complain of multiple symptoms, running the gamut from headaches to gastrointestinal problems to pelvic region disorders to cancer.[6]

Victims of sexual abuse are twice as likely to be abused again. One researcher concluded that "the incest experience itself could have stripped away some of the victim's potential ability to protect themselves.... Men appear to be selecting previously victimized females for further…victimization."[7] In my own experience, this is precisely what happened. A parish priest—who was privy to my father's shameful acts—also sexually molested me.

Also important to recognize when working with survivors of early childhood sexual abuse is a high correlation between traumatic stress disorder and memory disturbances later in life. An example of this occurred when I was in my thirties. My husband and I were mountain climbing enthusiasts and we had just returned from a big climb in the Himalayas. We were climbing in the Sierra Nevada Mountains near Lake Tahoe, an area we considered our own back yard. We were on the first pitch; I was above, belaying him on a rope in case of a fall, when— with no warning—he fell. I could not hold onto him, and, to my horror, I could do nothing but watch as he fell fifty feet to the ground below. Lying at the bottom, he did not move. I feared he was dead. Trying to get the attention of a hiker or climber, I screamed for hours. Fellow climbers finally heard me and we began a long rescue, littering him out over steep, rocky terrain to a waiting helicopter.

By the time he was released from the hospital one month later, I could not recall a single detail of the accident. Meanwhile, I displayed all the symptoms of traumatic stress disorder: loss of appetite, insomnia, phobic reactions (I became very afraid while driving) and frequent anxiety attacks that left me unable to speak. During my husband's extended recovery, I became the sole breadwinner in the family. With stubborn determination, I muddled through, holding on to my sanity by a grim and meager thread. But my body betrayed me, manifesting the overload of stress in the form of one physical disorder after another.

Studies demonstrate that patients "began to get better when the source of their trouble was finally recognized."[8] We see this over and over in clinical practice. A particular case in point was that of Carrie, a twenty-eight-year-old history teacher. Divorced with no children, Carrie began to have "female" problems in her late teens. At twenty-five, she was diagnosed with uterine cancer and had a hysterectomy. The surgeon decided it best to remove her ovaries as well, for good measure. But from Carrie's perspective the doctors had not been able to cut "it" out. She continued to complain of pain in her pelvic area. A number of other problems nagged at her, including an eating disorder that would not quit. She was always very quiet during our sessions. One day, she suddenly started to speak with the voice of a little girl. She spoke about her uncle, who had terrorized her sexually when she was a child. After her truth burst out, Carrie's pain disappeared, never to reappear. Like many survivors, once she broke her silence, Carrie felt compelled to confront her perpetrator. This brought about a remarkable change in her sense of self. For the first time she could remember, she did not feel weak and powerless. Her eating disorder gradually improved. Today, she is happier than ever before.

In some cases, unfortunately, having memory of the events is not enough for healing to occur. Suzanne had full memory of the abuse she sustained at the hands of her mother. (According to statistics, sexual abuse perpetrated by women accounts for less than ten percent of all abuse.) When Suzanne came to me, she was desperate to find help for an inoperable brain tumor. I explained to her that the rage she held toward her mother was literally killing her. I suggested she develop the dispassionate eye that allows understanding from a larger perspective in order to begin the process of forgiveness and healing. At first, she was eager to change. In our sessions, she had the safety needed to express and release her anger and fear. She began a yoga practice and joined a therapy group for sexual abuse survivors. Her scans improved dramatically—the tumor began to shrink. But after six months, she phoned me to say she just couldn't forgive her mother for what she had done. She abruptly ceased her treatments and quit attending her therapy group. Less than a year later, she died.

-§-
Surgery can fail to resolve a problem if the dynamics that caused the problem in the first place are not also changed.
-§-

Even surgery can fail to resolve a problem if the dynamics that caused the problem in the first place are not also changed. One client, Molly, is a case in point. Molly was only seventeen when she came to see me. Her mother made the appointment. Six months before, Molly had gone under the knife to have her cancerous thyroid removed. After surgery, she underwent radiation therapy. But another cancerous tumor had been discovered in her throat, and a second surgery scheduled.

We met twice a week for over a year. During these sessions, I combined chelation with other healing techniques. At the same time, Molly began an intense nutritional protocol, which I recommend to all my clients to support their healing.

Molly's parents had divorced some years before. Her mother was loving but very strict. Molly was not allowed to date. I insisted that her mother receive counseling, as she was consumed with guilt about Molly's medical condition. As my work with Molly progressed, I gently insisted that Molly speak her feelings. She began to drop oblique hints about abuse. Her mother had established a code of silence, cutting Molly's self-expression off at the throat (fifth chakra). Having others, especially her mother, speak for her, was all Molly knew.

The key to Molly's recovery came when she finally gave herself permission to say that her father had sexually abused her. When she found her voice, she could not keep the family secret any longer. Speaking her truth reversed the family's silence about more than incest. It countered the family dynamic that disallowed independent thinking. With each word, Molly released the stifling pressure weighing on her throat.

Gradually, the entire family changed. Molly was able to be herself; open, aware and present. She could finally be who she really was—with herself first, then with her mother, and, finally, with the rest of her family. Eventually, mother and daughter were able to speak about the horrible events. A great renewal occurred between them, along with the emergence of trust and closeness. Both were relieved of the pressure of guilt—Molly's mother for leaving her daughter with her husband while she worked, and Molly of blaming herself for being too "seductive" at the age of eight.

After the second surgery, Molly again had radiation therapy and her doctors gave her a good prognosis. From an energy perspective, her throat chakra has now become open and vital and the energies of malignancy and cancer are absent from her energy field.

Sexual abuse is like an iceberg: we only see the very tip of the problem. Professionals in many fields—sociology, anthropology, psychology and psychiatry—have various theories about the cultural beliefs and practices that allow incest to occur. My personal experience—and the work I have done with clients—has led me to develop my own theory: one of compelling cellular memory, deeply imbued in mass consciousness. Perpetrators of sexual abuse have a myriad of motivations for their acts. In general, they report feelings of frustration and powerlessness, which lead to the need to exert power over someone less powerful. The child is abused and promptly represses the event. When that child grows into adulthood and either has children or comes in contact with children, the distant memory of those experiences comes to the surface. Often, the adult will be drawn to sexual experimentation with a child without having any conscious memory of his or her own early experience. Abusers often feel tremendous shame when they act on their feelings, knowing that what they are doing is wrong. The compulsion to indulge their fantasy can be overwhelming. Where the drive comes from, they know not.

During an energy session, the practitioner is often able to discern the ancestral history of the client and even the components of their DNA. Claudia's experiences are a good example of this phenomenon. She'd had a grade four breast tumor surgically removed. But the cancer recurred, metastasizing to her lungs and liver. Her oncologist told her she had six months to live. Dim memories of abuse at the hands of her father came to the fore during one of our sessions. Over a period of months, Claudia worked through her horror and rage and was able to forgive.

She elected to sit down with both of her parents and talk about the abuse. While her mother was very defensive and denied knowledge of the abuse, her father was honest—he admitted what he had done and expressed deep regret. He told Claudia about his own experiences of abuse as a child at the hands of both his father and his uncle before he emigrated from Sweden. This stirred up the entire family, and stories of abuse going back several generations were dragged out of the family closet and aired. The effect was to cleanse the entire family tree. Claudia's oncologist is encouraged by her declining cancer markers; her prognosis, while still guarded, has improved. When either a perpetrator or a victim of abuse brings forward the memory of the event for healing, the healing extends backward and forward in time, affecting the entire family tree.

Only total openness among family members can begin the healing of this sickness. Secrecy is a hallmark of abuse. The abuser either threatens or cajoles his victim into secrecy, frightening the child into believing that "telling" will cause the loss of one or both parents. It is not uncommon for a child to be told that he or she "will die if you tell." Mothers almost always deny knowledge of abuse by fathers. Mothers don't know how to deal with the situation, and sometimes choose to see no evil, despite deep inner misgivings. They then prolong the abuse and the secrecy surrounding it. None of the family members can heal, nor can ancestral patterns of abuse heal, so long as secrecy is maintained.

-§-

None of the family members can heal, nor can ancestral patterns of abuse heal, so long as secrecy is maintained.
-§-

For the most part, what a survivor wants is not vengeance, but simple recognition on the part of the perpetrator and complicit family members. Once the abuse has been acknowledged and recognized as a wrong no one wants to see recur, healing begins. But even without admission and forgiveness, the mere fact of bringing the abuse to the surface of one's own consciousness begins the healing of the ancestral pattern. At a deep level, we love our families, flaws and all; they are extensions of ourselves. We can never know ourselves truly until we can look at every moment of our own lives dispassionately. We are all a combination of good and evil, light and dark. As long as we live in a world of duality, we will continue to have the specter of sexual abuse. By looking honestly at our experience — the good and the evil we have suffered and inflicted — we can find the unifying principle that supersedes all. Only then can we live our lives from a place of wisdom, knowledge and truth. In the words of the great mystic poet, Jellaludin Rumi: "No matter how fast you run, your shadow more than keeps up. Only full overhead sun diminishes your shadow. But that shadow has been serving you. What hurts you, blesses you. Darkness is your candle. Your boundaries are your quest."

DEBORAH ANAPOL:

The Marriage of Sex and Health

S exual healing means many things to many people. For me, it's important to place it in the context of a multilevel process that encompasses mind, body, emotions, sex, and spirit. Sexual healing includes an individual's relationships with the different parts of oneself, with others, and with all of creation. It's one element of a whole systems approach that recognizes that treating an isolated symptom or problem is only partially effective at best and can actually be harmful. Instead, I consider the complete individual along with his or her family, community, and society. A holistic approach is especially relevant when dealing with sexuality in order to counteract our culture's tendency to split off sex from the rest of life.

Health is the natural outcome of fully allowing and integrating every aspect of self and opening to an experience of unity with others and with the Divine. Sexuality has the potential to put us in direct contact with our innermost core and thus can open us up to connection with all centers everywhere in the universe. Because Life relies upon our sexual energy to ensure reproduction, it's an extremely powerful force. It's also an area where many people experience conflict. So while I have a holistic orientation, I've come to focus my attention on sexual healing.

Until very recently, the concept of integrating the erotic into healing has been unthinkable. Yet in ancient times, healer/priestesses and priests attended births and deaths, presided over temples, and utilized erotic ritual as a tool for serving their people. One of the oldest surviving literary works, *The Epic of Gilgamesh,* tells the story of one such

Deborah Taj Anapol, Ph.D., has been working with groups and individuals exploring sexual healing, the union of sex and spirit, and conscious relationship for over two decades. She is based in San Rafael, California. She is an inspiring and controversial speaker who teaches worldwide. She is recognized as one of the foremost thinkers and writers on the subject of polyamory, and is the author of *Polyamory: The New Love Without Limits* (Intinet, 1997). She is currently at work on a book about harmonizing feminine and masculine energies. Information: www.lovewithoutlimits.com or phone (415) 507-1739. Photo courtesy of Morgan J. Cowin.

qadesha (literally *Holy One* but often translated *Sacred Prostitute*) charged with the transformation of the savage Enkidu, key to King Gilgamesh's quest for immortality.

In modern times, the splitting off of sex and spirit, not to mention body and mind, has led to a situation in which realistic fears of exploitation and manipulation have mandated a separation between sex and healing. As a result, licensing requirements for every profession, without exception, prohibit sexual contact with clients. In this climate, any use at all of erotic energy in healing is highly suspect. While sexual healing need not incorporate genital touch, this aspect of sexual healing is certainly the most controversial. Ironically, among those who can benefit most from hands-on intervention are the victims of childhood sexual abuse.

With researchers estimating that three or four out of every ten girls and one out of every seven or eight boys are sexually molested as children, it's not surprising that so many adults have sexual difficulties. Because of the shame, guilt, and secrecy associated with child-adult sexual contact, the elusive nature of pre-verbal memories, and the body-mind's tendency to repress traumatic incidents that overwhelm available resources for coping, it is common for adults who have been sexually exploited as children to find themselves fearful or anxious about sex without knowing the source of their difficulties. Instead they may report that they have difficulty staying present during sexual encounters, that they have little interest in sex, or that they are obsessed with it. They may feel numb "down there" or they may have difficulty reaching orgasm.

For example, one client I worked with intensively, was an attractive, healthy, successful man in his late forties who feared he'd never be able to create a satisfying intimate relationship. Matthew had been physically abused by his father throughout his childhood. Vague memories of sexual abuse by several male relatives, combined with experiences with partners who'd secretly had affairs, left him distrustful of both men and women, and insecure about his ability to perform sexually. Matthew reported that while he was able to become aroused once he'd developed some intimacy with a woman, he would suddenly go numb during sexual play. Feeling nothing, he would focus on satisfying the woman, but be unable to orgasm himself. Frustrated, he'd long ago shut down his sexuality entirely and immersed himself in his work.

Before consulting me, Matthew had been through many years of both group and individual therapies and had worked through much of the rage and fear generated by his early experiences. But he still carried tremendous sexual guilt and shame, along with confusion about his lack of sexual feeling and felt hopeless about overcoming it.

Unlike many men who confuse their need for nurturing with a need for sex, Matthew was well aware that what he needed most was loving physical contact without any expectation that he perform sexually. When I provided this, along with reassurance that having a connection between his heart and his genitals was a good thing, he eventually began feeling turned on. As I probed the meridians and the muscles where sexual tension is typically held, he deepened his breath and became aroused, but would then suddenly go numb and find himself dissociating. After assuring him that I did not find vulnerability and emotional expression unmanly, I encouraged him to pay attention to what he was feeling and thinking just before the numbness set in as I continued to explore his groin, buttocks, perineum, thighs, and lower belly. I also directed him to allow any memories or emotional reactions to surface and be expressed while continuing to stay erotically engaged. This was a completely new concept for Matthew, but he followed my instructions. Soon he realized that feelings of disgust and terror preceded the numbness and when he focused on these feelings, vivid flashbacks of early sexual coercion flooded

> -§-
> Chinese medicine, based on ancient Taoist teachings, has long prescribed different lovemaking positions for the treatment of specific ailments.
> -§-

him. I supported him to stay fully in his body as these feelings and memories surfaced, and encouraged him to express and release the held energy. He was amazed to find intense sensations replacing his numbness.

The Need for Hands-On Sexual Healing

The rationale for prohibiting sexual contact between client and therapist has been to prevent the therapist from taking advantage of the client's vulnerability and trust to satisfy the therapist's personal desires. While this type of abuse of power has been all too frequent in the past, attempts to deny clients access to potent and perhaps necessary treatment options are not always in the best interest of the client and limit the possibilities for effective healing. These taboos may actually increase the likelihood of damaging, misguided, or self-serving interventions because practitioners who lack relevant training in ethics and appropriate methods may find themselves venturing into these realms anyway.

After offering a training in sexual healing, I began hearing regularly from healing professionals, especially those who work directly with the body—energy workers, acupuncturists, chiropractors, massage therapists, nurses, and bodyworkers of all kinds. These healers can no longer deny that sometimes the bodies they are working on are screaming for help with the movement and integration of sexual energies. They are eager, sometimes desperate, for instruction in both techniques and ethical guidelines for responsibly addressing these situations.

For example, I received the following e-mail from a man who was cautiously investigating the relevance of sexual healing in his practice:

"My work is centered around balancing the body's energy field by unblocking and opening up the chakras. The results continue to be profound, even providing a way for one client to overcome cancer. Among my female clients, there has been severe wounding in the first and second chakras at the hands of men. My coaching to them is to bring this energy up to the heart chakra for forgiveness and release. From your experience, do you think working directly with the first and second chakras [located corresponding to the perineum and sexual organs] might be a significant aid in my work? Do you think people are ready for internal work at this time? Can you tell me how this work is performed? We are dealing with some very powerful emotions here, so what precautions are put into place for everyone's protection?

"I have already committed my life to the healing work, and I am quite effective with it. Although I do admit some apprehension regarding the internal work (*meaning inside the pelvis*) if I am guided to do this, I will follow that guidance. Thank you so much for considering and responding to my questions."

This individual subsequently participated in a training. My impression of an ethical, mature, and sincere practitioner was confirmed by his behavior and comments during the training. While some people who are drawn to sexual healing fail to grasp the importance of healthy boundaries and self-knowledge, this man clearly understood the sensitive nature of this work. There are many more like him.

The exclusion of sexual energy from healing may seem necessary, reasonable, right, and good because it is so basic to our culture's beliefs about healing. But this has not always been so and is an assumption many free thinkers are beginning to question. Given the basic identity of the life force energy and sexual energy, one might conclude that trying to restore health when it is forbidden to utilize the sexual energy of either the patient or the health care practitioner is inefficient at best and foolhardy at worst.

Precedents exist. For example, Chinese medicine, based on ancient Taoist teachings, has long prescribed different lovemaking positions for the treatment of specific ailments. In the Victorian era physicians treated women suffering from "hysteria" as a result of sexual frustration with specially designed vibrators. The separation between sex and healing has been gradually breaking down since the sixties. Contributing factors are: the renaissance of midwifery and more natural birthing procedures, the introduction of sex therapy by Masters & Johnson, the growing acceptance of sex surrogates in clinical practice, and the surge of interest in Taoist and Tantric sexuality. However, as a healer on the cutting edge of this transformation I'm well aware we have a long way to go!

Nevertheless, having seen the evolution of massage from its association with tacky massage parlors to a respected therapeutic medium utilized in hospitals, health spas, and doctor's offices, I am optimistic about the future of sexual healing.

The Sexual and the Erotic

While I have been using the words "erotic" and "sexual" interchangeably thus far, it would be useful to get more specific about what each implies. Sexual could be considered to refer specifically to the genitals, whereas eros indicates erotic love, or a fusion of heart and genitals. Further, eros suggests a way of being which encompasses union, or longing for union, with all of life. The erotic includes the sexual, but is neither defined by, nor limited by the sex organs. The urge to merge can take many forms. Thus love of nature, or the cosmos, or the Divine, may be suffused with erotic energy and accompanied by sexual arousal, but have nothing to do with direct genital stimulation. Indigenous cultures throughout the world share this erotic appreciation of nature, as do poets as diverse as Walt Whitman and Rumi.

In his book, *The Love Cure: Therapy Erotic and Sexual* (Spring, 1996), John Ryan Haule boldly argues that while sexual interaction is rarely an appropriate part of therapy, good therapy is necessarily erotic. Haule is quite unique among Western psychotherapists, in daring to assert that "We need to know if there is, in fact, anything in the nature of therapy, as the structuring and unfolding of a self, that excludes all forms of sexual involvement." (p. 124) His book is an illuminating and provocative exploration of this issue.

Haule makes the distinction that "the erotic refers to the energy of an interpersonal field when a sense of we-ness comes forcefully to presence and that the sexual involves an impulse to embody that we-ness in a genital manner." (p. 55) He traces the confusion between sex and eros to the ancient Greeks: "To some degree, whenever we speak of 'the erotic,' we refer to Eros. But even the Greeks did not name the same psychic force every time they invoked the god. In the earliest texts he is the Son of Chaos and represents the attractive force behind friendships, marriages, and the creation of cities. Later he is the Son of Aphrodite and embodies lust." (p. 22)

Interestingly, the Hindu god Kama, who is clearly related to the Greek Eros, exudes chaos and lust simultaneously. He comes from a culture with a tradition of transcending of dualistic thought and whose religious icons symbolize the union of sex and spirit.

Haule makes an excellent case for the efficacy of consciously including erotic energy (in other words, empathy, compassion, and attraction) into the relationship between any type of healer and patient. He even puts forth very specific guidelines which could be used to determine whether sexual contact would enhance the efficacy of the treatment. As radical as this might be, it is quite another matter to consider beginning a healing relationship in which both healer and client agree that sexual contact of some type will be part of the treatment. This last possibility is still so radical that to the best of my knowledge there are no published guidelines for when it might be appropriate.

However, pioneering sex educator, Dr. Joseph Kramer, of the Institute for the Advanced Study of Human Sexuality, is now offering an academically accredited graduate course in sexological bodywork which is also a professional/vocational course certified by the state of California. This is the first time in the US that a government body has put its seal of approval on a course that uses sexual arousal as a healing modality, according to personal communications I have received from Dr. Kramer.

My Own Path

Sexual healing emerged as my path over thirty years ago, long before I fully understood all of the implications of such a groundbreaking concept. As an undergraduate at the University of California, Berkeley, in the early 1970s I participated in a new interdisciplinary program called Theme House in Community Health, which led to my doing an internship at a community run clinic known as the Berkeley Women's Health Collective (BWHC). I soon became involved with a BWHC educational project known as Women's Self Help. Who knew that twenty years later, former porn star and sex educator Annie Sprinkle would turn our format into performance art!

-§-
Breaking the taboos against telling the truth about our fears and most intimate experiences, as well as sharing information about what works and what doesn't, are most powerful tools for healing.
-§-

The Women's Self Help classes we offered included information about women's reproductive systems, fertility, birth control, and sexually transmitted diseases but the most dramatic aspect consisted of group instruction and practice in the use of a speculum, flashlight, and mirror to examine the cervix (entrance to the womb) as well as the vulva (outer genitals). I've never forgotten the looks of wonder and awe on these women's faces as their hidden parts were revealed and they were able to view the mysterious entrance to the womb for the first time. I was so impressed by the power of this simple, innovative strategy to free women from shame, embarrassment, and confusion about their sexuality that I undertook a research project to see if these classes positively affected general body image and self-esteem. They did! As I look back I see that this lesson went deep. Hands-on experiences and peer group support are very potent tools for sexual healing and central to my teaching to this day.

A year later, as a clinical psychology graduate student working at the University of Washington Psychology Clinic I learned about other innovations in sexual healing—Masters & Johnson's sex therapy, and the use of sexual surrogates. Masters & Johnson, the originators of clinical sex therapy had pioneered the use of non-professional surrogate partners for single clients who needed coaching in intimacy skills as well as overcoming specific sexual problems. While the clinic did not use surrogates, a student a few years ahead of me in the program had worked as a surrogate before entering graduate school and was excited about the effectiveness of hands-on treatment for sexual dysfunction.

My very first clients showed me the limitations of the Masters & Johnson approach. A couple came in with the complaint that the man had difficulty reaching orgasm. We knew that this was a much more common difficulty for women, and our supervisor was enthusiastic about this unusual case. We immediately began treating the symptom without much attention to their whole situation. His retarded ejaculation did indeed improve but we gradually learned of a much more serious problem—he was fantasizing about interacting sexually with his partner's seven-year-old daughter.

Around this same time I had a series of very profound erotic encounters with men I was close to which greatly expanded my ideas of what sex was all about. While it would be many more years before I was introduced to the concept of hands-on sexual healing, I began to realize that lovemaking could be a means of deep emotional release, altering consciousness and accessing a state of cosmic consciousness. Then, after reliving a traumatic abortion during an isolation tank session, I discovered that disturbing incidents left an imprint, or body memory, which could be released by consciously feeling the sensations the ego wanted to avoid.

What Is Sexual Healing?

Over the last thirty years I have evolved an understanding of sexual healing that encompasses three broad, interrelated categories of work.

1) Releasing genital armoring and regaining your capacity for pleasure.

Almost everyone who's come of age in our sex-negative culture has acquired at least some genital armoring. Genital armoring initially occurs when children are shamed or discouraged from touching their genitals, enjoying their bodies through masturbation and engaging in natural exploration with peers. It can also result from invasive medical interventions (e.g. abortion, hysterectomy, circumcision, or cesarean delivery) insensitive or unskilled partners, rough handling, overuse of vibrators, emotional trauma, and from unfulfilling lovemaking. The most dramatic and severe genital armoring is often a result of rape or childhood sexual abuse but ordinary people with no personal history of abuse can easily acquire enough armoring to drastically limit their sexual pleasure simply by being exposed to society's typical anti-sex messages.

The concept of genital armoring is derived from Wilhelm Reich's theory of body armoring. Reich believed that the muscular tissue of the body responds to emotional as well as physical trauma by tensing up in a protective reflex. Over time, these tissues become chronically stiff and hard, blocking sensation and energy flow in the affected area. Armoring is an instinctive protective device whose purpose is to defend against experiencing physical or emotional pain. It is the bodily equivalent of psychological defense mechanisms such as denial, projection, or repression. It is mediated by constricting the breath and by muscular contraction, both of which reduce our capacity to experience pleasurable feelings and ultimately lead to disease.

-§-
Almost everyone who's come of age in our sex-negative culture has acquired at least some genital armoring.
-§-

When body armoring occurs in the sex organs we call it genital armoring. Genital armoring in women can show up as decreased arousal, decreased clitoral or vaginal sensitivity, insufficient lubrication, hypersensitivity, absence of pleasurable sensation during intercourse, vaginismus, or painful intercourse.

In men, armoring can cause the penis to become insensitive, resulting in a need for intense stimulation in order to maintain an erection or reach orgasm. Conversely, armoring can create oversensitivity, premature ejaculation, retarded ejaculation, or a discomfort with being gently stroked. Armoring in men also manifests itself in the form of chronic tension in the anal sphincter muscles, involuntary erections, an attitude of sexual greed and the need for repeated genital stimulation. Men frequently have a lot of armoring in the heart area, as well. These last phenomena are common in women as well.

2) Utilizing sexual energy to revitalize, rejuvenate, and heal the body.

Leading edge health care practitioners and researchers are discovering what Taoist masters, Tantric adepts, and shamanic healers have known for centuries: Sex is not only pleasurable, it is good for you! Sexual arousal activates the endocrine system, which in turn contributes to cardiovascular health, enhances the immune system, elevates mood, and slows the aging process. Good sex can also improve your appearance, reduce stress, relieve pain, burn calories, and regulate the menstrual cycle. The basic concept involved in this aspect of sexual healing is that sickness and health are not the responsibility of medical experts; they come from within. By tapping into the innate wisdom and healing ability of the body via the breath and our sexual response, we create our own well-being.

The ancient Taoists understood that health results from raising and balancing the energy or life force within the body. Energy loss or blockage results in disease, aging, and ultimately death. Generating higher levels of sexual energy provides a means of clearing blocked pathways and directing more energy wherever it is needed for healing. In other words, sexual energy, life force, and healing energy all come from the same source and can be transmuted into one another. The Taoists determined that while sexual arousal can increase energy, excessive ejaculation depletes energy in men, as does excessive menstrual flow in women. Sexual healing

-§-
Sexual arousal con-
tributes to cardiovas-
cular health,
enhances the
immune system, ele-
vates mood, and
slows the aging
process.
-§-

thus encompasses teaching men how to orgasm without ejaculating, thus allowing them to prolong intercourse, be less goal-oriented and self absorbed, and fully satisfy a woman. Leisurely, unhurried lovemaking not only energizes the body, but also contributes to happier, loving interactions between partners.

3) Sexual healing is also about ending the war between men and women and learning to use our sexual energy effectively to nurture each other and experience a sense of unity with all of life.

The wound between men and women runs deep in our collective consciousness and often seems rooted in the very cells of our bodies. Men and women often find themselves polarized into opposing positions especially when it comes to sex, emotional expression, communication, and matters of the heart. The core of these differences is sometimes expressed as "men want hot sex and women want romantic love," when the truth is that both men and women long for satisfying sex and sustainable love. "Sleeping with the enemy" leads to conflicts and power struggles.

For many generations, men and women have been socialized differently and shamed or punished for exhibiting traits deemed inappropriate for their gender. By socializing women to repress their sexual desires and men their emotions, we have created a situation in which people often find it difficult to meet their needs for nurturing and erotic satisfaction.

Ancient traditions which honor the sacred union of male and female and recognize the importance of balancing the masculine and feminine elements within each of us, as well as in the external world, offer us a model for healing. Since our present culture has tended to elevate the masculine over the feminine, most people approach sex and relationship from a male point of view. We seek to balance this by learning to honor the deep feminine in a way that is not merely a reaction to or mirror image of patriarchal customs, but comes from an entirely different way of being.

The feminine inside of us wants the masculine, and the masculine wants the feminine. This is equally true for both men and women. When we create harmony between the man and woman inside of us, we attract harmony in our relationships. The same goes for conflict.

Getting masculine and feminine together can be tricky or it can be ecstatic—a joyful grand adventure. Most of us fail to recognize that this completion, this union of masculine and feminine energies happens inside of us, as well as outside. This incessant energy, this hot stream inside of us, is a force that's taking us somewhere. If we learn to surf it, we can enjoy the ride. If we struggle against it, we experience frustration and despair.

In the most basic sense, the flow of energy between the heart and the pelvis defines the masculine and the feminine. The masculine flow is in through the heart, out through the genitals. It's the exhale part of the breath. The feminine flow is in through the genitals, out through the heart. It's the inhale part of the breath. When we succeed in getting the polar opposites together—the masculine and the feminine—we feel great. When we can't, our hearts are cut in two. In sexual healing, as in any type of healing, the most potent ingredient is love.

A Vision for the Future

In our culture, the belief that children should be discouraged or punished for sexual curiosity, and that they should be protected at all costs from any exposure to sexual activity, is a strong one. Yet, three separate sources of information, suggest that this belief greatly contributes to our sexual wounding.

> -§-
> When we succeed in getting the polar opposites together— the masculine and the feminine—we feel great. When we can't, our hearts are cut in two.
> -§-

First, extensive research on the "Family Bed" demonstrates that infants and young children who sleep with their parents enjoy a variety of positive outcomes later in life, including greater comfort with their sexual identity, greater satisfaction with life, higher self-esteem, more comfort with affection, less guilt and anxiety, and more frequent sex.

Second, after working with thousands of people in several countries, that the majority of people attending sexual healing workshops have a deep, unsatisfied longing to see and feel their parents expressing physical affection and erotic desire.

Finally, while it would be naïve to assume that we can create a future that is a replica of indigenous, pre-patriarchal cultures, all indicators suggest that in societies where people lived in greater harmony with nature and with their natural bodily functions, sexual health was the norm. We can glean a few ideas from cultures like that of the ancient Hawaiians.

According to my library research, in old Hawaii, a boy infant was prepared for the future enjoyment of intercourse by gently blowing into his foreskin each morning.[1] Most likely, this treatment provided a secondary benefit of keeping the head of the penis clean and free of adhesions, which are often the rationale for infant circumcision (a common source of genital armoring). Later, when he entered middle childhood, he might be taken to a special temple or *heiau* for a ceremony in which the foreskin was slit (not removed as in circumcision) to allow it to slip back more easily during arousal. The priest and priestess might then suck the penis before applying healing herbs to the wound.[2]

A girl child would have mother's milk squirted into her vagina and the labia pressed together.[3] Again, this practice might well have hygienic benefits, as well, due to the immune enhancing properties of breast milk. Her *mons veneris* would be rubbed regularly with kukui nut oil to encourage attractively rounded curves and to bring out her passionate nature.[4] When both boys and girls entered puberty, they would be sent to the *heiau* or temple for an ancient rite of passage to help them adjust to the joining of Heaven and Earth in their bodies. This work included a special form of massage which continued day and night until their sexual, spiritual and creative energies were fully integrated.[5]

-§-
In sexual healing, as in any type of healing, the most potent ingredient is love.
-§-

These practices may seem strange, or even abusive, to those of us who've been raised in a sex-negative culture where parents believe it's their duty to discourage every vestige of their children's sexuality. But from the viewpoint of a sex-positive culture that values and honors the sexuality of both genders, Western customs of ignoring or even punishing children's sexual exploration might be considered neglectful and barbaric.

In contrast, the old Hawaiian practices of blessing and perfecting of the infant's genitals acknowledged the sacredness of procreation. The genitals of the firstborn child, whether male or female, were considered especially significant, a link between past and future generations.

As we consider the swing of the pendulum from ancient cultures who venerated sexual union as the source of life, as well as the symbolic representation of harmonizing masculine and feminine principles, to recent extremes of sexual shame, repression, abuse, and exploitation, it's clear that we must discover a middle way. I view incidents like this as hopeful signs that sexual healing is well underway. Perhaps our children—and our children's children—will come to experience sex as the simple, natural, and joyful gift that it is.

PART THREE

The Absence of Disease v. Vibrant Health

PAUL PEARSALL:
The Beethoven Factor

Fifteen years ago, they had to bring me back to life. An opportunistic virus had taken advantage of my immune system—left defenseless by the poison of several series's of what they called "scorch the earth" chemotherapy. Whole-body radiation had left me with loose skin hanging over protruding bones, and so weak I could barely swallow, or lift my arms. I had lost control of my bowels and, struggle as I might, I could not draw enough oxygen into my lungs to stay conscious. Stage IV lymphoma had sent millions of carnivorous cells to feast on my body, and a soccer-ball sized tumor in my pelvis left me crippled and howling in pain. I never recovered from my cancer.

If you're wondering how someone who died could be writing these words fifteen years after his death, it is because I am not a cancer survivor. Instead, I'm a cancer thrivor. By a mysterious blend of smart doctoring and nursing, a bone marrow transplant, wonder drugs, a loving family, prayer, genetic reserve, random good luck, and the influence of my ability to consciously choose to make my crisis into a catalyst for a change of consciousness, I did much more than recover. I learned that there is an immense amount of cosmic joy to be discovered amidst the chaos of life's local pain.

Like anyone willing to tap into it, my "thrive-ability" is due to my stress-awakened capacity for savoring every moment of my living far beyond what I might have imagined before my "death." I will never again miss the opportunity to drink deeply from the ocean of oxygen in which I had nearly drowned. I relish every chance I get to enjoy a full, slow inhalation, and lingering exhalation. I can smell and taste the air I've been

Paul Pearsall, Ph.D., is a licensed clinical neuropsychologist. A former chief of the positive psychology clinic at Sinai Hospital of Detroit, he is now a clinical professor at the University of Hawaii and on the board of the State of Hawaii Consortium for Integrative Health Care. He recently received the Scripps Medical Center "Trail Blazer in Medicine" award. He has authored over 200 journal articles and 15 best-selling books. His most recent book—*The Beethoven Factor: The New Positive Psychology of Hardiness, Happiness, Healing and Hope* (Hampton Roads, 2002)—studies people who have thrived through crises.

allowed to breathe again as if it is sweet nectar. Remembering the dimness of my suffocation, I relish every opportunity to gaze lovingly upon the faces of my family as if each glance could be my last. I am much more interested now in savoring my life than saving it.

I caution those who have made themselves too busy and distracted to marvel at, luxuriate in, and relish the moments of their living. They are wasting the time of their lives. I warn them that they may be languishing through their lives by leading hectically active but empty lives. I invite them to know that they don't have to wait to almost lose their life to discover they were never fully living. Like the many other thrivors I have interviewed, I am eager to tell the world that there is much more available to us than survival.

The Silent Epidemic

Through my own return from death from cancer, and my subsequent interviews of hundreds of persons made stronger by their adversity, I have discovered the miraculous but ordinary magic of what I call *The Beethoven Factor*,[1] the human capacity for creativity in the context of adversity and extreme personal growth not only through but also due to stress. I have learned that the major affliction of our time is not depression about our past or anxiety about our future. It is not the presence of negative feelings, but the lack of daily elevation from positive ones, that is robbing life of its joyful spirit.

-§-
"We do not really think, we are barely conscious, until something goes wrong."
—C. S. Pierce
-§-

I suggest that we are becoming a generation of languishers, survivors of what even we ourselves describe as "the daily wars."[2] We are living our lives more like uninterested mechanics than fascinated artists. Psychologist Corey Keyes describes languishing as leading a life of going through the motions without abundant positive emotions. He says that it has become the new silent and debilitating epidemic in the United States, and is experienced by three of every four Americans.[3]

Languishers are not mentally ill nor mentally healthy; they just "are." They are surviving by mistaking an intense life for a zestful one. The process of healing from a major illness, or other life-catastrophe, through crisis-induced awakening, can help us become born before we die. This is what I mean by The Beethoven Factor approach to healing.

Don't Call Me a Cancer Survivor

I always cringe when someone refers to me a cancer survivor. I have learned through several crises in my living and dying that merely surviving wastes an immense amount of mental, physical, and spiritual energy.

In my interviews with hundreds of thrivors through adversity, I have seen firsthand that each of us has within us a capacity to grow because we have suffered. In fact, it seems from my research that one purpose of life's tribulations may be to jar us from our languishing and elevate us to celebration.

I hope experienced thrivors will share what they know about the Beethoven Factor. That's the name I've coined for the stress-induced growth of the kind shown by Beethoven's ability to compose his Ode to Joy while facing his impending death, while he was in physical and emotional pain, and profoundly deaf. I hope those of you who have felt the power of the creative spirit to lift the emotional darkness of life's worst moments will come

-§-
"A man can be destroyed, but not defeated."
—Ernest Hemingway
-§-

forward with the news that it is not only the sick and suffering who are living in such darkness. I hope you will tell what you know about our innate psychological immune system that allows us to not only be up to the tasks of our crises, but to become inspired by them.

Healing and the CIA

CIA, as I am using these letters here, represents "Crisis Induced Awakening." I used this CIA code when I was in the bone marrow transplant unit. A few us made small cardboard badges, with "Member of the Cancer CIA" printed on them, that we taped to our hospital gowns. I used this anagram to remind my fellow cancer patients and myself that our cancers were offering us the choice of our lifetimes. We could hope to survive our trauma or choose to become more consciously creative because of them.

In my interviews with those who showed the thriving response, I seldom encountered an example of a vibrantly creative and spiritually energetic person who was savoring life who had not known crisis-induced awakening. My research on thriving indicates that we may not be as fully conscious and spiritually awake as we can be unless and until something goes dreadfully wrong. It may a purpose of terrible suffering to offer us CIA, the crisis-induced awakening necessary to be able to savor the simple grandeur of daily living. It is the opportunity and perhaps even the duty of those who have grown through despair to share their revelations. They can help us stop the silent epidemic of languishing.

Full Catastrophe Living

Psychologist Jon Kabat-Zinn coined the phrase "full catastrophe living."[4] He was referring to fully embracing life not because it is easy, but because it can be such a wonderfully terrible adventure. Researchers

Carol D. Ryff and Burton Singer write: "good lives are about the zest that comes from effortful, frequently challenging and frustrating, engagement in living."[5] In other words, the good life is as much about the terrible as it is the terrific, and about misfortune as well as good luck.

Author Bruce Russell wrote that the good life is one of constant challenge and not a journey of deliciously ripened fruit dropping effortlessly into one's mouth.[6] Chinese novelist and political prisoner Jian Bingzhi wrote that the good life is about personal growth through life's adversity and not sitting blissfully while plucking the harp. Thrivors know that the good life results from fully engaging with life's troubles and becoming more creative because of them.

-§-
"It's never too late to be what you might have been."
—George Eliot
-§-

I coined the phrase The Beethoven Factor to reflect the dynamic nature of thriving described above. Listen carefully to his Ninth Symphony and you will sense the kind of joy to which this ode was composed. It is a joy of full appreciation of the dramatic ebb and flow of life, from great happiness to deep sorrow; from life's joyful beginnings to it's ever-pending endings. Thriving is falling joyfully into the natural rhythm of life and being as awed as we are shocked by the bad times in our lives.

An Arrogance of Agony

I have been fairly challenged by some who have read my book *The Beethoven Factor*. They ask if I am suggesting that someone who has not gone through a major adversity is somehow less awake and fully alive than someone who has. With full admission of my bias as someone who has known severe pain and great loss in his life, my answer is, "Probably." Thriving is a choice, not an automatic response. While we all have the thriving response within us, it is up to us to actuate it.

Just because a person has known the worst of life does not mean she has found a more creative, more engaging way to live her daily life. Sadly, I have interviewed some sufferers of severe pain who were spending all their energy surviving. They said things like, "I'll be back to normal in no time," or, "I will be living in recovery for the rest of my life," or "I am a survivor. It takes all I can muster to do it, but I will survive." Such persons seem on the road to recovery but not on the path to flourishing. On the other hand, someone who has not yet faced a major life-challenge may have chosen to savor life much more than someone who goes through a crisis and comes out of it a survivor living in perpetual recovery. That being said, my personal experiences with my own life-trauma, and my research on stress-induced growth indicates that, when it comes to know-

ing how to savor life, it seems that zestful life-savoring is much more frequent among those who have grown through the worst life has to offer.

Some of my colleagues in the new field of positive psychology feel
that my position regarding CIA is too extreme and therefore limiting.
They say that I am wrong when I say that to know the heights of the
human experience, one must know its depths.[7] They
suggest that the savoring response can be learned
without running the gauntlet of life's travails and
through other means of heightened awareness. I
assert that the epidemic of languishing has become
too widespread and deep, and that our modern
world has too long lulled us into to a hectically busy

> -§-
> "If you think you can,
> you can. If you think
> you can't, you're
> right."
> —Mary Kay Ash
> -§-

but distracted and empty lifestyle. Most of us seem to require a spiritual
shock to help us realize our savoring response and need something to go
wrong before we decide to try to set our life right.

Healing as Flourishing Through Pain

Because of the pathology bias that exists in modern medicine, much
more is known about our vulnerabilities than our strengths. The new field
of positive psychology is attempting to address this imbalance.
Researchers in this field suggest that growth because of suffering can lead
to increased adaptability and some of the following strengths:

- New perceptions of our self and our place in the world

- Feelings of being stronger we than we ever imagined

- Feeling more self-assured and less fearful

- Enhanced "benefit-finding" skills due to extensive practice
  in looking for the slightest sign of good news and hope

- Development of a reasoned optimism beyond
  blind faith or a feigned positive attitude

- Increased self-trust in our capacity to not
  only survive but thrive through crises

- New awareness of our vulnerability, leading in
  turn to cherishing our present life-situation

- Seeing and seeking new opportunities that may have
  been missed in our distractions prior to our trauma

- Pursuing what we "always wanted to
  do" but failed to take the time to do

- Increased value placed on, and appreciation
  for, significant others in our life

- Greater self-disclosure and emotional expressiveness due to our increased valuing of the moments we have to live

- Decrease in being too busy to love and too tired to care

- Lowering of our "humor threshold" for more easy and hardy laughing

- A new, more adaptive philosophy of life, including taking things easier, and acting on a renewed appreciation for those things and people most important to us

- Increased spirituality, and a search for deeper meaning and comprehensibility

- Decreased fear of death, replaced by more fully engaged living[8]

The changes outlined above have led some researchers to juxtapose the concept of PTG–Post Traumatic Growth with the more well-known pathologically-oriented concept of PTSD–Post Traumatic Stress Disorder.[9] PTG involves more than bouncing back or recovery. It is the Beethoven Factor in action, a thriving response to trauma through a deeply felt and long-lasting redirection in the path of our life.[10]

Those of us who have suffered great pain know only too well that the clichés of a constantly positive attitude and only thinking "good thoughts" can be not only frustrating but also depressing and even angering. As one of the founders of the new positive psychology, Martin Seligman points out, being a thrivor instead of a survivor is much more than happiology. It is making a courageous and difficult conscious choice to gain because we have lost, to more fully indulge in life's simple pleasure because we have known severe pain, and to become more alive because we have been so close to death.

-§-
"Because I remember, I despair. Because I remember, I have the duty to reject despair."
—Elie Wiesel
-§-

Thriving is much more than learning to smell the roses; it's yearning to plant and care for them. It is not just watching rainbows but being in awe of a powerful storm. It is construing our life from new perspectives with different and more challenging horizons. It is realizing that, no matter where we think we are going, we will never get there until we are more fully here.

Turning Points

The Beethoven Factor is the ability to turn a tragedy into a turning point. Positive psychologist Elaine Wethington points out that thriving through crisis is about learning new things about ourselves, both about the good and the bad.[11] For survivors, life-crises such as cancer or the loss of a loved one are more life scars than turning points. Their crisis dictates their emotional tone and colors their consciousness forever. Thrivors do not deny, or fail to fully experience, the fact that tragedy has heaped damage upon their body, mind, and soul. They decide, however, to make their tragedy into a catalyst for unprecedented growth and creativity in their life. Their crisis does not cause them to "become" anything, but it does result in them turning to new ways of becoming.

My interviews with thrivors indicate that it was their creativity in the face of crises that distinguished them from survivors. In their unique ways, each of them chose to become an artist. Like most of the world's greatest artists, their pain became fuel for a flourishing imagination. They changed from a mechanic's to an artist's view of life.

Why Beethoven?

"Why in the world did you choose Beethoven?" asked an editor who turned down the opportunity to publish *The Beethoven Factor*. "I know he was a creative genius, but his personal life was a mess." I answered, "That's exactly why I chose him to represent the thriving response."

I did not choose Beethoven's creative adjustment to his deafness and other difficulties to represent my study of thriving because he was a well-adjusted, mature, stable, always cheerful man. I did not choose him only because he turned the crisis of his profound deafness into a new, gleeful and upbeat way of viewing the world. I did not choose him only because, deaf and dying, he conducted the premiere of his Ode to Joy. I chose him because he was also a flawed and ordinary man who came through his suffering to give us, through his music, what his biographer Maynard Solomon called a "counterbal-

-§-
"The world breaks everyone, and, afterward, many are strong in the broken places."
—Ernest Hemingway
-§-

ance to the forces of disintegration" and an "apocalyptic call for the suppression of doubt."[12] Like others who transcended survival, Beethoven was an ordinary man who chose art over survival.

Solomon writes that Beethoven's life crises somehow, "provided the kindling for the blaze of his imagination."[13] At the most difficult time in his life, and with his most precious faculty abandoning him, no hope of finding lasting love, and suffering from several illnesses, he chose timeless creativity over survival. This is the process of going beyond recovery and survival to creative thriving and savoring.

Beethoven knew he was running out of time. He had to make a decision all of us will face sooner or later in our own lives. Solomon writes, "Beethoven had to decide how he was going to spend his remaining time on earth, whether to try to fill the dwindling days with simple pleasures or to pursue his dedication to great artistic challenges, or even raise the stakes in his creative exertions. Predictably, but not without scorching conflicts, he opted for art against life."[14] This is what I mean by the Beethoven Factor: opting to continue to create our life and all life rather than merely sustain it. Solomon's phrase, "opting for art against life," captures the creative essence of the Beethoven Factor and the thriving response.

An Ode to Thriving

Survivors show us how we can "take it and make it," but thrivors shows us how we can "create it." Survivors show us how we might save our life, but thrivors show us how we might savor it. Beethoven's "Ode to Joy" is a celebration of both new beginnings, and endings. Even as he composed his Ninth Symphony, he was never sure how it should end. He contemplated several finales and agonized over the use of voice over instruments. Showing the total absorption characteristic of thrivors, his wrestling with the creative elements of his composition seemed to make time, and fear of its end, disappear.

Solomon writes, "Beethoven chose art over life precisely because, for him, art provided plentiful compensations here and hereafter. Through music, Beethoven cold locate and limn realms of permanence, constantly renewable, impervious to forces of decay and disintegration."[15] Beethoven's choice not only helped him thrive but also resulted in a gift for the world.

Solomon beautifully describes Beethoven's example of thriving and his gift to all of us. He writes, "Through his music, he could create impregnable, unified structures; describe endless forms of transcendence over hostile energies; inscribe narrative of return, refinding, and rebeginning; forge a channel between himself and a forbearing deity; invoke the healing power of music. He could declare himself and us victors in every deadly game, create ecstasies so powerful that they momentarily eradicated fear or at least made it endurable."[16] To feel invulnerable, safe from hostile energies, to feel victorious even in the face of life's random unfairness, and to know joy and freedom from fear (or at least able to prosper through it), these are the paths to a truly miraculous healing beyond survival.

-§-
"What doesn't destroy me strengthens me."
—Friedrich Nietzsche
-§-

A Thrivors' Hall of Fame

Consider the following list of persons who were healed and made more whole despite and particularly because of their suffering:

Lance Armstrong: He thrived through cancer, to achieve unprecedented success in bike racing, and to inspire other cancer patients.

William Carlos Williams: He suffered a severe stroke and subsequent emotional breakdown, only to later write great poetry and win the Pulitzer Prize for his work *Pictures from Brueghel.*

Nelson Mandela: He emerged from years of imprisonment and torture to become a leader for freedom, democracy, and the rights of the oppressed.

Pierre-Auguste Renoir: Unable to walk, and with fingers twisted by arthritis, he attached a paintbrush to his hand and painted some of the world's most memorable works, including (at age seventy-six) "The Washerwoman."

Henri Matisse: Suffering from heart failure, gastrointestinal disease, and with his lungs failing, he placed paintbrushes on a long stick and painted from his bed. His style created an entirely new field with a unique combination of color and form.

-§-

"Life is a daring adventure or it is nothing at all."
—Helen Keller

-§-

Enrico Dandolo: While serving as a peace ambassador to Constantinople in 1172 A. D., he was blinded in both eyes by the emperor's guards. Twenty-nine years later, at age ninety-four, he led Venice to victory over Constantinople, and at age ninety-seven was appointed chief magistrate of that city.

Sister Gertrud Morgan: She devoted her entire life to establishing and running an orphanage in New Orleans named Gentilly. When she was sixty-five years old, a hurricane destroyed her orphanage. She then returned to her interest in painting. Her works are displayed in museums around the world.

Ding Ling: (A pseudonym used by Chinese novelist and radical feminist Kian Bingzhi.) She was imprisoned from the ages of sixty-six to seventy-one, during the Cultural Revolution of the 1970s. Upon her release, she went on to write some of her most highly praised works. She wrote an inspiring novel describing her banishment to China's northern wilderness.

Helen Keller: Blind, deaf, and mute from nineteen months old, she wrote and published (at age seventy-five) her book Teacher in honor of the woman who helped her thrive through her suffering.

Jesse J. Aaron: A descent of slaves with a Seminole Indian grandmother, he too worked at slave labor. Throughout his life he cared for his disabled wife and had to spend all of his meager funds to on surgery to save his wife's sight. In poverty, he offered a definition of what I am calling the Beethoven Factor. He wrote, "It was then that the Spirit woke me up and said, 'Carve wood.'" He went on to become one of the most respected wood sculptors in the world.

Hardiness: The Art of Giving Up

Those who thrive through crisis display four major characteristics. The first of these is hardiness, a resilient spiritual and mental energy that allows us to construe crisis into challenge.

In Western culture, strength tends to be seen exclusively as personal power. Millions of dollars have been spent purchasing audio and video-tapes offering guides to perseverance and victory over all odds. Healing has often been seen as tapping into this kind of power by surviving against all odds, by succeeding in the struggle against disease and hardship.

We are told that cancer "survivors" have successfully engaged in a "battle" against cancer and those who succumbed to cancer "lost their bat-tle." Hardiness is seen as never giving up. The credo in business and sports is, "Quitters never win and winners never quit." Survivors are seen as bat-tlers who never gave up. Thrivors have learned just the opposite approach to crisis. They have discovered that sometimes it is having the energy and wisdom for "enlightened quitting" that is the quintessential act of healing.

-§-
"If we had no winter, the spring would not be so pleasant; if we did not sometimes taste of adversity, prosperity would not be so welcome."
—Anne Bradstreet
-§-

Positive psychologists Charles S. Carver and Michael F. Scheier write, "A critical role in life is also played by doubt and disengagement—by giving up."[17] Thrivors are not always fighters. Beethoven himself often expressed self-pity and a willingness to throw in the towel. He saw his newfound creativity as a form of informed enlightened surrender to his inevitable suffering and impending death. He sought help for his deafness from skilled physicians, and quacks. He finally gave up. He devised ways to compose his music from his heart and watch it with his eyes. He developed the skill of watching the bows of the violinists, and assessing their movement to determine the volume, pitch, and tempo at which his composition was being performed.

Carver and Scheier point out the importance of enlightened quitting as a form of hardiness: "The problem is how to know when something is truly unattainable. In truth, whenever the issue arises, it is impossible to be certain of the answer. To persevere may turn out to be glorious stupid-ity. To give up may turn out to be tragic loss. Whether the answer comes from a divinity or from a lifetime of experience, the ability to choose wise-ly (or at least believe that one has chosen wisely) and follow one's choice is also an important strength."[18] Being a wise quitter is a key.

Happiness: The Art of Mirth-itation

The happiness component of thriving healing is related to what posi-tive psychology pioneer Mihaly Csikszentmihalyi calls "flow."[19] Flowing is so totally immersing ourselves in an activity that we lose all sense of self, time, and place. One of the best forms of flow I have discovered to be characteristic of thrivors is their practice of "mirth-itation," a mindful escape through the use of humor.

There is evidence that hardy laughter directly results in positive changes in our immune system and general physiology. Even so-called "black humor" or the German *Galgenhumor* (laughter from the edge of the grave) can allow us to lose ourselves by dallying for a while in the absurd, finding temporary respite from the intensity of our challenge by seeking the silly. Every thrivor I interviewed seemed to have honed their sense for the silly. By doing so, they seemed able, at least temporarily, to side-step some of the pain of their condition.

The patient in the room next to mine at the bone marrow transplant unit was an experienced mirth-itator. He was a grocer, a huge man whose laughter could be heard down the entire hall. He was even sicker than I was. Few nurses and doctors thought he would live much longer. I wheeled myself into his room one evening to discuss the Beethoven Factor. He was wearing one of our homemade CIA pins on his hospital gown. I asked him if he had any advice regarding thriving when someone is fairly certain his or her time is running out. He thought for a while and answered, "Yes. I do. Don't buy green bananas." We laughed so hard that a nurse came running to see why two dying men were creating such a ruckus.

> -§-
> "To live is the rarest thing in the world. Most people exist, that is all."
> —Oscar Wilde
> -§-

When the grocer and I discussed our shared laughter the next day, we both agreed that we had not felt so relaxed and unafraid as when we shared our hardy guffaw about the green bananas and the message of living in the present. Even as we faced the most dreadful situation in our lives, we had found a few moments of escape from the place, time, and body that was so terribly frightening. The grocer did not survive, but his spirit thrives in all of us who knew and loved him. To this day, whenever I see a bunch of green bananas, I smile broadly and think of him.

Healing: The Art of Making Mountains out of Molehills

The word "healing" is used in two ways. One is to endure a disease or life-problem while the challenge runs its full course, even if this trauma eventually ends in death. The other meaning is taking steps to survive a disease or trauma. Thriving involves a third perspective on healing, to become more creative and grow because of a life-challenge and to find new and more creative meaning in life because of our suffering. This third approach to healing is characteristic of thrivors.

Research Aaron Antonovsky writes about a sense of coherence as essential to healing.[20] He refers to finding meaning, comprehensibility, and a sense of manageability when confronted with a severe challenge. One way thrivors do this is by what positive psychologists call "benefit finding" or sometimes "benefit reminding."[21] This is intentionally seeking gains, growth, and enhanced interpersonal relationships because we have been faced with a challenge. Forcing such an approach on a suffering person can easily backfire and lead to resentment by those who feel their pain and dire circumstances are being minimized, but voluntarily electing to look for gains in our pain can have positive healing influences beyond survival.

Hope: The Art of Putting Yourself Down

Psychologist Martin Seligman is a pioneer in the research on optimism and hope.[22] He has pointed out that an optimistic outlook is typically characterized by not taking things personally, not seeing negative events as pervasive in one's life, and not considering the down periods in life to be permanent. It is clear that persons who think in this way can adjust better to the bad times in their life, but thrivors often go a step further regarding these Three P's of Personal, Pervasive, and Permanent thinking.

My interviews of thrivors indicate that their optimistic view is characterized by a unique slant on the Seligman Three P's. They often highly personalize the negatives in their life and go searching for ways in which they can grow beyond the flaws and limitations they identify in their new way of thinking about themselves and their life. They see negative events in their life as having pervasive consequences and decide to attempt to make wide-sweeping changes in how they live and

-§-
"Cancer can be a turning point, but only for those who choose to turn."
—Larry LeShan
-§-

see the world. Finally, they see negatives as highly permanent signs that call for a new broader and more creatively adaptive life-perspective and explanatory system.

Seligman suggests that a constructive healing process might include rational self-disputation. When things go wrong for us, he suggests that we engage in rational argumentation with our "negative critical self" as if that self were a stranger irrationally attacking us. This has been highly effective for children and adults alike, and thrivors also use this process. They are persistently engaged in self-disputation and arguing against the limits imposed by their take on their crisis and any obstacles within their thinking and self-talk that prevent an upward psychological trajectory.

More than twenty years ago, I interviewed a twelve-year-old girl who had been repeatedly molested by her stepfather throughout her childhood. She had dropped out of school, experienced severe depression, and seemed to have given up hope for a quality life. Her capacity to thrive through her horror exemplifies the Beethoven Factor and its hope component.

-§-

"Everything ends. Beethoven knew that. But he also demonstrated that something remains."
—Maynard Solomon

-§-

She told me through her tears, "I keep thinking it was me. I think I brought it on me. He told me it was my fault because I tempted and teased him and he couldn't help it." She had come to me clinic for help and I told her that she had to argue against that part of her self and that she was not responsible in any way for what had happened to her. She answered. "I guess you mean I should start putting my bad self down." I answered, "Exactly. As if it is stranger saying stupid untrue things, argue against that part of your self."

Thrivors' Groups

Over her course of treatment, that girl had shown the hardiness, happiness, healing, and hope of thriving. I met her again recently when I went to the symphony; she was the orchestra's first chair cellist. She noticed me at a post-concert party. She introduced herself and gave me a long hug. She whispered, "Remarkable, isn't it, what the human spirit can make out of a disaster." After embracing me, she called her husband and three children to her side. She laughed, winked, and said, "May I introduce you to my own little thrivors' group."

I first recognized her earlier, during the concert, when the conductor called her to the podium and handed her the baton. Life often offers delightfully mysterious coincidences, and this one brought me to tears. She smiled and announced that she would be leading the orchestra in the final movement of Beethoven's Ninth Symphony, his Ode to Joy.

GERALYN GENDREAU:
Vital Catastrophes

A long-haired, elegant-looking man, whose voice came from some-where behind his navel rather than his throat, stood at the front of the room wearing nothing but a royal blue Speedo. "They must be trying to mimic the weather pattern in Calcutta," I thought. Ten minutes into the ninety-minute yoga class I began to fear asphyxiation and moved to open the window just a crack. Half the people in the class turned to look at me and scowl.

"Standing head-to-knee pose," the teacher commanded. He stood on one leg, extended the other in front of him parallel to the floor, flexed and gripped his foot, and pulled his upper body down, draping it over the extended leg. Watching this, I began to wonder what in the world I had got myself into. And this was but the fifth in a twenty-three posture series.

Suptavajrasana, Sanskrit for standing head-to-knee, required all the strength and balance I could muster just to get into. When I heard the instruction, "Now hold for one minute," a crotchety voice in my head said, "Right." As the class wore on, the crotchety voice grew louder and louder saying, "Just walk out of here and never come back. They don't know you, nobody cares." When the class finally ended, I left the building wondering where I might find a yoga studio with a truly beginning-level class.

But as I walked up Columbus toward North Beach for a post-yoga cup of coffee, something unusual happened. Houses I'd walked by dozens of times captured my attention, enchanting me with their intricate Victorian architecture. Colors on the houses seemed unusually bright, as

Geralyn Gendreau, MS, is a licensed therapist, poet, lifestyle consultant, and profes-sional muse. In 1987, she broke her neck in a bodysurfing accident and had a dra-matic near–death experience. She is a master yoga teacher and blackbelt martial artist by day, a performing artist and ecstatic poet by night. Both on stage and with clients, she works to ground the light of pure genius to sculpt a more balanced world. As founder of Svelte International, she employs practical mysticism to help people break free of the food and weight trap for good. Find her on the web at www.svel-teinternational.com. Photo by Michael Buchanan.

though the pigments in the paint were leaping off the building. As I walked across the grass in Washington Park, greeting people with a soft, easy smile, a lovely euphoric feeling pulsed through my body. The instant I stepped into the Bohemian Cafe and smelled the coffee, my desire for a double-shot latte vanished. I ordered it anyway, purely out of habit, but this time specified, "Decaf, please."

I felt deeply relaxed the rest of the day and had more mental clarity than usual. By evening, a slight soreness had crept into my back and legs. I fell asleep easily, nonetheless. When I awakened at six o'clock the next morning—surprised at having slept through the night without my usual 2 AM snack—I found myself pulling on a pair of yoga pants. Thus began the draw of that ancient art and science, and my first step on the road to embodied morning prayer. Six—often seven—times a week for the next twelve months, I zigzagged down the famous Lombard Street for morning yoga class.

Once a year had passed, I stopped attending class as my body had developed a rudimentary vocabulary and wanted to speak for itself. Today, my yoga practice knows no time or posture limits, and flows together in an ecstatic yoga dance, but it is built on the foundation of attending hot yoga class every morning for a solid year. Spontaneously arising, on or off the mat, yoga is now a vital thread weaving through every day, making life itself a breathing prayer.

Making major lifestyle changes is not always easy. But inside each of us, there lives a pure genius, ready and willing to align and direct our vital life-force—if only we consent. We can show our consent—and fuel our intent to make changes in our lifestyle—by engaging in a daily morning ritual. The yogic term for day-by-day integrative, self-transformational practice is *sadhana*. Most spiritual traditions suggest some type of intentional morning focus. It can begin with the simplest of disciplines: waking up in the morning and sitting still for twenty minutes of quiet time. At the start, participation in a group activity can be helpful. The support of a community—whether a health club, prayer circle, therapy group, or twelve-step program—can make all the difference. Old habits die hard, and sometimes our entire mindset needs revamping. Going it alone can be difficult, if not impossible. Regular class attendance was vital my first year practicing yoga. I had fallen out of the exercise habit, and my body was in the de-conditioned aftermath of a serious injury.

-§-

Inside each of us, there lives a pure genius, ready and willing to align and direct our vital life-force.

-§-

A body-surfing accident had left me with a crushed and fractured cervical spine. I was lucky to be walking. Prior to the accident, I'd been training for my black belt in Sun Moo Do, and eclectic Korean martial art that blends Taekwondo, Hapikido, T'ai Chi, Shiatsu, and meditation. On top of that, my goal to compete in a triathlon before turning thirty had me logging ten hours of cycling, running and swimming each week. Imagine the shock to my exercise-addicted body upon suddenly finding itself bolted into a "halo," a traction device that not only immobilized my neck, but made it impossible to walk briskly or even raise my arms above chest level. Caged for five months, my muscles atrophied and my body grew fleshy. I lost all stamina and strength, but—worst of all—all interest in exercise.

Over the next several years, I exercised my mind instead of my body while training to be a psychotherapist. By the time I completed my masters degree and the three thousand intern hours required for licensing, I'd become alienated from my body and its natural rhythms. I weighed 175 lbs., quite a load on a 5'2" body. To make matters worse, I was diagnosed with an "incurable" thyroid condition. For some unknown reason, my body was making antibodies that attacked my thyroid gland. My doctor could give me no explanation as to why. All he could offer was a fancy name—Hashimoto's—and a prescription. The name of the disease was terror enough, conjuring up images of a samurai soldier holding his long, curved sword to my throat, frightening my poor little endocrine gland half to death. Thus was my state when I started yoga practice.

-§-
It takes twenty-one days to make or break a habit.
-§-

One Saturday morning, my yoga studio held an open house to introduce a special guest physician from Calcutta. The doctor gave a talk on the health benefits of Hatha yoga, then opened the floor to questions. When I asked about my thyroid condition, his face looked grave. "This one very difficult," he said in an Indian accent, "how often you practice yoga?"

"I've been coming every day for two months," I said.

His face lit up. "Ah, this very good. You keep doing yoga daily, work deeply in throat in lying poses. After six months, you cut medication by one-quarter. Then every two months, cut by one-quarter again. You will be fine."

Although the process was not as simple as he outlined, I was eventually able to stop taking synthetic thyroid. Like so many stress-related autoimmune disorders, my condition required a change in lifestyle. Understanding the body as a self-regulating, self-repairing, cooperative organism is crucial. If we view disease as a signal from the body that something has run amok, and we begin to listen deeply, illness can be a remarkable catalyst for change.

In my case, listening to the message of a hypothyroid condition led me to look deeply into complex fear-based emotional, mental and physical patterns. I felt unworthy, unloved, and—at times—angry as hell. An undercurrent in my psyche of "I'd rather die" came into the light where it could be unraveled and understood. Finally, and most importantly, my slumbering will—the source of all power in the human personality—had to be awakened and rallied in service of my desire to live a vital, healthy life.

Since lifestyle choices readily become risk factors associated with heart disease, cancer and autoimmune disorders, it is important to consider how we move toward change. The "old habits die hard" admonition must be challenged. I offer clients this suggestion: "It takes twenty-one days to make or break a habit." Initial efforts pay off as new neural pathways are formed in the brain. New habits begin to feel good in no time at all, allowing a natural momentum to take over. The progression from conscious effort to unconscious competence can take as little as three weeks. The activation and development of will is essential to progress when making lifestyle changes.

Whether the goal is healing a specific illness, improved overall health, weight loss, freedom from emotional and mental stress, or full self-realization, strengthening the will is a critical first step. In *What We May Be* (Tarcher, 1983), a practical guide to psychosynthesis techniques, Pierro Ferrucci states: "The will in its true essence can explain a host of human attainments, while its absence can account for legions of psychological disturbances." I venture to add, a lack of *aware will* lies at the root of many physical problems.

-§-
Repeating the same sacred verse day after day turns even the simplest prayer into a living spiritual spring, quenching many an un-named and un-namable thirst.
-§-

Consider the condition of your will. Do you regularly do what you truly desire, from the core of your being, simply because you decide? Or do external circumstances and old habits keep you slogging around in the quicksand of indecision and half-hearted commitments? The discovery and development of will taps an under-used energy source that can provide the needed fuel to reach your goals. "The will is our greatest ally," says Indian scholar Ecknath Easwaran.

Here are some simple, day-to-day practices for activating and strengthening the will:

- Do something you have been putting off

- Postpone something you do impulsively

- When presented with a simple decision, be decisive

- Eat slowly, chewing each mouthful 30-50 times

- Change a routine way of doing something

- Make a plan and follow through with it

- Do something you did not think you could

- Drive the speed limit on the freeway

- Do something difficult without complaining

- Say "No" when you mean it, but it would be easier to say "Yes"

One of the best ways to jump-start the day and engage the will is to get up out of bed immediately upon awakening, splash some cold water on your face and sit down for a morning meditation. Activating the will in this way gives access to it as an energy resource by starting the day with a jolt of its power. During this period of meditation, Easwaran recommends slowly reciting a chosen prayer. Repeating the same sacred verse day after day while quietly resting attention in the heart turns even the simplest prayer into a living spiritual spring, quenching many an un-named and un-namable thirst.

-§-
We gain personal freedom, unimagined power and effectiveness when the will is entrained to the heart, fired by passion, grounded in the body, and aligned with the highest good for all.
-§-

As someone who spent years debilitated by an "eating disorder" and periods of depression, I claim some authority about the intricate process of awakening the will. Few would disagree that to live our full potential we need an aware, awake will. Ferrucci says, "the will is, more than any other factor, the key to human freedom and personal power." But will, by itself, may not be enough. I would amend Ferrucci's statement this way: We gain personal freedom, unimagined power and effectiveness when the will is entrained to the heart, fired by passion, grounded in the body, and aligned with the highest good for all. More simply stated, will is the key that opens the door to genius.

From a body-mind-heart perspective, when changes in lifestyle are wanted, the will must be engaged in a powerful, even heroic way. Old habits are to lifestyle change as gravity to a rocket. Just as the space shuttle needs an explosive fuel source to break free of earth's atmosphere, humans need a superior energy source to break free of die-hard habits. Genius is that superior energy source. Genius comes when will is fueled by desire and sparked by imagination in a ritual, day-to-day manner. Without an aware, awake will, desire and imagination can feed a downward spiral. We call this depression. Therefore, all three components become crucial: will, desire and imagination. Ritual activates this powerful inner trinity, contributing to the upswing in well-being and unveiling our genius.

Lest the word "ritual" bring to mind pictures of elaborate ceremonies conducted by candle light, let me clarify. Anything done repeatedly is a ritual. Brushing your teeth in the morning is a ritual. The sequence by which you accomplish any repeated task is a ritual. What I invite my clients and yoga students to create for themselves are intentional morning rituals, designed to align their thoughts and actions with their innermost desire.

It is far too easy to get out of bed in the morning and fall head-first into the hectic stream of never-ending demands served up with the sun-rise on a daily basis. The world at large is governed by the notion, "There's not enough time." Taking an interlude for prayer, meditation, and listen-ing to the heart, we step into the timeless dimension. This sets a different tone, inviting tranquility to rule over frenzy. Morning quiet time becomes a vital and effective counter-balance to the weight of modern life. From there, we build, adding a series of sun salutations, or a brisk morning walk. Such rituals quickly become delicious soul food. The benefits reach into all areas of life: home, work, relationship, creativity, and spirituality. Establishing a morning practice is a beautiful way to become intimate with our genius.

Ending the day intentionally is just as important as how we wake up. Taking a few minutes just before bed to review the day is a lovely way to clear the mind for restful sleep. An exercise I often recommend involves sitting at the edge of the bed just before climbing in and reviewing the days events from the most recent backward in time to the first action taken in the morning. The review should take no more and no less than three minutes. For those like me, oft-times possessed by the monkey mind—jumping up and down and tearing up the bed the minute my head hits the pillow—this practice can pave the way to a night of restful sleep. We give the playful monkey a little bedtime romp through the day just passed and assign it three tasks—to highlight unfin-ished business, appreciate the grace and beauty of life's little miracles, and express gratitude for any personal success. At the end of three minutes, make note of anything that requires future attention and lie down for a blessed night of rest.

-§-
A bed-time plunge into the biochemical bath of gratitude turns sleep time into a peri-od of subtle, conscious metamorphosis.
-§-

I like to think of my morning meditation as a catalyst, my evening meditation as forming my overnight chrysalis. Grateful, appreciative feel-ings trigger hormonal secretions that are far more conducive to regenera-tive sleep than the biochemistry of anxious, unintentional mulling-it-over-into-the-night. A caterpillar goes into a chrysalis and liq-uefies before emerging as a butterfly. A bed-time plunge into the bio-chemical bath of gratitude turns sleep time into a period of subtle, conscious metamorphosis. I call it butterfly medicine: turning the spiritual admonition "Die while you're alive and discover how to live" into, "Liquefy at night and spread the wings of genius when you awake."

Beginning and ending the day in an intentional way has a potent effect. Rather than being ruled by inevitable day-to-day challenges, we set a context of our own choosing. We approach each day as a canvas on which to express our life as art. Over time, this intentional focus generates a tremendous sense of awe at the promise each day holds.

But sometimes even the most carefully laid plans fail. Mike knew he had to make major dietary changes after being diagnosed with adult-onset diabetes at age forty-two. A first-time father to an infant girl, health and longevity suddenly became his top priority. An account executive in a high-tech company, he made a major stress-reducing change in his work life by accepting an assignment that allowed him to work from home three days a week. Doing his best to cut down sugar intake, he applied his gourmet cooking skills to keep the dinner menu interesting. He started on a walking program, and over a two-year period lost thirty-five pounds. But every time he indulged in his favorite forbidden food — coffee ice cream — he suffered tremendous guilt. To his way of thinking, eating ice cream was linked to potentially depriving his daughter of a father. Tears came to his eyes as he told me this. Then, at forty-six, he had the surprise of his life when a minor heart attack sent him to the hospital for heart bypass surgery. At four years old, his daughter came close to losing her dad.

-§-

The hurdle in front of Mike was one many must face when attempting to make major lifestyle changes: gaining the full support of loved ones.

-§-

When I began consulting with him, the hurdle in front of Mike was one many must face when attempting to make major lifestyle changes: gaining the full support of loved ones. Mike's wife wanted nothing more than to help him live a heart-healthy life. But whenever she did the grocery shopping, she would buy their favorite ice cream as well as Mike's other nemesis: cheese. Although incredibly supportive of his dietary changes, she saw no reason to give up her favorite foods. Looking into Mike's reluctance to ask his wife not to bring home these particular foods, we found that he had unrealistic expectations of himself. His belief system said he "should" be able to resist the urge to eat the high fat foods his wife kept in the refrigerator. But experience showed that he could not. Recognition and acceptance of this fact was a "reality check" without which Mike could not see what he needed to do: ask his wife for her full support, and agree on what that meant in practical terms. Mike's wife subsequently agreed to stop bringing home frozen desserts except when he was away on business, and to buy only low-fat cheese. She has since joined him in his morning meditation practice and now has a reason to look forward to his trips out of town.

Deciding to redesign your lifestyle — or being compelled to, as the case may be — can present any number of stumbling blocks. Taking the bull of ingrained habits by the horns can backfire. Perhaps a diet is broken with a massive sugar binge. Perhaps a three-day cold usurps that new exercise regime and the couch potato within gains the upper hand. Perhaps our vow to live within our means to reduce the stress of unwanted debt is foiled by that credit card. What to do when the all-too-human tendencies toward self-sabotage, backsliding, or denial take center stage and hijack the momentum we have built toward our goal?

One highly effective approach I have worked with both in my own life and in coaching others involves taking time out for a "reality check" like Mike did. In *The Path of Least Resistance* (Fawcett, 1989), Robert Fritz says, "Those who have become fluent in naming reality have the best chance of moving to their next step and creating what they want to create." Knowing "what's so" — and *simultaneously* choosing what you really want — sets up creative tension. Imagination puts that tension to work when we assign our inner eye the task of painting a clear vision of what we wish to birth. The discrepancy between what a reality check reveals as true-here-and-now and the vision of what you really want generates polarity — and a unique, alchemical tension. We can harness that tension like a natural resource, or a supernatural resource, as the case may be. Fritz calls this dynamic "structural tension," a distinct and superior structure to the merry-go-round of conflict so many people get stuck in. I have found his approach quite useful for igniting genius and attaining desired results.

-§-
Not only are we God's favorite rosebush, we are "the love of God's life."
-§-

In the upper corner of your heart is an anatomical structure known as the synoatrial node. It is the place where the heart beat originates, though the source of that pulse cannot be verified by science. In heart-meditation, I like to focus there, as though drawing near a doorway to the divine. Allowing attention to settle in this spot affords our genius a unique perspective, especially when absorbed in personal concerns. The juxtaposition of our desire for change with the unchanging, ever-present Source makes our efforts sacred and honors the paradox of what we are: an infinite soul within a finite physical form. Seeded by the Divine, life is a growing concern, and not only are we God's favorite rosebush, we are "the love of God's life," as I wrote in this little poem:

And the words made flesh in your body are these:
All is well.
You may at times hit patches of confusion
wherein you cannot render this truth
and distortion takes over your knowing.

Fear not, or if you must fear, do so quietly and get some rest
for your innermost can never be lost.
You are love from skin to bone marrow.
Be released from fear and not knowing.
Live in the stream of grace that has always, always carried you.
For you are the love of God's life.
Embody this truth,
it will lead you to freedom.
This is your promise.

Kay Weinshienk:

Matrix of the Health Awakened

Within each of us there is exists magnificent intelligence — the creative force that is continuously manifesting our growth and health. It may be more accurate to say that we exist within it, for this is the same creative force which gives life to all that is animated in the natural world.

When I put my hands on a patient during a treatment, I know that I am holding something miraculous. I become as quiet in myself as I can, and I listen with all my senses. I feel with my hands, through my arms, into my heart, and with my whole being.

People have a natural wish to move toward health — to live in a state of love and freedom — with a feeling of well-being. A few years ago, I treated a woman named Sandra, who had been in an automobile accident five years before. Her head had been caught between the door and frame of her car as it rolled into a ravine. Since the accident, she had suffered from daily migraine headaches which were completely debilitating. Her life had been reduced to sheer survival of the pain, and a search for a way out.

When I placed my hands on her head, I felt the tremendous compression forces which were still present in her system. I could feel in her body the wish to be well, and behind that, the power to restore wellness. This power is held in the matrix of the health. On a sensory level, I want to be in communication with it, arouse it, and engage it. I listen, watch, and let it show me what needs to happen to restore function and freedom of

Kay Weinshienk, DO, grew up in Colorado where she spent much time in the Rocky Mountains developing a deep love and respect for the natural world. She is a graduate of the University of New England College of Osteopathic Medicine, and did her residency in Osteopathic Manipulative Medicine at St. Barnabus Hospital New York. She is actively involved with teaching and lecturing on Osteopathic principles to medical students. She has a practice in traditional Osteopathy in Sonoma County, California, where she lives with her husband and two children.

motion. In this case, the base of Sandra's skull was compressed and restricted in a way that interfered with normal physiological function. After a few treatments, the intensity of her headaches was greatly reduced. Within three months they were a thing of the past.

Healing is a force through all of nature. The health is always there. It wants to be seen. What I bring to a treatment is my willingness to engage the health. I open to make contact with the intelligence manifesting the health. It's been waiting to be seen as it truly is. When I see it, it sees me seeing it. I bring a receptive, open awareness which recognizes the wholeness of the person I am treating. Recognized, it awakens and emerges in response.

-§-
What I bring to a treatment is my willingness to make contact with the intelligence manifesting the health.
-§-

Consider taking a walk in the woods. You step into the forest very early in the morning just when the sun is coming up, and you start to get a feel of everything around you, everything that holds you. The coolness of the damp air on your skin, the soft earth, the presence of the trees with their branches swaying slightly, the birds starting to wake up and sing. You are exploring — you don't know what you are going to find. If you are fully open to your senses, the forest will show you how miraculous it is. It is as though your presence there, your open quiet attention, your appreciation of its magnificence, all combine to arouse a response — so the forest unfolds its beauty for you.

The Body's Exquisite Design

The human body is exquisite in its subtlety and complexity. It is a dynamic living system which senses and responds, grows and adapts, dances and sings, continually renewing itself. If you look closely enough into the physiology of the body you can just barely begin to understand what a remarkable achievement it is.

Consider the heart. It is the first functional organ to develop in the embryo. Long before the embryo is recognizable as a human form, the cells which will become the heart gather like a crown on the embryo's "head." They coalesce and form into an early heart. Then, before the third week of development ends, the embryo bends forward and the heart is enfolded within the future chest. The curved form of the aortic arch in an adult stands as a spatial reminder of this early process.

Over the next weeks, as the developing embryo raises its head, in the space between the heart and the brain, the face is formed. I once attended a talk by a Tibetan nun. I watched as she touched her hands first to her forehead, bowed down, and brought them to her heart, and then, with her hands still at her heart, raised her head. I was struck by how her ritual gesture echoed the embryonic journey of the heart.

We've all been stunned by the beauty of the human eye. The cornea is the one-millimeter-thick layer of tissue that covers the eye. With its crystal transparency, it forms the actual "window" through which we see. Unlike glass, however, it is flexible, resilient to compressive force, and — when cut or abraded — will heal quite rapidly. How many naturally occurring substances are transparent and self-healing?

The very unusual characteristic of transparency is achieved through a remarkable microstructure. The substance of the cornea is comprised of millions of collagen microfibers of varying diameter (21–65 nanometers, much smaller than the wavelength of light). They are organized in over 200 micro-layers (lamellae) in such a way that all fibrils in a particular layer have identical thickness. The lamellae comprised of thinner fibrils lie toward the front of the eye.

-§-

Healing is a natural process by which living physiology is continually guided by the innate wisdom and intelligence within the body.

-§-

Within each layer the fibers are all exactly parallel. Neighboring layers orient to each other — always at wide angles. It is this subtly detailed and mathematically exact arrangement that allows light to pass through without distortion. For most people, it retains this amazing function throughout life. When inflamed or injured the cornea becomes white and opaque; we can peel off a piece and examine its structure under the microscope. It is only in the state of perfect integrity that the cornea takes on the quality needed for its function, that of invisibility. Remarkably, this amazing structure is created from scratch, in the dark!

Another example: In a lecture I heard recently, a geneticist spoke about how every human cell contains six billion base-pairs of DNA (the genome) — a number he said is equal to the number of letters found in two full years of *Wall Street Journals* — a massive amount of information. But sequencing the genome doesn't answer the question of interest to me. What and where is the intelligence or guiding force using and directing the use of this information? It's an important distinction, because the body is enormously intelligent. It makes choices, thousands of choices per second. The more closely I look, the more I see it as a divine creation. It is intelligence itself manifesting in form.

By training, I am an Osteopathic physician. One of the principles of Osteopathic philosophy is that the body is a self-healing, self-regulating system. Healing is a natural process by which living physiology is continually guided by the innate wisdom and intelligence within the body. A surgeon is comfortable making an incision because she has certainty in her knowledge that the body will know how to heal it. And there is a greater picture, for the body is only one aspect of the whole.

Another fundamental principle of Osteopathy is that the human being is a unity of mind, body, and spirit. This is often misunderstood to mean that mind, body and spirit are connected. In reality they are aspects of the complete human being; they are one and the same, expressions of an indivisible whole. To move toward complete well-being, we must cultivate an awareness that brings harmony to the dynamic interplay of these three aspects of the Self.

Perception

Our body is an extremely sensitive sensory instrument. Most of the time it is never trained and developed as such. Infants in a nurturing environment naturally start to develop their sensory capabilities. Young children notice sounds, sights, and smells with curious fascination. They feel and respond to subtle changes in the world around them and in the emotional states of important people in their lives. They sense their aliveness, and it gives them great joy.

But our educational system is lacking in courses that help us develop our sensory capabilities. When children start school, the emphasis very quickly becomes a focused development of the intellect, the abstract skills of written language and mathematics. For most human beings, the development of refined sensory capabilities is stunted and may never be fully experienced.

-§-
For most human beings, the development of refined sensory capabilities is stunted and may never be fully experienced.
-§-

Yet we can develop our senses further, extending our ability to perceive. I have a creek near my house where a giant bay laurel tree fell over many years ago. Its huge trunk lies on the ground, but with its roots still in the creek the tree has continued to grow. The branches come off the fallen trunk and reach vertically toward the sky. There are two branches that grow side by side, both about an inch in diameter. One branch bursts into a small leafy umbrella about twelve feet up. The other ends in barren tips, for that branch has died. Any person who wraps her hands around these branches simultaneously will feel the difference between the two. One is surging with vitality, with the cool living sap under its bark. You can feel the life, the health inside. The other branch looks the same but feels altogether different. It is dim and dry, with no vitality there. It is not alive, not expressing the power in the tree. If we take the time to be still and listen, and practice a good deal, it is amazing what subtle and delicate input we are able to perceive.

When I was in medical school, I heard a lecture by an E. R. physician with an interest in photography. He had just returned from Mexico, where he had been photographing a full solar eclipse. While there, he befriended a NASA photographer—with all his hi-tech equipment—on a similar mission. He showed us the resulting photographs from both his camera and the superior NASA camera. He also showed us an artist's rendition of what they had all seen through a pinhole in a box. The amazing thing was that neither camera had managed to capture the fullness and color of the light halo that had been visible to the artist's unaided human eye.

There are many types of motion in the body. The most obvious ones we observe as we move our bodies through space: the swinging of the limbs, turning of the head, swaying of the hips. Our muscles also move us in finer, more precise ways, the way our spinal muscles adjust to keep our posture upright and balanced as we walk over uneven ground, the way a painter holds the brush when giving detail to a masterpiece.

There is also the motion of our breathing, most easily seen in the ribcage, but also moving our diaphragm, our heart (which sits directly on the diaphragm), our throat, and all of our internal organs right down to our pelvic floor. In fact, if you look closely enough, you'll find that almost all of the body moves in some way as a response to the motion of breathing.

-§-

If we take the time to be still and listen, it is amazing what subtle and delicate input we are able to perceive.

-§-

The breath is unusual as one of the most basic of biological functions in that it is under both unconscious and conscious control. Breathing is just given to us to do; it happens automatically whether we are aware of it or not. The autonomic nervous system adapts the rate and depth of our breath to keep pace with the body's requirements. Our breathing also tunes to our emotional state. Whether we are running or sleeping, frightened or joyful, our breathing responds automatically.

But our breathing is also under conscious control. We can choose to breathe slow or fast, shallow or deep. We can even hold our breath for a period of time, stopping it altogether for a minute or more. But eventually the physiological imperative to restore this function will drive us to take our next breath. If someone were determined to hold his breath indefinitely, he would eventually lose consciousness and at that point the unconscious control system would start him breathing again. Because of this dual system of control, breathing may act as a bridge or window between the conscious and unconscious self.

In addition to these obvious motions, there are many other internal, less visible motions as well—the pumping of the heart and circulation of blood through the vascular system, the change in size of arteries as their muscular walls dilate or contract to regulate blood flow, the coordinated movement of the esophagus as it carries food to the stomach, the peristaltic motion of the intestines, the movement of lymphatic fluid carrying the metabolic waste products of the cells back into the venous circulation, and the release of glandular secretions. The nervous system not only moves electrical currents, but also brings nutritive factors to the tissues through neurotrophic flow. There are many more. The whole body is in motion, down to every cell. There is a tremendous biochemical and electrical metabolic activity occurring continuously on a cellular level.

A thorough knowledge of anatomy and physiology is the foundation for the practice of Osteopathy. The founder of Osteopathy, Dr. Andrew Taylor Still (1828-1917), was a man of both science and philosophy. He discovered Osteopathy by studying the laws of the natural world, and developed it as a science to heal the afflicted. There are approaches in Osteopathy that interface with some of the less obvious motions and forces within the body. Osteopathy in the cranial field stems from the insight and intense work of William G. Sutherland, DO (1872- 1954), who as a medical student viewed a disarticulated skull and noticed that the articular surfaces between the bones looked as though they were designed for motion. He spent the next thirty years of his life studying and researching the implications of this observation, and continued to work throughout his life teaching the clinical applications of his discoveries.

-§-
Because of this dual system of control, breathing may act as a bridge or window between the conscious and unconscious self.
-§-

We have twenty-nine bones in the head, not including the teeth, all of which have complex three-dimensional shapes. They live inside of interconnected membranous envelopes, a membranous system which also encloses and supports the central nervous system, which is protected and nourished inside a waterbed of cerebrospinal fluid. There is an inherent motility of the central nervous system, and a fluctuation of the cerebrospinal fluid. The sutures between the cranial bones retain some flexibility throughout life. This whole integrated system, always in motion and responding to life, is a powerful interface to work with in the therapeutic process.

Why Do We Have Disease?

If we are truly self-healing and self-regulating, then why do we have disease and dysfunction? There are many ways disease may come to us, derailing the health in the human system. It may happen through physical trauma, emotional abuse, chemical poisoning, malnutrition, grief, poor lifestyle choices, ongoing stress, or inherited behavioral and genetic tendencies. In most cases I see disease as an aberrant pattern that is taken on by the body and central nervous system, or by the mind and emotions.

When I was a child, I saw the boy who lived next door attacked by a dog. A stray dog was loose in the neighborhood and had started a vicious fight with the boy's dog in his front yard. He was trying to break it up when his right hand was bitten and torn open around the thumb. The boy came back from the hospital with an impressive number of stitches, and his hand held up near his chest. He was a young teenager at the time, and

I was younger still, but I found it curious that after the stitches were out, he always held his right arm with the elbow bent at about ninety degrees and the hand hanging around the chest. Even two years later, when his family moved away, he was still carrying his right hand in this position.

When he was bitten, his peripheral nervous system sent messages to the central nervous system saying, "We're attacked, we're torn, we're in pain." The central nervous system sent messages back to the hand saying, "Draw back, recoil!" It's hard to appreciate the tremendous speed with which things happen on a cellular level in the body. The release of phosphate from the ATP molecule, a chemical reaction that provides energy for cellular processes, occurs ten million times per second in every cell. Ten million times! I can't even begin to grasp the speed of that; it's happening so fast. Our nervous system works at this level of tremendous speed. For this boy, the message to draw the hand back was sent down the nerves in the arm millions if not billions of times. Directly after the injury, other messages told him to keep the hand up to ease his pain and swelling.

> -§-
> The memory of dynamic perfection is alive within the matrix of the health.
> -§-

Unfortunately there was never an input made to override this dysfunctional pattern, and after a time the nervous system decided that this was where the hand belonged. It reset the neutral resting position for the limb with the elbow bent at ninety degrees and the hand held near the sternum.

In an ideal situation, there would be an intervention that restores the normal freedom of motion and function of the limb. The intervention might have been the boy's own awareness saying, "Hey, I don't want to walk around with my hand in this funny position, so I'm going to pay attention and work to bring it back to normal."

If he had seen a skilled practitioner shortly after the injury, it would have been easy to re-establish the original position and dynamic function of the arm and hand. If he were to walk into my office today, thirty years later, I believe we could still establish the original function in the limb because the memory of dynamic perfection is alive within the matrix of the health. It may be hidden, or overridden by the noise inherent in the unreleased resistance of the stress response, but intact nevertheless. I would predict that there would be other dysfunctions with the arm and hand, set up within the aberrant pattern of injury. It might take a lot of work to unwrap and disengage all of the adaptations and compensations established over thirty years. But without intervention, the patterns may become fixed for life.

This is a simple example of how the body can take on a dysfunctional posture. Consider the implications for the complete human being, the intellectual, emotional, spiritual "posture" of a whole person. On any level an aberrant or imbalanced response to stress may result in dis-ease.

Healing and the Therapeutic Process

It is a relatively small percentage of Osteopathic physicians who practice traditional hands-on Osteopathy. For those who do, Osteopathy is taught in an oral tradition, passed on directly, experientially, from physician to student. I've had many wonderful teachers throughout my training. Much of my understanding of the therapeutic process I have learned from my work with James S. Jealous, DO, through his biodynamic approach to Osteopathy. The bulk of my practical skills I've learned while treating my patients.

A few months ago, a seventy-seven-year-old man, Russ, came to my office and told me, "I'm just all falling apart." In the past five years he'd had three joint replacements and two abdominal surgeries. Although his mind was sharp, his body was failing. He no longer had the dexterity in his hands to dress himself, his balance was poor and he walked unsteadily with a cane. He was being treated for heart arrythmias. His spine was bent forward. He used to be six-foot-three, but he told me that after his last surgery, he was looking his five-foot-four wife in the eye. He had pain here, there, and everywhere. He was fearful about his future, scared by the way his life was heading downhill so quickly.

-§-
**Awareness often
retreats from an area
that has been injured.**
-§-

For Russ, there is a lot of active work we can do to get things going. We want to create more space, more freedom in his musculoskeletal system. We need to wake up the spine and mobilize the rib cage. This will help get the diaphragm moving which will allow more breath and improve fluid dynamics, including circulation through the heart. Systematically, we restore blood flow to nourish the tissues and restore the function of the lymphatics so the tissues can be cleansed. As we restore structural dynamics, nerve conduction and neurotrophic flow is improved.

Awareness often retreats from an area that has been injured. Russ's awareness has significantly neglected his body over the years; he has become tight and stiff. We want to bring awareness back into his body, so that he can live in it in a more full and connected way.

We start the process. On Russ's third visit he comes out of the treatment room standing much straighter, and proudly puts his chin on top of his wife's head.

With my hands, I challenge his system to see how it will respond, where there is an opening, a vitality that will engage with me. Initially, I find mostly his restrictive pattern, but I feel through that pattern, into something much deeper which still moves with its original dynamic freedom. Within this field of underlying vitality or potency the health operates. It is that which we wish to arouse and unveil.

As we work together, another important change takes place. Russ begins to believe, actually observe, that he is moving toward health, living a more functional and comfortable life.

Russ continues to make steady progress. The dexterity in his hands is vastly improved. He can dress himself, including socks, shoes and buttons. He can use his computer. He stands tall and upright. He feels stronger. His arrythmias are gone. His balance is better and he's walking confidently. He recently told me, "I've become my own man again."

Osteopathic treatment is an intervention which aims to restore function as directed by the health, to rekindle the ability of the health to manifest. It is an intervention, a "breath between" the unmanifest and manifest body, which arouses a memory of original perfection, and allows it to go to work.

Like many people in our culture, I grew up trained to ask, "What is wrong with this picture." Much of Western medicine asks the same question, looking for the problem, the disease. Healing is also about asking the question, "What is," and acknowledging any symptoms of illness, but it is also about *looking through the contracted self* to see the continuously manifested health. It also asks, "What is working? What is right?"

Healers are people who see integrity and beauty unfolding in the world around them, in the world which holds them. The power to heal exists within every human being. My skills as an Osteopath help me sense the motion inherent within the body, and make contact with the living substance of the system's innate intelligence. When I see it go to work, I stand in awe. It is truly miraculous. I can invite it into presence, call to it, but to have that call answered is always a gift.

LION GOODMAN:

Dorothy and the Disowned Very Bad Awful Feelings

Dorothy feels afraid and powerless, and she doesn't like it. Mean old Elmira Gulch is threatening to take away her dog Toto, Dorothy's closest friend and companion. Aunt Em and Uncle Henry are too busy counting chicks to be bothered with her predicament. Zeke insists she be courageous, even though he's afraid. Hunk tells her to use her brains and gives her wise council while fumbling every move he makes. Hickory is too self-absorbed to care about anyone but himself. Despite Dorothy's pleading, Aunt Em cuts her off and scurries away, telling her to stop imagining things and find a place where she won't get into any trouble. Elmira takes the dog away to be destroyed, but her selfish plot is foiled by Toto's quick escape. Dorothy feels she has no choice but to run away from home.

Dorothy is desperate. She feels alone and frightened in a dangerous, uncaring world, and she doesn't want to feel these very bad awful feelings. She decides to utilize one of the most successful strategies for avoiding them: running away. This is not only a classic children's story, but also a classic psychological stance we take toward our very bad awful feelings. We will do anything—even create a completely delusional world—in order to avoid feeling uncomfortable. This is the insidious realm of disowned experience.

At age thirteen, while showing off for my father, I dared a sequence of three flips on our backyard trampoline. On the third flip, I opened my tuck too early and my forehead hit the mat. My body continued its trajectory over me. I heard a crunch and felt pressure and a twist of my neck as

Lion Goodman is an executive coach, author, workshop leader, public speaker, and businessman. He coaches chief executives, managers, and entrepreneurs, helping individuals achieve extraordinary success and happiness. His workshop "Everyday Awakening"™ is offered worldwide. He is a licensed teacher of The Avatar® Course, an internationally acclaimed belief management and consciousness training program. He earned a degree in Consciousness Studies in 1975. His stories, articles and poetry have been published internationally. His full information is available at www.everydayawakening.com. Photo by Jack Gescheidt.

the back of my head touched the middle of my back. My body lay still as I went into shock. I had come very close to snapping my spine in two. Fortunately my back was only traumatized, not broken. I felt okay a few days later, although my enthusiasm for the trampoline vanished.

Nine years later, while attending the University of Colorado in Boulder, I was chosen to participate in a demonstration of Rolfing, a connective tissue massage therapy also known as Structural Integration. After stripping down to my underwear, I was led onto the stage to stand next to a wrinkled, white-haired, eighty-year-old grandmother and originator of the technique, Dr. Ida Rolf. In front of her audience of three hundred people, Dr. Rolf pointed to my back and identified various imbalances in my posture. She then asked, "How did you injure your back here?"

-§-
We will do anything, even create a completely delusional world, in order to avoid feeling uncomfortable.
-§-

Not, "If," but "How?" Speaking into the microphone, I told the story of my tangle with the trampoline. She then laid me on a low massage table and began pushing her strong hands, knuckles, and elbows into my body, stretching my tissues and changing my structure with each powerful move. I breathed deeply as the intense manipulation opened something deep inside me. My body began to vibrate with a subtle electric buzz, and my nose started to tingle. The tingling sensation slowly spread to my entire face, head, and chest. Ida slipped her fingers beneath my back and pushed up into a spot below and between my shoulder blades.

A bolt of lightening shot through me, as if she had plugged my toes into a 220-volt power outlet. A fire rushed up my spine and out my head. I remembered the entire trampoline accident as if it were happening in that moment. Instead of going into shock and feeling nothing, as had happened nine years before, I heard the crackling sound of bones twisting in the wrong direction, and felt the folding of my neck and upper back. I could feel my vertebrae crunching into each other, and began to sob. The trauma that had been stored in my body for nine years flooded through me. I curled into a fetal position, crying like an injured child. Huge waves of energy flowed through me, so powerful that I couldn't move.

Ida covered me with a sheet and put a loving hand on my shoulder. Between my sobs, she told the audience, "Those of you who are therapists will recognize this as emotional trauma release, normally coming after months and months of therapy." Opening my eyes for a moment, I saw hundreds of people staring at me, mouths agape. "The hell with them," I thought. "I'm going to feel this fully. So what if I'm crying in public." It was not one of my most glorious moments in front of an audience, but it was a glorious moment of release. After that night, I felt more alive than I had felt in nine years. Feelings in my body and my heart were more vivid than I could ever remember. Had the trampoline trauma remained stored in my tissues, it might have later turned into back problems, emotional distance in my relationships, or disease somewhere in my body.

When very bad awful things happen, whether by threat, stress, injury or disease, the nerves send signals to the brain and the surrounding tissues to indicate something is wrong. We experience most of these signals as pain. In the case of emotional stress or trauma, we usually experience it as overwhelming, something we cannot handle. Dorothy felt it as panic and the associated need to escape. These feelings are the result of a chain of hundreds of thousands of chemical and electrical events, including those that stimulate repair of damage. Pain is an important signal to receive and welcome, but we don't always receive the message. We don't like to be uncomfortable, and we don't like pain, whether physical, emotional, mental, or spiritual. We resist it. We seek to dull it, or extinguish it completely. We intellectualize it away by labeling or analyzing. We try to fix it, desperately seeking change or solutions. We may try to ignore it by distracting ourselves, or pushing ahead with other activities. We may suffer silently, enduring it, or we may talk endlessly to others about it. We sometimes use alcohol or drugs to numb ourselves out. We rely on our favorite addictions of choice—for some it is food, for others sex, TV, or work. We will do anything to resist the pain, even to our detriment. But whatever we resist will somehow persist. We will experience it eventually, sooner or later, one way or the other.

-§-

Getting injured or creating a bigger problem is another convenient way to avoid unpleasant feelings.

-§-

Getting injured or creating a bigger problem is another convenient way to avoid unpleasant feelings. Dorothy went so far as to get hit on the head, commencing a shamanic journey involving tiny people she could tower over, an emerald city with infinite delights, and vivid manifestations of her many sub-personalities: a simple con-man portraying himself as a powerful wizard, a lion with no courage but much false bravado, an empty kettle with no heart and a steely personality, and a stuffed doll with little brain but lots of bright ideas. Instead of being ignored and unseen, she became the subject of everyone's attention.

Had Dorothy lived through the 1990s, receiving the benefit of psychotherapy and the human potential movement, she might have sat down with her family to express how frustrated, afraid and unloved she felt. Auntie Em, Uncle Henry, and each of the farm hands would hold her close, telling her she was truly loved. Someone would remind her that adults get busy, and sometimes forget to show their love. Children misinterpret this busyness, believing they are unloved or unlovable, and feel neglected or abandoned. (Unfortunately, this is also true of many adults.) Each member of her family would promise to do better, and someone would remind her to ask for what she wanted. "Feel your feelings as they come up," they would tell her, "and tell us all your feelings honestly." The story would be much shorter and far less interesting, of course, because Dorothy never would have left home or stumbled into Oz.

Six years after my near-naked on-stage demonstration of emotional trauma release, a young man who was traveling with me pulled out a gun, aimed at my head, and shot me—four times. I had learned by this time that any resistance to an experience only delays, and often exacerbates, suffering. The first bullet felt like a baseball bat to the top of my head, yet it shocked me into a state of hyper-awareness. When I realized my companion intended to kill me, I decided to face my death with presence and courage. I relaxed completely. I was determined to die well, fully awake to whatever might happen.

The absence of resistance saved my life. My relaxation was so deep that the fourth bullet pushed my head to the side, allowing the bullet to glance off at an angle. Resistance in the form of fear or anger would have locked up my neck; that counter-force may well have allowed the bullet to shatter my skull. I not only survived, but as Dorothy did, received my own initiation into another world. The full story, "A Shot In The Light," can be found in the international best-seller, *I Thought My Father Was God... and Other True Tales from NPR's National Story Project* (Henry Holt, 2001), and in the film, "The Kindness of Strangers," directed by Claudia Myers.

-§-
We have two options when faced with an unpleasant experience: we can experience it very intensely for a short amount of time, or we can experience it faintly for a long period of time.
-§-

Whenever we experience a trauma, shock, or injury, the natural response is to contract inward to protect ourselves. When the difficulty is over and the body has recovered, we should ideally return to an open, relaxed posture. Cats and dogs demonstrate this natural principle: when they get hurt or injured, they first shake themselves or jump around, discharging the energy generated by the trauma. They then stop eating, curl up, and rest or sleep for extended periods of time. After their body has healed, they return to their natural feline or canine behavior. Humans, however, have the option of disowning their experience.

The most severe shocks and traumas—especially repeated or sustained traumas such as sexual or emotional abuse, or the experience of life-or-death conflicts such as war—cause the temporary contraction to become permanent. The body is unable to relax back into trust and openness. A defensive posture becomes a fixed way of life. The holding pattern becomes protective body armor against a dangerous world.

Every holding pattern, regardless of cause, restricts the flow of energy (including healing energy) in our body. Disease often results. Much of the work of healing involves returning to past experiences that have been avoided in order to re-experience them, or perhaps even to experience them fully for the first time. Body-centered therapies such as Rolfing, Bioenergetics, and Holotropic Breathwork can release the protective armor, allowing the natural flow of breath and movement to return. Psychotherapy aims at the same principle, targeting the release of emotions and memories, and the establishment of new patterns of behavior.

An even more effective method of release is to eliminate the beliefs and resisted experiences that created the persistent condition in the first place. In the programs I teach, called Everyday Awakening™ and The Avatar Course®, we use a wide variety of methods to root out unhealthy core beliefs and dissolve them, replacing them with more positive beliefs that will create our preferred reality. Dorothy's core beliefs included, "Nobody cares about me." She was released from her colorful delusion with her new belief, "There's no place like home."

We have two options when faced with an unpleasant experience: we can experience it very intensely for a short amount of time, or we can experience it subtly, in the background, for a long period of time. But experience it we must. If we put up enough resistance, another experience just like it will come our way. Distancing or disowning reality only delays our confrontation with the inevitable. Running away from a threat or a feeling prevents a full encounter with what we fear, but as Dorothy demonstrated in Oz, experiences tend to repeat themselves in our lives until we face them fully. When we do finally confront the dark force we've been avoiding, we tap into inner resources we didn't know we had. Our character is tested, and we find our courage, intelligence, and heart. Our greatest fears are often dispatched with nothing more potent than facing the naked truth. As very bad, awful and scary as they seem, witches and goblins that have prevented us from achieving our goals are dissolved by a splash of water: the willingness to experience them directly.

-§-
We have been given a simple, glorious and important assignment by the Creator: experience *everything* that comes.
-§-

We have been given a simple, glorious and important assignment by the Creator: experience *everything* that comes. You were given the gift of human birth in order to have unique experiences. Your job is to act as a nerve ending and give full attention and appreciation to your experiences. I like to believe that our experiences travel up the chain of being into the Infinite Mind of the Creator. When we dull, deaden, or numb our input signals, we cut off the flow of this information. If the information can't get through, it will wait in the background as an annoying little signal until it has the opportunity to be experienced fully. It's like the memory buffer on your printer which blinks a little light to let you know that it has stored the pages you sent. It waits patiently until you give it the attention it needs, replenishing its supply of paper so it can finish its assigned task.

Why would a benevolent God have given us the ability to experience a wide variety of feelings and then have us avoid them? To the Great Mystery, all experiences are interesting! This includes the very bad awful experiences of pain, trauma, injury, loss, tragedy, sickness, and death. The Infinite Mind does not have a human heart or human preferences. It wants to experience everything, always creating new possibilities along with its old favorites.

But humans have human hearts, and we have strong preferences. We resist approximately half of all our experiences—the difficult and uncomfortable ones. We believe that pain is bad. We believe that we shouldn't be uncomfortable. We resist these very bad awful feelings, pushing them away, dulling our senses, anesthetizing ourselves with our own version of the field of poppies enchanted by the Wicked Witch. The poppies of today are everywhere—as close as the nearest rack of convenience store snacks or the infinite distractions of the web and cable TV. They put us to sleep, separating us from our own (often uncomfortable) direct experience. Every disowned or refused experience, however, persists until experienced. Everything we resist does persist.

-§-
We resist approximately half of all our experiences—the difficult and uncomfortable ones.
-§-

If you have a persisting condition that you prefer not to have, including pain, disease, unworkable relationships, or a bad financial situation, there is something you are resisting. This is not to say there aren't things physically wrong with your body, brain or circumstances. Physical manifestations are the expression of our resistance. How do you know when you've stopped resisting? The rule is simple: *When you experience something fully, it will change or disappear completely.* If you're still experiencing something you don't like, there is more work to do.

If you wish to make a change, ask yourself these questions:

- What experience or feeling am I successfully avoiding by having this condition persist?
- What is the payoff I get from having this exact condition?
- What beliefs do I have that could create a condition like this?
- What beliefs would create the scenario I would rather have?
- Am I willing to change my beliefs?

Curiously, God would not have given us the ability to *resist* our experiences if she didn't want us to use this ability from time to time. Persistence keeps things in existence. Rocks resist erosion, so mountains last for millions of years. Life-forms resist being destroyed, so we avoid dangerous situations and survive.

We cannot change a condition we dislike unless we first take away our resistance to that condition. When the Wizard gave Dorothy and her crew the assignment to retrieve the broom of the Wicked Witch of the West, they resisted the idea and believed it impossible. But they then accepted the fact that it was the only route home. Here is a handy trick: If you have a persisting condition (a pain, problem, disease, or difficulty), begin by intensifying your resistance. Fight off what you don't like. Keep it away with all your strength. Consciously ignore it and deny that it belongs to you. Push it as far away from you as you can possibly push it. Do all of this consciously, by choice, rather than automatically and sub-consciously, which is what you have been doing.

When you are good and tired of what that resistance has created in your life, become willing to experience your resistance fully. Feel your resistance to the condition. Allow it to be there. Appreciate it as one more gift from God. Experience it, and glory in it. The cycle of resistance will be completed, and it can move on.

When you feel your resistance lift, become willing to experience what-ever you have been resisting. If you didn't want to feel the pain, let the pain in, and feel it fully. Let the discomfort come through the door like a welcomed guest. Offer it a cup of tea and appreciate it for what it is. If you have a disease, even a terminal one, appreciate it as part of God's plan, as part of your plan for your life. If there is persistent pain, open your arms to it and thank the Creator for this

-§-
All pain is growing pain when received and welcomed fully.
-§-

experience, sending it on to the Infinite Mind of God, since that is your role as a nerve ending—to experience and send the signal on to Source. Breathe into it. Breathe through it. Pain has a role, just as pleasure does. It is a signal that something is out of balance, dangerous, or beyond the edge of our safe limits. The body needs this signal in order to know how to heal. Receive this gift willingly, and let it play the role it is designed to play—prompting growth and healing.

All pain is growing pain when received and welcomed fully. This is true for emotional pain—those very bad awful feelings—as well as phys-ical pain, intellectual angst, and spiritual crisis. Appreciate the gift, wel-come it, and it will move through you more easily. Deny it, or resist it, and it will stick with you forever—or until you accept it as your gift and learn its lesson. Miracles can, and do happen. We can go home again—to our bodies, to our aliveness, and to the full range of our experience—recog-nizing finally that there really is no place like home.

Jim Gilkeson:

Exploding the Upper Limit of Healing

Healing processes change us. To a greater or lesser degree, they always entail a growth in our consciousness, which inevitably takes us beyond what we have established as our everyday reality. This subtly changes our worldview and the way of living our lives that we are most familiar with and propels us beyond boundaries where we previously stopped ourselves. As a result, healing that leads to growth often challenges the notion of "getting back to normal," or returning to the way we were before we started the healing process. By its very nature healing changes our view of reality, hopefully expanding how we experience our lives.

I know a healer named Virgil, and I'll go out on a limb and say that he's the genuine article. Virgil comes from Texas and, like it or not, he looks enough like Ronald Reagan to make you wonder if you have come to the right address. Virgil is in his mid-sixties and every morning he jumps up and down on his mini-trampoline several hundred times while holding a #5 can of Campbell's Soup out at arm's length in each hand. Try it sometime. Really gets the old ticker into high gear. He says it's better than jogging.

Virgil's healing sessions combine specific breathing techniques along with his own brand of subtle and not-so-subtle bodywork. He has an uncanny ability to track the subtle interior processes within people who come to him for help. No matter where they are in their journey, on his healing table he is right there with them.

I once had the opportunity to assist Virgil in some healing sessions. He begins with an outrageous prayer. Looking around the room like an

Jim Gilkeson, CMT, is a creative bodywork therapist, teacher and the author of *Energy Healing: A Pathway to Inner Growth* (Marlowe, 2000). A former brother in a semi-monastic spiritual order, Jim's background in meditation and spiritual practice and his love for experiential learning have made him keenly attentive to the developmental and initiatory dimensions of bodywork and energy healing. He has practices in San Anselmo and at Harbin Hot Springs in California and is working on a second book on energy healing. This material is a revised version of the chapter entitled "Progressive Healing" in *Energy Healing*. Photo by Kathy Evans.

orator addressing a huge audience, he says something like this: "In this healing, let us all come to a *new place,* one where we haven't ever been before." At this point, the person he is working on swallows audibly, or opens her eyes, and takes a deep breath. For a person coming for the first time for such a treatment, this moment is always a surprise since it is a clear statement that the object of this healing is *not* going to be a return to something that is already known, but rather a move into the unknown. A new place. It is outrageous because Virgil really *means* it.

From the vantage point of the person lying on Virgil's healing table, these words can be quite unsettling. Here is someone who may have driven across town or even from out of state, and is paying good money for a treatment. She has come in hopes of mellowing out or getting "energized" for an hour, only to hear from this Ronald Reagan look-alike that this healing business has to do with moving into a "new place." The first reaction may be alarm. If she has had some level of experience with healing and personal growth, she may also have an inkling that she will be encountering something from her own subconscious, perhaps shadow material that she had never dealt with until this moment. Just as with going to a new country or trying a brand new experience, people's reactions will vary, from anxiety and resistance to being excited by the prospect of a new discovery.

-§-

One does not become enlightened by imagining figures of light, but by making the darkness conscious.

—C. G. Jung

-§-

Most of us have inherited at least a certain degree of our ancestors' fear of the unconscious. This subterranean place within our own consciousness can at first seem dark and forbidding. Freud sought to release us from this fear by providing tools for exploring the human subconscious and demystifying the primitive impulses that so many generations of our ancestors had feared.

If Freud invented psychoanalysis, and saw dream analysis as the doorway to the unconscious, it was his cohort, C. G. Jung, who dared to suggest that the unconscious contained far more than clues to our inhibitions and repressions; it also provided clues to the spiritual dimension of our lives. Jung, who was a student of Oriental and Gnostic philosophy, introduced the idea (in the West) that remarkable wisdom, power and resources are contained in the unconscious or are accessible to us through our dreams and intuition. One of the greatest steps in healing is learning to trust, to say "yes" to these deeper personal processes, which, as we will see, becomes much more than managing symptoms and solving problems and "getting back to normal."

Our friend Virgil's healing sessions were not about getting back to normal so much as they were about peeling back the veil to an expanded view of his client's life. The whole atmosphere around his sessions was charged with the certainty that, more than anything else, the point was to move into a process of growth and change in which we become ever more responsive to life.

Two Modes of Healing

Healing is a natural process, but the reason it is natural is not because we have now decided to take herbal medicines instead of chemical ones, or that we seek the help of an acupuncturist rather than a surgeon. We are each born with self-healing capacities, as is every living organism. And this kind of healing goes on continuously, involving virtually every cell in our body and our whole consciousness. It is a movement—provided by nature—toward reincorporating parts of ourselves that weren't integrated before. Those who find a way to appreciate that movement and participate in it are often awestruck at how it goes on constantly throughout our whole body and consciousness.

In this regard, I wonder if we are not doing a disservice to the idea of natural or holistic healing when we call it "alternative." Maybe we need to shake off a certain kind of thinking, or at least stand it on its head. It is good to remind ourselves that these are among the original healing modalities. Not only do they have their own historical developments, which in many cases predate our modern technological medicine by millennia, but they also make use of the natural elements of our planet: fire, air, earth and water, the animal, mineral and plant kingdoms, and the self-correcting power of nature within us, represented in the way the energy of life flows within and around living beings. Our body heals itself every time we scratch or scrape our skin.

-§-
Progressive Healing: Focuses on moving forward.
Regressive healing: Focuses on returning to previous ways of being.
-§-

In light of the vastly different healing modes that have developed, I find it helpful to think in terms of "regressive healing" and "progressive healing." These are represented by two different attitudes that are sometimes on speaking terms with one another, but usually are not. As the words themselves imply, regressive healing focuses on returning to a previous way of being while progressive healing focuses on moving forward.

Regressive healing refers here to a program of bringing symptoms under control so that the sufferer can make a speedy return to his previous state, that is, to whatever he viewed as "normal." For example, the stressed out stockbroker goes to his doctor and gets a prescription for high blood pressure medication—but returns to the same stressful work environment. By contrast, progressive healing refers to processes that, by their nature, carry us into new ways of being, presumably a way of being that is more in harmony with our inborn, self-healing capacities. For example, our same stockbroker discovers he has high blood pressure, gets medication for it but begins questioning fundamental patterns in his life: Why he feels so driven toward financial success, why he chooses to work in a pressure cooker environment that he knows is killing him.

The progressive path is colored by the belief that even our really horrible experiences serve a necessary purpose: our difficulties are part of a process of growth and insight. In fact, what we often find is that some of our most painful experiences were the only way we could have gained access to what we needed to heal in our lives. An example of this kind of progressive healing—a move into a new place—is found in the following passage from a lecture by German homeopath, Jürgen Becker and is used by permission. The case study he refers to below, which I translated, was of a Greek woman who had come to him because of a heart condition.

-§-

"Things fall apart, so they can 'fall together' at a higher level of order."
—Marilyn Ferguson

-§-

I saw her only twice; once when she came for her initial consultation, during which I gave her a single dose of medication, and another about four months later when she back came in order to tell me what had happened.

This was a pious, strictly brought up Greek Orthodox woman. She was educated, a scholar. She told me that she had experienced a "healing." She told me of two dreams that came in an exact rhythm—fourteen days after taking her first dose and then fourteen days after she took her second dose.

The first dream was this: She encounters a young man, handsome, beautiful even, immaculate, wonderful, her ideal of a man with whom she would fall in love. If she were to encounter such a man in real life, she would immediately say "that is the right man for me, this man and no other."

But he is the Devil. You can't see it by looking at him, no hoofed feet, no horns. He looks perfect, but he's the Devil. She is deeply unsettled by this dream, in which she finds herself falling in love with the Devil.

My impression, again, was that this woman was extremely pious and strictly brought-up, and in her faith there is the idea of Deadly Sin. Once one has committed a Deadly Sin, once you have yielded to fleshly desire—the first time you don't take this rigid, unyielding posture—Deadly Sin immediately enters in and you are damned for all eternity. And so this deep longing of hers for the beautiful young man who is also the Devil is absolutely forbidden, a Deadly Sin. This dream caused a huge upheaval in this woman.

This first dream was not her healing experience, but rather it thrust her into the core of her problem: *fear of deadly sin before God Almighty.* If you live in such a state, what kind of image of God do you have? Probably as the kind of God who sits on high, swinging an ax, saying, "Only the one in a hundred, only the one in a thousand who is worthy, will I allow into heaven. But everyone else gets eternal damnation! You're going to have to take the *full* consequences of each and every little tiny thing you ever did wrong! Each time you ever had a bad thought — and remember, *God sees everything* — you will pay for each thing! It is hopeless. No matter what you do, no matter how much effort you exert to do everything right. You might succeed in some things but as soon as you make even one little error, you will have to face the *full consequences.*"

And that will go on eternally. No mercy, right? Apparently this woman was confronted with just this in those fourteen days. After that exact period, the second dream came: A bright shape made of light comes toward her and she recognizes it as Jesus. Jesus speaks to her very gently, "Hello, Elisabeth." And that was all. This was the healing moment she was talking about. [Apparently her heart symptoms improved dramatically afterward.] Redemption.

-§-

"It is our lot, if we are honest, to live in duality and paradox. The dialogue of those paradoxical elements is the stuff of life."
—Robert A. Johnson

-§-

It happens like that. There is no way that most of us could possibly produce such an experience. But *this* woman could. Her inner situation was such that this was what she needed. The form in which it appears makes no difference.

I have always found this case history to be a wonderful example of progressive healing. This woman's inner struggle was part of the background of her illness, but it also turned out to be what brought her to the threshold of change. Chemical intervention might have managed to calm her outer symptoms and helped her to get back to normal, but it was her dramatic dilemma and its resolution in her dream encounter with Jesus that transported her into something very new indeed. What could be more beautiful?

The Longing of a Drop of Water For the Ocean

What is the "motor" behind progressive healing? The very nature of being alive seems to insist that we grow and that our worlds expand, whether we consciously want that to happen or not! In my work with clients and as a workshop leader, I get to watch the kinds of transformations that come over people when they come, even momentarily, into a state of balance. It seems that when energetic balance is struck within us, we become receptive to fresh impulses that lead us into brand new experiences. The polarity principle, which has special meaning in the striking of that balance, is represented, one way or another, in all approaches to healing. While it is not a complex principle to understand, having a picture of how it works is important.

In its simplest form a polarity exists anywhere that we establish two points or poles: North and South; East and West; left and right; yin and yang; masculine and feminine; or positive and negative. When healers set out to understand what is causing a lack of harmony, or dis-ease in a person, they always run into the polarity principle. Whether they are making sure that the right gods are propitiated, yin and yang are balanced, chakras and energy streams are unobstructed, vertebrae are aligned, diet is balanced, or pH-levels are properly adjusted, there is an intuitive awareness, at the very least, that balance is essential. The paradox and mystery of spiritually-active approaches to healing is that when the natural polarities that influence us come into balance, our consciousness can move completely *beyond* polarity, and a very different balance, one that is more complete, will enter the picture.

-§-

In energetic treatments, whether we use our hands directly on or just off the body, we are enlivening and bringing balance to the place where the body and the psyche meet.

-§-

In any healing activity, an ancient and universal spiritual instinct seems to be at work. Healing is at its best, and is the most elegant, when it involves the merest nudge to the system. The healer who is adept in subtle healing thinks in terms of giving a nudge to one single log that is the key to freeing the logjam, allowing the stream to flow freely again. At the opposite extreme is the guy who uses dynamite to free the logjam. The stream may flow freely again but in the process the riverbed itself is damaged, creating a whole new set of problems. The healer knows instinctively that imponderably tiny things—the longing of a drop of water for the ocean, a touch or a word or a look of recognition—can tip the soul's scales toward balance and initiate a new cycle.

To test this principle of the power of the imponderably tiny to bring about balance, try this with a pendulum or a small weight on the end of a thread: get the pendulum swinging, then try to stop its swing by making big movements. The swinging only becomes more violent and out of control. Now try to minimize the swing by concentrating your thoughts on its settling down and becoming still. In no time at all the pendulum will settle down, no longer vacillating between the two poles of its arc.

In polarity energy-balancing therapy, in which we place our hands on pairs of energy-active positions—"polarity positions"—on either side of the body. Then we simply allow the energetic exchange between our hands to take place. In time, the energetic system of the person receiving the treatment will naturally shift into a balanced state, and this brings with it a host of effects including the release of tension, relaxation, energization, and faster recovery from injuries and diseases.

But the question that kept me busy was: Why do people also regularly experience flashes of *insight* during treatments, and an infusion of new energy which seems to carry them forward in their lives? Polarity-style treatments make use of "energy-active" positions on the body. These energy positions are part of the etheric, the layer of energy activity immediately surrounding and interpenetrating the physical body. It has a number of very distinct qualities. It responds to all kinds of energetic influences; among them are color and light, sound, geometry, touch, and emotion. In my view, healing the etheric is one of the first important tasks of energetic healing because this is the layer of the energy field that creates the living energetic link between your physical body and the other dimensions of energy and consciousness around and within you. Just as important, this layer we call the etheric is the *storehouse of the subconscious mind* and an energetic link between the body and the psyche. As a result, in energetic treatments, whether we use our hands directly on or just off the body, we are enlivening and bringing balance to the place where the body and the psyche meet. The result can be a sense of tapping into wisdom both personal and beyond the personal.

-§-

Regardless of the subject, balance comes only when both sides are given their due.
—Robert A. Johnson

-§-

Julia, who had recently married, was in a conflict about whether or not she was ready to have children. Her husband grew up in a culture where it was expected that they would start a family immediately. Julia's new family situation created a lot of pressure for her because she no longer felt free to make her own decision on this important issue. During an energy work session to release tension in her back and shoulders, her whole body suddenly relaxed. She wept with relief as a new insight broke through in the process. She realized that her own mother had been extremely ambivalent about having children when she was in her early 20s and had bowed to external pressure to do so. In the process of the polarity release Julia not only released her body tension, but also understood that she had been given an "assignment" to learn to do something that her mother had never learned to do, namely, make sure that if there were to be children, it would be at a time of her own choosing.

Julia's husband and his Latino family didn't suddenly change their attitudes about a woman's say in having babies. But now through the connection and synthesis of the poles within her, Julia's balance and insight opened her to something new about her own strengths and potential to resolve her conflict. Just as with meditation and prayer, the polarity process in energy work can:

- invoke heaven
- call in energy from other dimensions
- invite insight
- create that "third point" that changes everything
- ignite the creative process

CHAPTER SIXTEEN

Constellation

Five hundred years ago, Renaissance philosopher Marsilio Ficino described illness as a form of "monotheism," that is to say, a person's life comes to be dominated by one god, their imagination fixed in a single kind of consciousness. Ficino's examples included ailments, expressed in astrological language, such as depression (a domination of Saturn), obsession with relationship and sexuality (a domination of Venus), and choleric aggressiveness (a domination of Mars).

-§-
"Many men are scared of women and many women are scared of men, [but] what they are actually scared of is themselves."
—Bob Moore
-§-

Nowadays we might say that a person is "stuck" or "hung up," has neuroses, fixations, obsessions, they are living a kind of one-sidedness, they are out of balance. Ficino's idea was to find a way to offset the one-sided tendency by inviting in an opposite kind of spirit, while at the same time experiencing the dominant spirit in great depth.

He prescribed a whole array of "remedies," including specific activities, foods, wines, objects of contemplation, music, sex, and contact with nature—not as an attempt to repress or get rid of the problem (or dominant spirit, in Ficino's terms) but rather to invite a healthful *constellation of influences* in that person's life. This creates the kind of environment which the soul needs in order to balance and heal itself, and continue its progress.

Ficino obviously sensed that the tension between natural polarities—all the different conjugations of masculine and feminine—is the medium for healing, and, with the *restoration* of that tension, its close relative, creativity. For when male and female interact, they create, whether literal physical offspring, the million objects and activities that our wishes and thoughts give rise to, or a means of moving into other dimensions of consciousness. Male and female can only be separated on a physical level. If we try to keep them apart, we eliminate the means by which we can experience what is beyond the physical.

The most basic and inherent spirituality of energy work rises out of its capacity for creating meaningful constellations of the forces that act on us. Energy work, in particular the polarity-type treatment, becomes an art of skillful placement, a *feng shui* of the inner world. Though very simple, it can be one of the most important tools in a healer's bag because it offers an opportunity for a subtle kind of Ficinian constellation. When this type of treatment is used with some understanding of how to find and make good contact with the polarity positions, and when it is done with a decent amount of care and consciousness, the results are often quite impressive. This relaxation and mobilization of energy guides the system toward release and shift of consciousness to what is beyond polarities, and here, something very important happens. We take a quantum leap out of the ruts we have been caught in.

Breaking out of the "Symptom/Misery/Stupidity Cycle"

The "monotheistic stuckness" described by Ficino is a repetitious pattern like what psychologists John Dollard and Niel Miller, in their reformulation of the Freudian concept of neurosis, called the Symptom/Misery/Stupidity Cycle. Symptoms, and the misery they cause, cycle again and again because there is, at the same time, a shutting down of what Dollard and Miller refer to as "higher thought processes." This shutting down is the "stupidity" part of the cycle: without the intelligence and fresh impulses from higher dimensions of consciousness, usually in the form of what we call "catching on," or having the "light go on in our head," we literally don't know what to do. As a result, we tend to fall back on what we have done in the past and make the same mistakes over and over again, perpetuating the cycle. Graphically, it looks like this:

CONFLICT
Inhibition about expressing anger or any response which will reduce tension

REPRESSION
Thing stops, reducing cues for higher mental functions, i.e. intuition and higher consciousness

STRONG DRIVES
Fear and Anger

"SYMPTOM/MISERY STUPIDITY/CYCLE"

MISERY
High level of (repressed) anger and fear

SYMPTOMS
Physical, emotional, mental, social, spiritual

STUPIDITY
Unawareness of the meaning of symptoms, i.e. not getting message about what to do

The "Symptom/Misery/Stupidity Cycle": This is how psychologists John Dollard and Niel Miller reformulated the Freudian concept of neurosis.

Dollard and Miller's explanation of the Symptom/Misery/Stupidity Cycle begins with the repression (or "repressed expression" as I prefer to call it) of a strong drive, such as that of an emotion like anger or fear. Let's say a child is angry with his parents, but has real reasons to fear the consequences of expressing the anger. Odds are against the kid in a fight, so self-preservation means repression. The expression of the anger is shut down, but the anger is still there, of course. It goes underground where it creates anxiety in one form or another. We have the tendency to do things that reduce anxiety, and generally, the reduction of anxiety and tension feels good, so we do them. But if this means further repressing the anger (which caused the anxiety in the first place), then the thing that is done to reduce the tension is continued as a neurotic symptom and is difficult to give up.

Energy healing practices that succeed in balancing our polarities interrupt the Symptom/Misery/Stupidity Cycle. They set us up for an influx of energy and intelligence from a transcendent level of life, which is not caught up with our problems. This type of transcendent experience has the potential to break us out of ruts because it emanates from dimensions of life that are not on the level of the problem. This is basically what is meant by the "strengths perspective," which says that we are barking up the wrong tree when we try to solve a problem on the level of the problem. It is better to go to an area of strength, find access to our source of inner wisdom, and approach the problem from there. If you are in balance, and can operate from such a position of strength—even for a short time—you have a better chance of effecting change than if you remain stuck in the Symptom/Misery/Stupidity Cycle.

-§-
An idea or an insight doesn't come from a single happening, it requires a meeting to alter perspective. Often it takes a while for the events to collide, but when they do it is inevitable that a change will follow.
—Nick Bantock
-§-

Healing, in all its more eloquent forms, sets the stage for inspiration to enter our experience. Something new is born. It is this influx of spirit, the breaking through of life from a bigger world, that gives us renewable chances, not only to break free of the Symptom/Misery/Stupidity Cycle, but also to find ourselves, express our gifts, do what we've come here to do.

This journey of transformation—from problems to exploration to experience of transcendent realities—is what progressive healing is all about. The polarities at work in our bodies and psyches create all kinds of conflicts when they are out of balance. Once in a healing balance, however, they provide fertile ground for our inner growth and draw to us what we need in order to be more sure-footed and confident as we find our way home.

PART FOUR

Healing and Consciousness

JOAN BORYSENKO:

Strategies For Managing Your Mind

Y ou can change your habits and learn to manage your time, but without learning to manage your mind, inner peace is impossible. Even when you're sitting in a comfortable living room, surrounded by loved ones and trying to relax, your mind is capable of producing outrageously stressful mental movies. You probably create them several times a day, perhaps without even noticing what you're doing. The key to making your mind your ally, rather than your enemy, is to become aware of how you produce and direct your very own cinema of the absurd. Then you can choose to run a different feature. Awareness and choice are the keys to mental peace.

Here is how the average stressful mental movie gets produced. I was on my way to facilitate a weekend workshop at a cozy conference center in upstate New York. It had just snowed, and the trees were bowed to the earth, shaking off their frosty offerings in a light breeze. The sunlight sparkled off the flakes, and the world was enchanting in its beauty. I was in the moment, feeling spacious and present. My body was relaxed and comfortable. Then I had some constricting, afflicting kinds of thoughts: What perfect skiing weather. I moved to Colorado to spend more time outdoors. Everyone at home is probably out enjoying the snow. I'm on my way to spend the weekend teaching indoors. Poor, poor pitiful me. I'm so busy.

One moment I had been peaceful, expansive and present, thoroughly enjoying life; the next I was feeling deprived, crabby, and stressed. Nothing had changed except my thoughts, but that's where we live the majority of our lives. Much of the time, the suffering and

Joan Borysenko, Ph.D., has a powerfully clear personal vision—to bring science, medicine, psychology and spirituality together in the service of healing. Her brilliance as a scientist, clinician and teacher have placed her on the leading edge of the mind–body revolution, and she has become a world-renowned spokesperson for this new approach to health, sharing her pioneering work with a gentle graciousness, enthusiasm and humility. She is the author of the best-seller *Minding the Body, Mending the Mind* (Bantam, 1987) and eight other books. This chapter appeared initially in *In Light Times,* and is used with permission of author and publisher.

busyness we feel has very little to do with the reality of the situation. It's a direct result of our thinking.

The Buddha had a great analogy. He said each of us has some suffering, like a cup of salt. If you choose to dissolve your salt in a small bowl, the water will be undrinkable. But if you dissolve it in a lake, the water will still taste sweet. The mind, and how you deal with your thoughts, is the equivalent of the bowl or the lake.

Life is filled with very real suffering. God forbid you or a loved one gets seriously ill, a child dies, your business fails, divorce rips your family apart, or you're betrayed by a person you trusted. These things happen because they're a part of life. As you get older, you realize there's no magic amulet or formula that prevents suffering. Bad things routinely happen to good people. Suffering is part of the human condition. You may wish this were not so. There are plenty of books that trade on that hope, dispensing advice on how to think, eat, pray, and behave in order to avoid suffering, but suffering will come just the same, in spite of your best efforts. The only thing you can really control is how you respond to life's inherent challenges.

-§-
The suffering and busyness we feel has very little to do with the reality of the situation. It's a direct result of our thinking.
-§-

However, there are two types of suffering: mandatory and optional. On my drive through the snowy countryside, there was no external cause for suffering. It was all in my mind. This made me recall that the original definition of yoga had nothing to do with stretching exercises. It was defined as learning how to control the mind and banish the afflicting thoughts that create needless suffering. Learning how to do that, said the ancient sages, is the most difficult of all disciplines. Learning to walk on water was said to be much easier.

Getting control of your thinking may not be easy, but if you want lasting peace, it's a worthwhile practice. As Pogo once said, "We have met the enemy and he is us." It takes consistent effort to overcome that internal enemy, but you can do it as part of your daily life. It takes no more time to use your thoughts well than it does to let them drive you crazy. The basic skills of awareness and choice are available to every person, in every situation, during every hour of the day and night.

For example, in order to stop my mind from creating suffering over its preference to go skiing, I had to notice what I was doing. That is awareness. "Uh-oh. I've lost it. I've made myself miserable." The thought of skiing started the process of woolgathering, or bringing up other thoughts about how busy I was. The next move in the practice of mental martial arts was to change my thinking.

Modern cognitive psychologists suggest you internally yell, "Stop it," then start in on a more productive train of thought. In the skiing example, I might have nudged my mind onto a better road by thinking, Next weekend I'll definitely go skiing with my family. I'm glad I remembered how much we love to do that. Today I'm going to enjoy my work. These thought corrections are called affirmations. I like to think of them as station breaks for the opposing point of view. This might all seem very simple, but it's not easy. If it were, we would all be yogis.

-§-

How to control the mind and banish the afflicting thoughts that create needless suffering, said the ancient sages, is the most difficult of all disciplines. Learning to walk on water was said to be much easier.

-§-

This week, notice your thinking and develop the habit of awareness. Witness your thoughts with the recognition that you are not your thoughts. They are just a mental movie, and you can make the choice to run another film. Try saying an emphatic mental "Stop it" when you feel tense and constricted by unproductive obsessing. Then substitute a train of thought that can be your ally in experiencing inner peace.

Taber Shadburne:
Radical Intimacy

Let's face it: we all yearn to give and receive love. We want to create deeper, more intimate relationships and true community. We are dogged by a nagging sense of isolation. And yet, upon investigation, we discover that we're in pain because we've shot ourselves in the foot. We, ourselves, sabotage the openness we want—with our own defensive conditioning, old patterns of fear, dependency, and blame. How can we drop this rusty armor, that we may, at last, see each other clearly and hold each other closely?

There is a way of using communication as an interpersonal meditation and our relationships as a spiritual path, transforming the challenges of closeness into a vehicle for growth. Working together in this way, we notice how we separate ourselves from each other, and how the barriers to intimacy we've erected darken our lives. By telling the truth about our insides, we finally see these walls and battlements, and help each other dismantle them. Sharing ourselves with others, we reveal ourselves to ourselves, bringing what was hidden into the light of shared compassionate awareness.

In this way, the pain and conflict that intimacy inevitably brings to the surface become a source of creativity, a womb for the birth of a new way of being. Gradually, Love becomes effortless—our birthright, our own true nature.

My first serious relationship was hindered by a fear of conflict and big emotions. We unconsciously avoided the hard stuff, which meant that a lot of the soft, squishy stuff got buried along with it. Consequently, our

Taber Shadburne helps people transform their lives. He facilitates bringing meditative awareness to the messy, juicy stuff of life—emotions, relationships, conflict, conversation, love and intimacy. His teaching and psychotherapy integrate Buddhism,
psychology, and conscious communication. He's completed two years in residence at
Dharma Rain Zen Center, dozens of silent meditation retreats, and serious study of
the world's mystical traditions, as well as an M.A. in Counseling Psychology, training
as a Community-Building facilitator by M. Scott Peck's F.C.E., and certification as a
Radical Honesty Master Trainer. His web site is www.tabershadburne.com.

relationship was plagued by a mild sense of boredom. When we did argue, it was a long, dry, lawyerly affair that went in circles, leaving us both frustrated. Though most pronounced in my relationship with my girlfriend, this pattern also marked my interactions with friends and family.

Later, the pendulum swung—I got in touch with my passionate side (boy, did I ever!), and with a whole new set of problems. I went from cold anger to hot anger, from dry arguments, little of the time, to *fighting, all* of the time! This new relationship was *anything* but boring. Its plague was blame, hostility, and high drama. Of course, it was juicier—there was some great makeup sex—but that didn't compensate for all the wear and tear on our nervous systems. We loved each other, but we had a hard time. Again, I replicated this pattern in all my other close relationships—except for the makeup sex part!

I do not regret these experiences. Rather, I am grateful for them. With the help of wise teachers, I've found my relationships with lovers, close friends, and family—though often challenging—to be a powerful training ground, a means of awakening from the trance of old pain and conditioning. It was through these relationships that I learned (and am still learning) to use communication as an awareness practice. Through this practice I transformed these relationships. Through my relationships I am transforming my life.

-§-

"Out beyond ideas of right-doing and wrong-doing there is a field. I'll meet you there."—Rumi

-§-

My passion is to help others to transform their lives. After years of slogging through the trenches myself, and of helping others to do likewise, I've learned something wonderful: The raw energy brought up by close relationships can be harnessed, and conflict can be used creatively, as a means to a deeper love and freedom than we have ever known.

The Noble Truth of Suffering

Being human is often painful. Even when we manage to escape the more intense forms of suffering, we often experience a vague dissatisfaction. And it pains us to see others suffering. These facts, faced squarely and accepted, are what the Buddha called, "the noble truth of suffering." The good news is that we create most of our own pain. We're the authors of our suffering, which means we can learn to write a new story, one with a happier ending.

We humans are endowed with amazing minds, which turns out to be both a blessing and a curse. The same mind that allows us to cure diseases and write poetry also enables us to torture ourselves in ways that are, quite literally, unimaginable to the other animals. The way we torture ourselves requires imagination. Our minds are powerful, but they often turn on their owners. Like the other animals, we are motivated largely by fear, aggression and greed. But whereas your dog's greed and aversion are straightforward and easily recognizable, you can use your frontal cortex to elaborate, multiply, rationalize, justify, and disguise your fear and greed into sophisticated forms way beyond poor Rover's reach. Consequently, his suffering is rudimentary — short-term and instinctive, none of the complicated, chronic stuff. Only we intellectual creatures are capable of that.

For you and I have thinking at our disposal. We can — and do — artificially divide all of our sensory experience into discrete mental categories, labeling all which might bring us pleasure as "good," and all which might bring us pain as "bad." Then we can proceed to create purely mental abstractions, wholly imaginary "good" and "bad" "things" to fear, resent, and crave — "things" like: "Not living up to my full potential," or, "Finally finding the true love I so richly deserve," or, "The precipitous plunge in value of my stock portfolio," or, "Success," or, "Failure," or, "The American coup d'etat perpetrated by that bastard Bush and his cronies," or, "The good old days," or, "The future." Our advanced intellectual capacities allow you and I, unlike the mere brutes, to kick back in an easy chair, safely ensconced in our comfortable homes, and work ourselves into a foaming rage, a paralyzing panic, or a suicidal depression — *all with no unpleasant sensory input whatsoever.*

> -§-
> The raw energy brought up by close relationships can be harnessed, and conflict can be used creatively, as a means to a deeper love and freedom than we have ever known.
> -§-

We live as if in a warehouse full of countless dusty maps and globes, most completely erroneous. We spend our lives poring over them and congratulating ourselves on having seen the world, never realizing what wonders lie beyond the walls; never realizing that we live within walls at all. But our self-congratulations ring hollow, and we are troubled by a gnawing sense that something is wrong with our pictures — we secretly doubt our delusions. Instinctively, we yearn for the wide-open spaces.

Not that maps are bad — far from it. When heading off into the wild blue yonder, having some accurate maps in your pocket is handy. But not all maps are created equal. An inaccurate one creates problems. Even an accurate map's usefulness depends entirely on where you want to go. And even if your map accurately describes your intended destination, if you just spread it out and sit on it — thinking you've arrived — only to complain about what a flat and dreary territory it is and certainly not worth the trip, you're lost. No map can substitute for its territory, any more than eating a menu will satisfy your hunger. A map is just a map — no map is ultimately real.

CHAPTER EIGHTEEN

In my work with individuals who are in acute emotional pain, often the first layer we need to work with is their shame about finding themselves in this situation, their embarrassment about needing help. They are suffering under the delusion that they *should be happy,* and that their depression, anxiety, or whatever indicates a *lack of moral fiber* or *willpower* on their parts. This misguided belief is a completely inaccurate map of reality.

Or some that I meet find themselves working very hard to achieve certain goals and their lives, but finding the whole process tedious and joyless. In exploring together, we find that the goals they've been pursuing are ones that were handed down to them, goals they thought they *should* adopt, not ones which describe where they, themselves, *really want to go.* They've been navigating with the wrong maps, maps of the wrong territory.

-§-

Our advanced intellectual capacities allow you and I to kick back in an easy chair, and work ourselves into a foaming rage, a paralyzing panic, or a suicidal depression—all with no unpleasant sensory input whatsoever.

-§-

And I often work with spiritual seekers— those who know where they want to go, and possess some pretty sophisticated maps of the territory, but who sometimes forget (as do I, and everyone I know) that their maps are just that: only maps. And so they subtly torture themselves with spiritual ideals and beliefs about how they, as good seekers, *should* be. The biggest hindrance to waking up is often our attachment to our *ideas about* waking up.

But we find our own beliefs and ideas very compelling, so through the combination of our craving and fearing, and our getting lost in thought, we find ourselves in our La-Z-Boys, thumbing through a pile of maps, reacting to some with insatiable longing and others with abject horror, suffering from alternating fits of fury, nostalgic depression, and panic.

Close relationships frequently exacerbate this predicament. They have a way of bringing up the messy stuff. Upset leads to conflict. Conflict leads to blame. And blame leads nowhere—real fast. So what are we to do? How will we ever get out of that damn chair?

The Noble Truth of the End of Suffering

The solution to the problem of suffering is simple. If actually applied, it leads to freedom. Not only that, this doorway out of suffering is also the doorway *into* love and bliss. Although well-known to the mystics of various traditions, it is so contrary to common practice, and so rare in society at large, as to seem like a secret, esoteric wisdom.

The simple secret does not require extensive intellectual study (though acquiring *some* new maps helps), but actually practicing it is challenging. You have to live it to learn it, and it takes work to gradually get it in your bones. This is a lifetime project. So if, upon reading it, you say, "Oh yeah, I do that all the time," or "Okay, I'll do that from now on," then either you're the Buddha's second coming, or you're delusional—you've snatched the map from my hand and sat on it.

The secret? Simple: *Love whatever is arising in this moment.* This is not as simple as it sounds. It's like learning to ride a bike: "Okay dear, just hold the handles and push the pedals with your feet..." And fall over...a few hundred times. Love requires much practice, and is widely misunderstood. (The fact that we use the same word to say, "I love you, Dad," and, "Oooh Honey-britches, I love you," and, "I just love ice cream!" is a sad commentary on the subtlety of our culture's distinctions in matters of the heart—the Eskimos' 986 words for snow, and our one for love. Bleak.)

-§-

The fact that we use the same word to say, "I love you, Dad," and, "Oooh Honey-britches, I love you," and, "I just love ice cream!" is a sad commentary on the subtlety of our culture's distinctions in matters of the heart— the Eskimos' 986 words for snow, and our one for love. Bleak.

-§-

To truly Love (I will capitalize our term, distinguishing it from codependency and ice cream lust) is a learned skill, an acquired capacity. It's not some sappy feeling or sentimentally significant attitude. It can be fierce, as well as tender. It opposes nothing, even hatred (our own or another's). This Love is the larger context, the sentient space within which all else unfolds. It is of a higher order than either anger or affection, and as willing to kick over the money-changers' tables as to turn the other cheek. This Love is guided not by ideas of right and wrong, holy or unholy, spiritual or unspiritual, but rather by a deep listening, moment by moment. And because it embraces what *actually is,* rather than being seduced by delusion, Love requires true seeing.

Love requires *present-centered awareness,* being awake in the here and now, consciously noticing the flow of experience. But what *is* experience? What can one notice? An old Buddhist formulation says we are aware of *sights, sounds, smells, tastes, bodily sensations,* and *thoughts.* That's it. Period.

But then Love has another requirement: learning to stop *condemning* and *approving* what awareness finds, learning to drop our *judgmentalism.* We interrupt our habit of hating or fearing some experiences and clinging to others, cultivating instead a *willingness* to be with whatever shows up. We can call this capacity *compassion, a basic friendliness* toward all experience. Love needs both these wings: wakeful attention, and compassionate *in*tention.

Figuratively, we could say that whereas awareness is a function of the mind, friendliness is a function of the body; whereas awareness is an action of the head, compassion is an action of the heart. Taking a few breaths, you invite your body to expand, making room in your chest and belly for the sensations of this moment. With awareness, you see the truth of what your experience *actually is;* with compassion, you *feel it.* You relax, welcoming the uncomfortable sensations, freeing the pleasurable ones.

This Love transforms everything it touches. When we stop ignoring, denying, rationalizing, justifying, condemning, judging, or resisting our experience, bringing it into the warm light of compassionate awareness, evolutionary growth happens naturally. You may have heard the adage: "That which we resist, persists." I would add: That which we know, grows. That which we Love, evolves.

-§-
The elements of experience we can name are those same things the old Buddhists said we could be aware of: *sights, sounds, smells, tastes, sensations,* and *thoughts.*
-§-

Loving whatever is arising can be practiced not only as a silent sitting meditation (which I highly recommend), but also as a moment-to-moment way of being, at all times. Not only can yoga, t'ai chi, and tantric sex be approached in this way, but so can eating, brushing your teeth, and taking out the trash. And relationships — particularly the intimate communication they entail — provide an especially potent, juicy (if also challenging) form of this meditation.

Meditating Out Loud

Ordinary conversation, even when "pleasant," tends to work against awareness practice. The way we usually talk, and the things we usually talk about — other people, other times, moral or aesthetic evaluations, abstract concepts — distract us from noticing what's happening here and now. Generally, most folks would consider communicating about "whatever is arising in this moment" to be rather weird. Needless to say, "I'm feeling slightly nauseous, and having the thought that your shirt is hideous," is not a topic for polite conversation. And "I missed some of what you said, because I'm having a sexual fantasy about the babysitter" would be considered in bad taste. Consequently, we avoid all such unpleasantness and our conversational conventions support us in doing so. We avoid the truth of what's really happening.

But the convenience of constant distraction comes at a grave cost: you cannot Love that which you are avoiding (or *one whom* you're avoiding). Distraction prevents you from Loving what is. It keeps you from *Loving yourself.* Or anyone else. You can't be friendly toward that which you are busy hiding from awareness — your own, or another's.

Whereas ordinary conversation directs our attention to the conceptual *content* of thinking, conscious conversation points us toward witnessing the *process* of experience. Noticing the elements of experience, we name them as they occur, doing our best to hold it all with compassion.

This is more of an art than a science. Conscious conversation cannot be reduced to a technique, because consciousness is not a technique. Unfortunately, when you talk to the intellect about awareness, intellect quickly converts awareness into something static—a new belief system, say, or a method. Awareness is much bigger than that. To make room enough for awareness, intellect has to get out of the way. Intellect, however, usually requires some persuasion. So I'm writing this essay. And now I'll get a little more prescriptive, but only with this caveat:

-§-
This kind of communication not only heals conflicts, but also creates alarming degrees of intimacy, for those thrill-seekers who are into such terrifying delights.
-§-

The skills required for meditating out loud are like those required to ride a bike—you can't learn them from a book. They're best learned by having someone running along beside you, holding your seat. Intellectual understanding is merely a preliminary step, opening the way for the real method of transformation. The real method which is not really a method. The un-method of awareness, however, is the only way beyond the morass of moralistic mind.

Awareness Out Loud: Naming

In order to accurately describe your experience, you must first notice it. Then comes the skill of *naming* what you notice. Naming is not *interpreting*, though the thinking mind has a hell of a time distinguishing between the two. In naming, one strives to be as non-interpretive and as *descriptive* as possible. *It is finding the simplest, the most accurate (and morally neutral) labels with which to describe the elements of your experience.* To interpret is to evaluate and make meanings about one's experience— usually without consciousness of even having done so. You can, however, name an interpretation as an interpretation, in effect saying, "Please allow me to show you the map I'm carrying."

Saying, "You have wounded me deeply with your callous insensitivity" is not naming. And it's not *true*. Ever. It's truer to say, "I'm *feeling* tight in my belly and chest and hot in my face, and I'm *thinking* you're an insensitive jerk."

Naming is *an attempt to use words to point directly at the truth of experience.* The elements of experience we can name are those same things the old Buddhists said we could be aware of: *sights, sounds, smells, tastes, sensations,* and *thoughts.*

By learning to speak in this way, you start distinguishing between your experience of sense-based reality and all the meanings you make about that reality, which in turn shows you how arbitrary and imaginary your interpretations usually are. Meditating out loud teaches you to better see what is actually arising, moment to moment.

-§-
Compassion is used to balance the desire for authenticity with the desire for connection, the need for courage with the need for acceptance, one's own need for expression with the other's need for listening.
-§-

And this is very useful, since arguments are mostly about whose interpretation is the "true" one, who's "right" and who's "wrong," whereas the actual reason for the argument is that the combatants are feeling big, uncomfortable emotional energies in their bodies (fear, anger, grief) and are trying desperately not to experience them.

We work to disown and avoid actually feeling our emotions. They scare us. Even the yummy ones often scare us. We avoid the depth of our affection, appreciation, attachment, and attraction. Naming, however, invites us to befriend our feelings. And the radical openness, honesty and directness of this kind of communication not only heals conflicts, but also creates alarming degrees of intimacy, for those thrill-seekers who are into such terrifying delights.

Compassion Out Loud: Honesty & Empathy

This practice requires not only awareness, but also compassion; not only right use of the head, but also right use of the heart. If awareness, distinguishing perceiving from interpreting, and the technicalities of naming are the head's contribution, the heart is used to sense what aspect of experience is most important and useful to name at any given moment. (And whether it's important to name anything at all. Or whether there might be more benefit in closing one's mouth for a while. Or talking about the weather, telling stories, or cracking jokes.) Compassion is used to balance the desire for authenticity with the desire for connection, the need for courage with the need for acceptance, one's own need for expression with the other's need for listening. We use the heart to find the *spirit* of naming.

The wisdom required for this practice is better gained through skilled coaching, but here are some guidelines:

Set the stage: permission and preface. Ask the other if they would be willing to listen to you talk about your thoughts and feelings and/or to talk about their own. Share your intent: to describe your *own* experience and/or to *listen* to theirs; to move through and let go of any feelings that are in the way of closeness; to learn; not to control or make the other wrong; to understand each other and arrive at agreement; to address desires; and so on.

Start where you are. If you are nervous to start an intimate conversation, name that. If you're worried about hurting feelings, name that. If you're afraid of the other's judgment or anger or that they'll go away and hold a grudge, name that. If you're livid and want to hurt or blame the other, but are committed to working not to, name that.

Listen to your body. Keep checking in with your body, noticing your sensations — it's the ultimate authority on what really needs to be said and whether you are speaking skillfully. If you are, your words will help your feelings move and resolve, help your body open and relax.

Communicate with the intention of changing yourself, not the other. You may have a preference (maybe a strong one!) that they change in some way, but name that as such and see if you can hold it with some detachment. Choose the intention of self-revelation, rather than trying to be "right" or control the other person.

-§-
We drop our painful attachment to habitual, unconscious ways of being and arrive together in the truth of the present moment, the only place where love and truth are ever found.
-§-

Don't interpret. *Name*. Describe the sensations in your body: "I'm tight in my belly." Describe emotions as emotions: "I'm sad" (or mad, scared, happy, or lusty). "I'm feeling devastated" is an interpretation masquerading as a feeling. Ditto with: "I feel that you..." Describe behaviors in concrete, neutral language: "I'm sad that you will be gone for a week," not "I'm sad because you're abandoning me." (This person is probably also mad. "Abandoning" is an interpretation with moral connotations and "because" blames the other for one's feelings.) We can also name thoughts, but as thoughts: "I'm thinking you shouldn't have left the cap off the toothpaste."

Name feelings first. When you're emotionally charged, give your attention to that before traipsing off into the land of interpretations. "I'm tight in my shoulders and I'm mad! I'm hot in my face. I'm mad at you for making those plans without talking to me first!" By bringing compassionate awareness to our emotions, we soothe ourselves. We may need to shuttle back and forth between feelings and interpretations, but give priority to clearing emotions first. Put more passion (and possibly, more volume!) into emotional expression, naming interpretations with a more neutral tone. Preface interpretations with: "I imagine..." or "I'm thinking..." or "My judgment/assessment/interpretation/story is..." and similar clear labels.

Name what matters most. Notice the thing that you are most nervous or hesitant to say, the piece which feels most embarrassing, vulnerable, or risky. That's probably the most important part. Be willing to scare yourself. Be willing to look bad. Be willing to have the other get mad at you or feel hurt. Be willing to risk actively creating your worst nightmare, and then feeling your way through it.

Name everything that matters. If you're feeling lusty, and also afraid of being perceived as obnoxious, name both. And if you're also feeling afraid of being perceived as lacking confidence and wimpy if you're not obnoxious *enough,* name that too. If you're mad at someone, and afraid of talking to them about it for fear of losing their friendship, and feeling guilty for being so petty, yet convinced that the best way to deepen intimacy is to talk about this stuff, name it all. Name mixed emotions, contradictory ideas, ambivalent feelings, and inner conflicts.

Work with tone of voice and body language. Sometimes we use all the right "spiritually correct" language and still communicate blame or disdain with our voice or facial expression. Or we speak in monotone about something which we feel strongly. Try to make what you're saying and *the way you're saying it* line up. When you notice a mixed message slipping out, break it down and name the parts. Use a tone of voice and body language which is passionate enough to actually reflect what you feel in your body. Aim for congruence.

Listen deeply and express empathic understanding. Listening is not the same as waiting to speak. It is working to get yourself out of the way, allowing yourself to be affected, resonating with the other. Empathy is then skillfully communicating that understanding and emotional resonance back to the other (without commentary), providing an accurate and loving reflection.

Ask for what you want (and what the other wants). See if your conversation has uncovered any desires, and make the appropriate requests and offers. If in conflict, don't try this while you're still upset—angry requests don't work too good. Don't ask in order to control. Ask like you're asking for a favor, ready to hear yes or no. "I want you to..." is not a request—technically, it's a description of an emotion-thought, though it's usually delivered more as a demand. "I request that you..." is not a request—again, it's a demand in disguise. "Do you want to..." is closer, but no cigar (technically, it's an inquiry as to the other's psychological state). A true request is a question with a yes or no answer, which contains something like: "Would you...?" "Will you...?" or "Would you be willing to...?" (Although requests are often implied with tone of voice, true requests are more open, direct, and vulnerable, better for dissolving fear and creating intimacy.)

You may also realize that you want to make an offer. Use words like: "Would you like me to...?" "Do you want me to...?" or "How/when/ where/who/which/what would you like me to...?" A true offer is for the sake of the other, with no expectation that it be accepted or reciprocated.

As we pursue this mutual meditation, embracing all the messy, juicy stuff of relationships, we surrender to the power of intimacy to call up old pain and neurotic beliefs. These outcasts, once invited into the space of shared awareness and compassion, are transformed. Gradually, we drop our painful attachment to habitual, unconscious ways of being and arrive together in the truth of the present moment, the only place where love and truth are ever found. Sharing in this way, we create a deeper intimacy — with each other, and ultimately, with the ground of Being itself. Those who have walked this path together, who have known and helped each other in this way, find themselves in a field far beyond ideas of right-doing and wrong-doing. They find themselves in a new land. They find themselves in Love.

Tom Stern:
Changing Faces

The masked stranger, razor-sharp knife in hand to execute his bloody deed, leaned over the sleeping girl to more closely ponder exposed lines for his deep cuts. Respectful of Leader's determination, four other masked figures revealed controlled excitement with but the slightest narrowing of their eyes.

Wordlessly, calm and steady-handed, Leader plunged his blade deep into the girl's face and carved smoothly downward, pulling as hard as through rawhide until his blade split her upper lip. Without hesitation, he jammed a pair of pointed scissors into the groove where gums join face, spreading tissues and cutting as he went, advancing his scissors until their tips stretched the skin just beneath her eye.

I sponged away gouts of blood while Leader peeled skin from bone until her left face flapped limp and he could repeat the assault on the girl's right side. In ten minutes, Leader created a disfiguring wound beyond what any person would be able to salvage. What had once been Josephina's face now hung as two bleeding flaps, a detached nose, and no upper lip. Why had the girl let a stranger do this to her? Why was I there?

Slowly, with the utmost precision, Leader ran more than a hundred fine sutures into lip and face, gradually closing the gaping distances between the left and right flaps. Time flew by, as I stood amazed at the accuracy of his stitches. Ninety minutes later, the girl had something new, something she had never possessed in all of her twenty-two years:

After growing up in North Dakota and central California, Tom Stern, MD, matured into a national record holder in swimming before graduating from Stanford University. He picked fruit with migrant farm workers, rode the railroads of America as a brakeman, and discovered gold on a remote island in the China Sea. He has practiced with the Berkeley Family Practice Medical Group for thirty years, and is Assistant Clinical Professor at UCSF School of Medicine. He has traveled to Asia over 50 times, and written two novels, *Gold Fever* (AEI, 2001) and *Vatican Gold* (AEI, 2003). See www.tomstern.com. Photo by Phillip's Photography.

An upper lip without a broad split in it all the way to her nose. Her harelip was finally closed.

That night, making rounds in the rickety hospital high in the mountains of a remote Philippine island, while I visited Josephina in her hospital bed, I unwound her bulky dressing and smiled at the single, thin line that closed the hideous harelip, present since birth. When I put my large mirror in front of her face, she touched her cheek with her brown hand. Her eyes wide, she blinked to be sure she saw her own reflection, then began to weep with joy. When she could control her sobbing, she crossed herself, and murmured, "Thanks, Lord."

-§-
At age 7 I had my first dream of practicing medicine on the world's poorest, farthest away, and most needy people, for not a single centavo of money.
-§-

Overwhelmed by her exultation, my own heart felt as if it would burst with a sublime mixture of compassion, satisfaction, humility, and thankfulness that I had been able to help poor Josephina. When twenty village Girl Scouts in their cute little outfits arrived to serenade the children in hospital, I sat beside Josephina and bawled, face down, into the torn sheets of her decrepit hospital bed.

When I visited Josephina a year later, red lipstick and a dab of make-up over her thin scar erased every vestige of her former ugliness. She had become beautiful, and acted as if she knew it. "I have a boyfriend," she said. "And he kisses me." She knew that I understood the enormity of that simple statement. Something so normal for other people but denied her until now was miraculously hers.

Before, no boy had ever kissed her lips. Instead of being allowed to walk to elementary school with all of the other Filipina six-year-olds, proud in a regulation blue skirt and starched white blouse, she had been kept inside the flimsy hovel her family called home, her harelip a mark of shame. Other village women whispered, "Her mother must have thought of sex while pregnant," or, "Beware of Josephina and her evil eye."

For me, the experience of helping Josephina completed an entire cycle of life, one that began at age seven. That's when I had my first dream of practicing medicine on the world's poorest, farthest away, and most needy people, for not a single centavo of money.

My parents were playing bridge at the house of a doctor friend, Dr. Gough. They stashed me in his library instead of hiring a babysitter. I picked up hardback called *Burma Surgeon* by Gordon Seagrave, a missionary surgeon. Already deep in Burma, Dr. Seagrave joined the US Army when World War II blew up around his work. The book told his stories of volunteer medical service. Here, in bamboo lands teeming with underprivileged humans, the purity of altruism shone out.

Fifteen years later I graduated from Stanford University. I was so undecided about my future that I matriculated at Stanford Law School. One night, in a dream, I remembered *Burma Surgeon*. A woman I recognized as Dante's Beatrice from *The Inferno* reminded me, "You know you really want to go to medical school, like the Burma Surgeon, so that is what you should do." I felt vibrations, as if from a large bell, tolling in me, its resonance shaking answers loose from some deep conscience within. To my mind's utter surprise, but with an inevitability I recognized as originating from my heart, I promptly changed to medical school for the long haul of immersion into modern medicine.

When I finished training, I began in practice, married, had children, bought a house, made and lost money, and worked very hard — but I felt that my life lacked salt. I always knew I could never feel complete until I had acted with the altruism of my hero, the Burma surgeon.

When I was forty-five years old, with two decades of medical practice under my belt, Yolanda, my remarkable Filipina wife, was working with a large organization, The Federation of Philippine American Chambers of Commerce of the United States of America. She suggested I initiate a plastic surgery project in the Philippines. I did not hesitate a single second. By that time I had developed the connections and financial ability necessary to tug a large project into port. With the help of many friends and benefactors, I piloted this project to first docking two years later, and it has continued for three weeks each year since. The harelips of more than one thousand people who are the poorest of the poor have been repaired. The Governor of one Filipino province told me, "All the children of my province have been operated on successfully. Our Congress has passed a special bill making you an 'Adopted Son' of our island." Mission accomplished, we began work on another island.

This visit, after operating on Josephina, we had to rush. The volunteer team that had flown out from the US had only had nine full operating days, and we could not possibly complete surgery on all of the children who stood in line outside the clinic, hoping to have fortune smile on them just once. To improve our efficiency, we brainstormed ways to create more surgical slots: quicker turnaround time with the instruments, bringing patients up from deep anesthesia so they wake simultaneous with the last stitch, and assigning volunteer orderlies from the enthusiastic community to move patients about the hospital. We geared up like an industrial assembly line.

By the twenty-sixth case of the week, after several days hunched over the operating table, my emotional state no longer retained the elation of the first case. I was griping to myself about the heat. My sandwich at lunch lacked enough mayonnaise, and contained my least favorite type of mustard. I missed my wife and kids. The nurse from Omaha was getting on my nerves with constant complaints about all things under the tropical sun. My wife's family wanted me to join them for scuba diving. My office in Berkeley reported a hair-pulling fight between one of the doctors and a female staff member. Most urgent of all, I suffered from cramps and explosive diarrhea. Several of the team did. Feverish and weak, Leader called for intravenous fluids to keep himself going. After we gave him a couple of bags of saltwater and sugar, he struggled upright and forced his body to walk to the operating room to perform more surgeries. I felt worn out by the constant worried questions from parents, especially pressure from those who wanted their child to be chosen. I flinched at the thought of making late rounds in a ward with thirty beds bursting with two hundred people; mothers sleeping on grass mats beside their daughters; fathers sitting silently all night on their son's beds; the horror and carnage of all of the blood and cutting, my shoes spattered with blood, needing to go to the bathroom again, but never finding one as clean as home.

-§-
The early thrill of helping a patient is such a familiar feeling that the doctor takes little note of it in the midst of his daily titanic struggle against sickness and death.
-§-

During my twenties and early thirties I studied in the philosophical school of G. I. Gurdjieff, a Russian mystic who emphasized self-honesty. His followers owned a large mansion in San Francisco where complex, dance-like "sacred movements" made up part of our training. It also included meditation, fine manual work at high speed, and group discussions about searching for awareness, for self-remembering, for the route to the moments when we live with consciousness of ourselves. Two days a week I devoted to this esoteric school until, worried about its cultish aspects, I awarded myself a diploma from Gurdjieff's Fourth Way School and departed. I concentrated on another invisible technique: scientific medical hypnosis, which I had studied at Stanford. After hypnotizing more than a thousand patients, I came to appreciate and respect the power of unconscious processes. We humans, like icebergs, have much unseen beneath the surface.

That sweaty day in the Philippines, at the end of the fortieth operation, I recognized what was going on inside my heart. When people speak of "heart" in a poetic sense, they mean the emotions mysteriously but cross-culturally felt in the chest. Why do Americans, Cambodians, Brazilians, Jews, French, Kenyans, and all others have the identical experience? Surely it involves pathways of the nervous system common to our species, perhaps some accelerated network for emotions — they seem both faster and subtler than muscle reactions. The difference suggests separate mechanisms. Perhaps there exists an unnamed locus of heart muscle that senses emotions and is our True Heart. But until someone can prove otherwise, I believe we only know our world through the nervous system, and it was in my nervous system that I detected a problem developing.

Below my power of conscious resolution, a new force, negative and initially nameless, was intruding on my experience. It made a languid entrance over the course of a few days, spreading fog-like through my brain. My elation over Josephina became humdrum on children equally worthy. "What neurophysiologic process is this?" my inner scientist wondered. Then I recognized what had deflated the sublime to the routine, with a victory of brain over heart. *Habituation.* The specific characteristic of the nervous system that complicates the life of the healer's heart, and indeed the lives of all hearts.

What is habituation, neurophysiologically? For two months, while I rode locomotives and switched boxcars for Southern Pacific Railroad to earn money for medical school, I slept in the back seat of my 1959 Chevy Bel Air. I parked next to a noisy canning factory in Tracy, California. One Friday night, a lightning bolt knocked out electrical power. The din of the twenty-four-hour cannery stopped, and I woke with a start, jolted from sleep by the silence. Hard-wired to detect changes, *Homo sapiens* naturally become inattentive to repeated experiences — sounds, sights, smells, temperatures — that hold no threat. Instead, our nervous systems dedicate premium energy to line detectors, motion detectors, gradient sensors, change sensors of every form. Any sudden change could mean death. In the world of survival of the fittest, the ability to discriminate danger equals success.

-§-
You no longer remember to smell the roses. You don't even remember you've forgotten!
-§-

But in the gentler world of the heart, habituation takes a horrible toll. You no longer appreciate a beautiful redwood tree after passing it six times. You lose your loving feelings because you've been with your spouse for so long that your nervous system doesn't detect her or him. You note a gradual decline in how much satisfaction you get from practicing medicine. You no longer remember to smell the roses. *You don't even remember you've forgotten!*

Surveys of career satisfaction show that at least one third of doctors wish they had chosen another profession. While most doctors begin practice with the enthusiasm of colts, in a few years too many of them age into workhorses, plodding with ears down, necks bowed into a feed sack. Doctors have high rates of divorce, suicide, and poly-drug abuse — alcohol, narcotics, amphetamines, and cocaine. What happened to their hearts? Where is that old vitality?

Doctors suffer because habituation has attenuated the joyful heart that comes from human contact with patients. The accumulated events of the practice aspect of medicine, especially the business and bureaucratic functions, are perceived as threats by the change detectors of their nervous systems. Their firing stimulates the brain to turn attention in that direction. For example, regulators from every government level threaten sanctions against physicians for a million potential violations. Patients write letters of complaint against 99.9 percent of physicians, because no one can please everyone, because no physician can be perfect all of the time, because some physicians are corrupt, because patients with certain types of personality disorders like to lie and make trouble. Every physician has people angry with him, if only as the target of misdirected rage by family members when a loved one's time has come. For their skills and sacrifices, doctors want to make a good living, though few become wealthy. When one rapacious CEO sold his health insurance company, he made $756,000,000. I calculated that had I begun practicing medicine 24/7 during the reign of Tutankhamen I in Ancient Egypt, I still would not have made that much. But being up all night with a desperately ill patient, or being on-call for 75,000 people in your city, with the telephone ringing like a banshee for seventy-two straight hours, with the constant attention to detail so as to do no harm to patients, with struggles with partners and employees…all these cause the change sensors to fire their alert warnings. By the time a physician has seen five thousand patients, the early thrill of helping a patient is such a familiar feeling that the doctor takes little note of it in the midst of his daily titanic struggle against sickness and death.

-§-
Make it a sacred habit to read one page daily of poetry, wisdom, religion, or other uplifting material.
-§-

At a later stage of the developmental arc of the physician's heart, he or she recognizes dissatisfaction but usually misidentifies the source of the restlessness. The doctor believes that a new specialty, a new car, a new spouse, a new religion, a new lover, or a new city will provide the salt he or she needs to taste life. In fact, because of the inevitable habituation of the doctor's nervous system to the subtle joys that emanate from the heart, he or she becomes inoculated against the joys that permeate life like gamma rays, building us up, nourishing us. Even if the physician recognizes the true source of his or her angst, the longing for wholeness, he or she does not know how to obtain the one nutrient that can satisfy: the magic the heart felt at the beginning.

Our eightieth case looked like all the others had begun to look to me, a member of a strange race with split lips and cleft palates that allowed Coke to come out of the nose when sucking on a straw. Francisco, aged four, looked a bit thin to me when I did his pre-op exam, but I attributed his lack of fat to his poor mountain village, which contained scant food and not a single obese person. Besides, his blood count and chest X-ray passed scrutiny. I picked him up from his mother and carried him to the operating room.

Just after Leader splayed Francisco's face open, the wild buzzing of an alarm told of a child's heart stopped cold. He was "straight-line" on the monitor.

"Asystole!" Anesthesiologist shouted.

"Damn!" I reached for the defibrillator paddles to shock Francisco back to life.

"Clear!" Anesthesiologist barked. "Do it now."

Paralyzed by a nerve-poisoning medicine similar to the feared *curare* used by Amazon Basin hunters, Francisco hardly flickered when I blasted one hundred and fifty joules through him. On the monitor? Nothing.

"Start CPR!" Anesthesiologist said. "I'll give him some bicarb."

-§-
Every physician has people angry with him or her, if only as the target of misdirected rage by family members when a loved one's time has come.
-§-

While Leader did his best to control bleeding, I pressed rhythmically on Francisco's chest. I imagined him dead, in a flimsy cardboard coffin on the shoulders of his family marching to the graveyard, a line of mourners walking in the rear. I felt I had killed him by not obeying the intuition I'd had during the pre-op that he didn't seem quite right. I imagined myself suffering over this error for the rest of my life. All of us, including Anesthesiologist, who had completed his flurry of injections, were very frightened.

"Hit him again, Tom. All three hundred joules."

I pushed both red buttons and saw a spark on Francisco's chest, a wisp of smoke, and the odor of scorched flesh. Nothing happened.

Anesthesiologist jammed a needle into Francisco's heart and gave him a bolus injection of adrenaline.

"Last time. Shock him!"

Zap! A miracle! A flicker of a beat, then a crescendo of normal activity. When Francisco's pump settled into normal rhythm at ninety beats a minute, sighs of relief exploded all around the room. Since we had already gone so far, Leader closed his lip with a first-class repair and led us into the hallway, where we all slumped on hard benches and sat as speechless as athletes after a great test.

But I felt absolutely crystal clear, once again in full contact with my physician's heart, my habituation of the past few days overwhelmed by the cosmic magnitude of Francisco's near-death. Gurdjieff used to say, "Stay aware that you and everyone around you will eventually die." But I say: Guard against excessively morbid worldviews. Take the flip side of that idea, and celebrate everyone on the great journey of life.

Whichever view is more correct, the scare over Francisco sandpapered my heart, polishing off the barnacles in a way that stayed with me for the remainder of the trip. I felt present, right there, sensitive to the situation, in a way that proved to me that habituation can be managed to some degree. The question I ponder is: What, short of such extreme shocks, can promote continuing sensitivity in the healer's heart? I boiled the choices down to four teaspoons of sugary medicine, to be taken one at a time.

Axiom I: First, the healer must *wish* to stay more in touch with the heart. If you lack that wish, ask yourself, "Why?"

Axiom II: Make it a sacred habit to read one page daily of poetry, wisdom, religion, or other uplifting material.

Axiom III: Learn how to still the mind enough to free yourself, however briefly, from worries. Many techniques—from meditation to Zen, from prayer to self-hypnosis to yoga relaxation, from aerobics to golf—can accomplish brief removal of all anxieties. I believe that a personalized series of lessons about how best to achieve a meditative state that works well for you would be helpful for most people.

Axiom IV: Do volunteer medicine for the joy of it.

Now in my thirty-second year of practice, what about my own healer's heart? From the time I read *Burma Surgeon,* my question was whether there can exist an act of utter altruism. When Leader struggled back to the operating room, an IV tube still dangling from his body, he answered my question for me. Everyone on the team gave their all. Now, when people ask me why I've given away so much of my time and money to help others, my best explanation comes from a quotation from *The Havamal,* the wisdom of the Vikings, collected in the ninth century:

Generous and brave men lead the best lives.

They have few regrets.

Deepak Chopra:
Healing Our Hearts

We have the deepest aspirations. We want to create a new mythology that says that peace and harmony and laughter and love are possible. That says that social justice and economic parity and ecological balance and a sense for the sacred and a universal spirituality irrespective of our origins are all part of the tangled hierarchy, the interdependency chorus.

Human beings have only existed for 200,000 years. For most of this time, we have been surrounded by predators. In order to survive, we have had a biological response, the flight/fight response. Because we have become so good at this flight/fight response, we have become the predator on this planet. We are the most dangerous animal.

That is not our whole history, however. Something very interesting happened to us about 4,000 years ago, when a few luminaries across the world appeared at once. They were the prophets of the Pentateuch, the great Greek philosophers, the sages of the Upanishads, the Eastern seers like Lao Tsu, Confucius and Buddha, and many others. They developed the ability to get in touch with the domain of awareness that is non-local, that transcends the space-time energy and everything that we can perceive with our senses.

The great English poet William Blake once wrote,

We are led to believe a lie
when we see with and not through the eye

Deepak Chopra, MD, has written twenty-five books, which have been translated into thirty-five languages. He is also the author of more than one hundred audio- and videotape series, including five critically acclaimed programs on public television. In 1999 *Time* magazine selected Dr. Chopra as one of the Top 100 Icons and Heroes of the Century, describing him as "the poet-prophet of alternative medicine." Dr. Chopra currently serves as CEO and founder of The Chopra Center for Well Being in Carlsbad, California. For more information you can visit his web site at www.chopra.com. This chapter first appeared in *Tikkun* magazine.

that was born in the night, to perish in the night,
while the souls slept in beams of light.

When we see beyond the physical we see into our souls.

We can go a whole lifetime without getting in touch with our souls. But once we get in touch with this presence, there is no going back. This soul place is one of knowingness, of light, of love, compassion, and understanding. Intention, imagination, insight, intuition, creativity, meaning, purpose, and decision-making are the attributes of this presence. When we get in touch with it, we have recourse to what is called the intuitive response, which is a form of intelligence that is contextual, relational, holistic, and nurturing. When I'm in this presence, and you are, we are in the same place.

-§-
Just because we are part of a collective insanity, we must not assume it is normal. It is the psychopathology of the average.
-§-

We see that we are part of a great chain of being where we interdependently co-create each other. There is more that we share than what separates us. We all seek love, we all seek self-esteem, we all seek creative expression, we all seek self-actualization—these are the birthright of every human being.

There is no more important task at this moment in our history than to get in touch with the sacred core of our being that is common to all of us. Our practical proposals will be effective only when we get in touch with our souls, and feel this fundamental shift in our hearts. If we can feel that shift in our hearts, if we can join together and be living examples of this shift, then the world will transform, because the world is as we are. The world is nothing other than the projection of our souls.

Just because we are part of a collective insanity, we must not assume it is normal. It is the psychopathology of the average. We can emancipate ourselves from this psychopathology through the realm of spirit. Even though we have interesting scientific insights, the religious traditions of the world have access to universal truths.

A friend of mine sent me an English translation of an Egyptian papyrus discovered in the 1940s. The language is pre-Babylonian. We don't know who the author is, but he or she lived in the time of Solomon. The author is talking to God and he or she says:

You split me and you tore my heart open and you filled me with love.
You poured your spirit into mine. I knew you as I knew myself.
My eyes are radiant with your light. My ears delight in your music.
My nostrils are filled with your fragrance. My face is covered with your
dew.

You have made me see all things shining. You have made me see all
  things new.

You have granted me perfect ease. And I have
  become like Paradise.

And having become like Paradise, my soul is healed.

-§-

**The world is
nothing other
than the projec-
tion of our souls.**

-§-

At this moment, there is a rift in our collective soul. But there is one
part of our evolution that says this rift can be healed. And if we heal it, we
will all move into that ecstasy which is nothing other than the exaltation
of spirit.

MARI HALL:

Gardening Well— Weeds and All

A traditional Sufi story goes like this: There once was a young man named Nasreddin who planted a flower garden. But when the flowers came up so did a great crop of dandelions among them. Wishing to eliminate the unwanted guests, Nasreddin consulted with gardeners near and far, but none of their solutions worked.

Finally, the young man traveled to the palace of the sheikh to seek the wisdom of the royal gardener himself. But unfortunately, he had already tried all the methods the royal gardener recommended to him.

Silently they sat together for a good long time. At last, the royal gardener looked at Nasreddin and said: "Well, then, the only thing I can suggest is that you learn to love them."

There is a space we can reach in our healing work where we forget where we stop and where the other person begins. I tell my students that this is the greatest gift we can experience, for it is the oneness of spirit that calls forth healing on all levels. We, as the person transmitting the energy and working with someone, also become the person being healed. The teacher becomes the student, the student the teacher and we are one. In this space of surrender, where all judgment has ceased to exist, we are simply and profoundly being one with all there is.

The key to achieving this oneness is surrender or, as the royal gardener said, "learn to love them." When we release our demands of how it should be; "No dandelions in the garden," we essentially surrender any reaction. Reaction is what keeps us separate form each other. This surren-

American Reiki Master Mari Hall is the founder and director of the International Association of Reiki based in the Czech Republic. Mari teaches Reiki and self-development courses through her Eagle's Path Training programs in Europe and the US. She recently introduced her new energy work ONE as a means to integrate more spiritual essence into our physical bodies. She is the author of the best-selling books *Practical Reiki, Reiki for Common Ailments, Reiki for the Soul* and *Reiki*. The story about Johnny is reprinted from *Reiki for Common Ailments* (Piatkus, 1999). Her website is www.wisechoices.com. Photo by Sonya Whitefield.

der and learning to love has been the focus of my own personal work, as well as the focus of the work I do as a teacher of the form of energy medicine known as Reiki. For in surrender we remember our light or divinity, which helps others to remember theirs.

Some of the work, in addition to Reiki that I have done in my own process of surrender, has been with reactionary patterns in my personality. These appeared like layers that could be removed, much like peeling an onion. As the layers of my personality were exposed, it took time to integrate what was newly presented. Gradually each aspect of my personality was revealed, layer by layer, until my center or the soul self was reached and my light could be fully experienced. This was a process into love. Accepting the dandelions of my personality was part of the surrender I needed to help me remember that love.

-§-
Each mask also can keep us from experiencing our own light and divinity. That is why we search outside ourselves first for the truth that lies hidden within.
-§-

In essence, the layers of the personality are like masks that we have created in order to survive, to have love and to be accepted. Each mask also can keep us from experiencing our own light and divinity, or rather from remembering that light. That is why we search outside ourselves first for the truth that lies hidden within.

What holds the masks in place are our thoughts, emotions, and the demands we place on ourselves about how we must be. This moves us away from our spiritual nature, and from our inner peace. We certainly do not need to experience the opposite polarity in order to come into harmony, or go from one extreme to another. We can move rather softly and gently into the center of who we are authentically, and in this place, our soul is open to the source. It has become the doorway for the spirit to move through us. Love and acceptance of ourselves transform and move us to this beautiful center of our souls.

Healing depends upon the extent of the problem and how deeply rooted it is. Each person is an individual made complex by reaction. I have found that Reiki helps us move into harmony in our minds, bodies and emotions, thus working on the root cause of physical illness. When our emotions and mind are harmonized, we have moved closer to our spiritual nature and certainly to the possibility of being one with each other. The essence of Reiki is unconditional love. It is the spirit of God that moves through us encouraging us to live. Spirit sources the soul; Reiki brings the spirit of God to humankind, and thus sources the being to come into complete harmony. It nourishes the soul.

This process always starts with us. Our inner reality is reflected in our outer world. If we cannot be one with ourselves, how can we be one with each other? This is indeed the challenge of the heart.

Personally I came to Reiki out of a need to find something that would help me in my own physical healing process. What I experienced as a result of my willingness to treat myself was nothing less than miraculous. After taking Reiki, my whole life changed. The deep depression that I had experienced so much of my life lifted. I was more willing to accept what life had brought to me. I took responsibility for myself. I saw beauty and love around me and experienced it inside me. I was living life. I felt whole.

After a year I was completely healed of my physical problem. It only seemed natural to turn this precious gift outward to others. The more I changed, the more I responded to others. I was no longer closed. The layers of defense that I had so carefully built up, one by one, were stripped away, as I continued to work on myself. My masks had slipped away. The deepest healing for me was not physical; it was emotionally and mentally. I began to have hope and trust in life. Even when things would occur that I would previously have reacted to, by closing up, or condemning, I saw as a gift to help me wake up spiritually. My life began to have a natural ebb and flow; I was swimming with life not against it.

My relationship with everything around me changed too. I began a search for what was working in my life, what I needed to let go of in order to support this newness in me. By being myself, I was witness to God's love, Reiki and humankind. I realized that I had held onto so much resentment that it had pulled me out of balance. I was righteously resentful; "After all," I argued internally, "look at the bad things that have happened in my life!" As I released this resentment, I could see things from a different perspective. I understood deeply that people react—and that their reactions give me

-§-
Needing something to make us feel complete is the mind's fear of the unknown.
-§-

the opportunity to react. Reaction is fear-driven, and it keeps us from living in the precious moment of now. I could see how the world was constructed by people who had forgotten their basic truth of oneness.

I have found that Reiki gives me the ability to process life events in a clearer, more objective way. By using Reiki on a daily basis to stay in harmony, I am better able to handle life's messages. I know that all events in my life are miracles—if I am open to receiving them. They are life's way of waking me up and inviting me to come back into the center, where love is. The more resistance I have, the more my ego is involved. I use Reiki to release my need to be right and safe. It is a process that becomes part of your life, like breathing. I am not separate from Reiki; I am Reiki, and it supports me to live a life with much more majesty and grace.

I moved quite naturally from my own inner work to include working with others. Yet there was still something more I wanted to express out of this newness I was experiencing. I had a need to pass this inner peace I had discovered on to others. The decision to work with others by becoming a teacher of Reiki was one of the single most important decisions I ever made. As I taught others, I could see how much of my personal ego was in place; I wanted the students to like and acknowledge me. Even with all the work I had done, the "I" of Mari was very present. How could I learn to feel safe enough to lose the self I had struggled so hard to define? All my life's experiences had made me who I am. And yet, to be a good teacher and therapist, it is the letting go of myself that clears a channel for this loving spiritual energy to be drawn through me, healing others and myself. The concept of only being the instrument is important in the surrender process, and certainly in the process of the work itself.

To see myself as an instrument does not mean giving away my personal identity. It creates a space for healing in and through me. I am an instrument, a channel through which energy flows. I am not the energy nor I do I hold onto it. The energy flows through me and yet it also helps me to be a better instrument. So therefore my job is to be the best instrument for the energy to flow through. This involves self-treatment. It is simply not enough to talk the talk of healing and harmony — it is most important to walk the talk. I must be an example of harmony, peace and oneness. As I began to peel this layer of the onion, I was forced to ask myself, "Am I congruent with the message of Reiki?" Honesty compelled me to answer, "No, I am not."

-§-
The only time we experience pain is when we refuse to learn the lesson of the particular pathway we are on.
-§-

Once I realized this, I quite simply prayed for direction. I asked to be given a chance to serve humanity and come into harmony with myself. I also prayed that I be given the opportunity to develop the ability to walk the walk and to talk the talk of inner peace and oneness. I was told to always be careful of what you ask for; you just may get it!

Little did I know this prayer would set my life on a course that would take me away from the safe world I knew, and propel me across the world, to Europe, to take up the walk. When we ask for change it can come in ways we might not expect! Will we answer when life calls? That is the question.

On the surface I may have said that I was ready for change in my life. I had prayed for "direction and opportunity," yet with direction came change, came fear. My mind had invested so much into the way I had become at that time. Change meant the unknown; change to what? My mind did not know how the newly changed "me" would be, or where this direction would take me. It attempted to hold onto what was known, even if it no longer worked in my life and had ceased to nourish me. In the ensuing inner struggle, I felt like a sweater that was unraveling.

Earlier in my life I identified several pathways to change. These pathways have helped me to understand the nature of what I am experiencing, and given me the perspective to stay in the process, rather than becoming so uncomfortable that I give up on myself.

The first pathway feels like we are pulling apart. It is like when we pull the yarn and unravel the sweater. In moments like this our lives seem to be unraveling. The puzzle that was so perfectly put together no longer looks right. We see where we have forced some of the pieces to fit in to place. All our energy is involved in keeping the status quo, and the effort simply becomes too much.

The second pathway involves knowing what we want. Once we understand that life is asking us to change then when we see doors closing and old ways of being no longer working, it becomes important to decide just what it is we want—and also what we no longer want in our lives. When faced with this sorting out process, sometimes it is easier to figure out what we do not want, what has to go. From what is left over, it is easier to choose what we want to keep.

The third pathway involves letting go. When we let go of the things we no longer want or need, it sometimes involves pain, especially if we have invested much energy into being right. Righteousness can bring pain, as we let go of the excess baggage in our lives. We must also lose the need to be right.

The fourth pathway is one of adjusting: Once we have let go of something, there is a time for us to integrate the change. We settle into this new space, and begin to feel what we want, rather than need. Needing something to make us feel complete is the mind's fear of the unknown. Very often if we are not careful we will bring our needs into our lives in the form of needy people. If this occurs we are just constructing the same old puzzle again. We need to take the time to allow ourselves to feel what we really want.

The fifth pathway is to surrender: We release all the endless questions and need to know. Instead we allow God to send to us what is truly important in this moment. We enjoy what life brings to us, rather than trying to make it like we think it should be. We see the gift in every moment and love accepting it. We now love the dandelions.

In the sixth pathway, we literally are drawn into the swim of life: We flow with life rather than trying to force ourselves upstream. We are supported where once it was a struggle. We have released our necessity to control. We are, in fact, "out of control." We enjoy the journey and take in all we experience. We are on our return back to the center and to God.

The only time we experience pain is when we refuse to learn the lesson of the particular pathway we are on. When we get fixed in our thinking, when we "know" how things ought to have turned out, then we often wish to retreat to the last comfortable place, or we refuse to go forward.

This is called resistance. Our resistance to change causes pain. I began to do research into how emotions play the biggest part in creating disharmony; that thoughts in the mind are actually secondary to emotions. The key was to re-pattern a person's emotional energy, which would in turn release the thoughts. I understood that the reason affirmations did not work sometimes was that people had not done the spiritual gardening work necessary to plant these new flowers or thoughts deep into their psyches.

I started incorporating a technique I learned to re-pattern mentally challenged children, before I learned Reiki. By incorporating a cross pattern with the use of Reiki, I could see how the body took the energy deeper into areas where there had been emotional fracturing. At first I started treating people with dyslexia this way.

What started as an idea for the treatment of common dyslexia led to years of work with people with motor neurological problems. I discovered that dyslexia is actually like being "switched off." It usually starts with a moment or moments of emotional fracturing. Furthermore, we can be considered slightly dyslexic on many levels. The specialized integration treatment I am writing about has helped people to reconnect body, mind and soul, to experience wholeness again. First I will share some of the stories and miracles that make this special integration treatment so beneficial to use.

Johnny's Miracle

I was visiting a family in the countryside of Scotland. One day, their young son John who was thirteen years old asked me if I had problems understanding things in school when I was little. I replied, "It is funny you should ask that, Johnny. I was just thinking how hard it was to get my mind focused on what the teacher said and what I tried to read in books. It seemed like there was a part that was missing, like a door I couldn't go through." It turned out that Johnny had a similar problem.

Synchronistically, I had been doing research into using Reiki with Whole Brain Therapy. I had strong impressions of how I might treat dyslexia and other problems. I was searching for people to work with, to see if what I suspected had some validity. I explained this to Johnny and his parents. I asked Johnny if he would be interested in helping me to find a way to help other kids that had the same problem that the two of us shared. He and his parents both agreed.

I treated Johnny once a week for one hour. Instead of having him lay on a traditional couch or massage table, I asked him where he would be comfortable. He said that if the weather was nice he had a special spot in the glen—a field that was "his" but he was willing to share. So off we would go, hand in hand, to his spot, with a blanket and something to drink.

When I was treating him with Reiki, he would talk about what he felt, and how the energy seemed to move. He was full of insight and could talk a blue streak. During the fourth treatment, he got so quiet I thought he had fallen asleep. I asked Johnny if he was sleeping. "Nope," he replied. "You see I am reading this wonderful book I found in the library of my mind, Mari. I have found the doorway into understanding. It's great in here and there are so many books to read."

My experience in working with Johnny became the foundation for a specialized integration work I began doing with Reiki. His miracle of "finding the door" helped many other people. John is now a neurologist, practicing medicine implemented with Reiki, in his clinic in western Scotland. He tells his story to the children he works with.

Sean Is Walking

I was asked to come and talk with a family on the outskirts of Edinburgh, Scotland. They had heard about my work with Johnny. Sean didn't have dyslexia. He had suffered a massive stroke, losing his ability to walk and talk. His left side was paralyzed. His doctors had given up hope, telling Sean and his family that he would never recover. When you are over eighty years old as Sean was, caregivers may tell you that there is no chance to recover. However, Sean and his family wanted to see if Reiki might help his problems.

Fortunately Sean could write with his right hand. It was a painstakingly hard process but his only way to communicate. He kept paper and pen with him all the time and had devised his own shorthand by the time I was asked to use Reiki with him. I asked him if I could use a particular process for brain integration I had used in the treatment of dyslexia. I had been seeing it benefit people with motor neurological problems. He replied that he had nothing to lose and everything to gain.

I worked with him five days a week for the first month. He would lie on his back while I treated his whole body in traditional Reiki positions. I then spent extra time using a special position that favored brain integration. The most notable effect Sean noticed was that he felt connected to his body and more clear. He said he felt he was working with the Reiki and not being worked on. When I said you are always working with the energy as you are using it, his written reply was, "Well, now I really know it from the inside out." His family took first and second degree Reiki trainings in order to work more closely with Sean. They took turns working with him twice a day. This became quality time for Sean and his family members. When I would stop by to see his progress, they remarked that they were actually enjoying this special time with him and were able to see how his body was changing.

He started talking in the third month, first words and then short sentences. After a few more months a speech therapist was called in to work with Sean. We celebrated each success. I continued to treat him two to three times a month. His body became suppler, and his left arm regained some slight movement. We ran energy through his limbs and cradled his head in our hands. The right side of his brain was the side that had been traumatized, affecting the left side of his body. Extra time was spent there. We often remarked that working with Sean was like connecting the dots in activity books that we had worked in as children. He was acutely aware when a particular dot had been connected. His eyes would light up as he said, Yes, that's the spot." I gave him a drawing of a human body and asked him to point to where he felt more and less alive. I asked him to show us how to work with him. He loved the integration position as he said he could feel how the energy pushed through into other areas. He told us that his body was feeling stronger.

After Sean had his stroke, the family had built a ramp from the back door, so that he could be wheeled into the back garden and be outside. As he started making improvement, his need to be outside became even greater. As he regained some use of his arm, Sean started learning to push his chair, using the wheels. His task, as he put it, was to get outside by himself. He was proud when he could roll his chair outside, and, in the months that followed, get back into the house. Each time was a victory, celebrated and savoured.

-§-
When we cease to demand, have surrendered, and are being one hundred percent in the now, then life works with us.
-§-

The treatments continued throughout the year and went on into the next. Both his family and Sean were convinced that there had been marked improvement and wanted to see what else would happen. Sean did first and second degree Reiki training in order to work on himself. He treated his own legs. A physical therapist had been working with Sean to keep his body from atrophying and he, too, noticed the changes in Sean's body. The doctors were also amazed at the changes, and suggested a more aggressive physiotherapeutic approach at the local center. He exercised there three times a week to strengthen his left leg as it started to come alive.

It was a beautiful day in the fall when I next drove to Sean's house. The air was crisp and clear. I had run through in my mind the progress he had made during this time, and felt he had made many miracles. I was inspired by his tenacity. I had used Sean's story in many of my Reiki classes as a way to bring home to the students the miracles Reiki can bring to us. I pulled the car into the drive and found his empty chair at the bottom of the ramp. I looked in the back garden, in Sean's special place, to see if he had been put in a chair there. No luck. I was in a panic. Where was Sean?

As I started to the house, I heard him laugh. I looked toward the door of the house and there he was, holding onto the metal railing, a look of great satisfaction on his face. I said, "What are you doing here all by yourself, Sean?" He said, "I am practicing my surprise for the family. I can walk ever so slowly, and I want to give them this as a thank you. Don't tell a soul."

Sean's birthday was November 1st. His family assembled for a luncheon celebration. I was asked to join them. After a lovely meal we went into the garden to enjoy the beautiful fall weather. Sean said he would roll down to join us, "in a shake." He had declined help, giving me a wink, saying would be along presently.

We all were talking when a hush came over the crowd. Sean walked out of the house and began walking toward us on his own. He stopped and said, "Since it's my eighty-third birthday, I wanted to give you all a present." What a precious gift it was to us all

-§-

There is a space we can reach in our healing work where we forget where we stop and where the other person begins.

-§-

to see him walking. We had been taught so much about ourselves all the time we had been working with Sean. Miracles had touched us all—Sean's triumph was the best birthday present I have ever witnessed being given. I've realized that the integration position is not just for dyslexia or motor neurological problems. We can use it to reconnect ourselves, and integrate our body, mind and soul for the purpose of living fully.

From Being Out of Sorts to Being Clear-Headed

Sometimes I get out of sorts. It may be when I find myself in a stressful situation. It may be that I am so busy that I have not given myself enough quiet time to reconnect. This manifests in me becoming edgy and not fully present. I become vague, forgetful and short-tempered. Even Reiki teachers can get out of sorts; we are human after all!

To remedy the situation, I lie down and do this integration technique on myself. Within a few minutes, I am more clear and calm. I feel reconnected on all levels, and more awake. There seems to be a common thread of experience in all cases where this integration technique is used; people have a sense of being fully at home in our bodies, clearer-headed, more alert, awake and refreshed. My suggestion is this: Use it on yourself and have your own experience, and then work with others. All you have to lose is being disassociated; all you have to gain is living fully! This photo (from my book *Reiki*, Element Books/HarperCollins) shows what the integration technique looks like when practiced on another person.

CHAPTER TWENTY ONE

Using the Integration Technique On Yourself

Lie on your back and cross your ankles, left ankle over right. Cross your wrists at the top of your head, right wrist over left. Place your hands on both sides of your head. Leave yourself in this position for approximately twenty to thirty minutes and then change the crossing to right ankle over left and left wrist over right and give Reiki to yourself for another twenty to thirty minutes.

When I work with clients I always take a client history detailing physical problems, the state of their emotions, and ask what issues they have been dealing with lately. Part of the work I do with clients is to ask them to do simple tests in order for them to feel where they may be switched off. I watch them walk and see how the body presents itself. I may also ask them to take their hand and touch their knee on the opposite side. All this when you have been trained helps you to see the disharmony in the body mind. Once they have been treated, they normally feel when there has been a shift in their energy. They will walk with more stability and feel better from the inside out. We do not tell — we give them opportunities to experience for themselves the effects of their work with Reiki. We often witness miracles.

What I have been given to realize is that all these moments of intuition or clear insight are all moments of oneness. When we cease to demand, have surrendered, and are being one hundred percent in the now, then life works with us. We are given answers and direction. Life is a series of opportunities to get out of our own way and reconnect to all that is divine. And because life loves us enough, all we need to do is show up and it is here supporting us to remember, even when we do not ask.

At the end of the day we have come back to the beginning. There is a space we can reach in our healing work where we forget where we stop and where the other person begins. It is the greatest gift we can experience; it is the oneness of spirit that calls forth healing on all levels. We as the person transmitting the energy, or working with someone, also become the person being healed; the teacher becomes the student, the student the teacher, and we are one. In this space of surrender, where all judgment has ceased to exist, we are simply and profoundly being one with all there is. There is nothing more satisfying nor more profound than to sit next to someone with your hands on them, and experience, one more time, this divine connection, both inside yourself and with others. It is truly inspiring, an experience that burns with light eternal and continues to challenge the heart to love.

KATHY O'CONNOR BURROUGHS:

The Scalpel of Intention

Pleasant Grove, Utah, September 2002: Leo can hardly believe it. The pain in his knees is completely gone. Two months ago, when he hobbled into the chiropractor's office, he'd given up all hope. X-rays had revealed all he needed to know: bone touching bone. The cartilage was gone. No wonder his knees hurt so much. Having seen it himself, he accepted that nothing could be done and scheduled the recommended knee surgery. At eighty-five years of age, he reasoned, what else could be done? The aging process takes a toll. After reporting all of this to his chiropractor, he hobbled into the adjusting room, saying, "but I sure could use a little tune-up on my back, Doc."

Leo's chiropractor suggested an experiment, a new technique that might reduce the knee pain. His doctor explained how, with this technique, he would talk to Leo's nervous system directly, asking what specific faults existed in its current operations. By making corrective statements to repair those operational faults, he would instruct Leo's nervous system to become aware of the degeneration and begin repairing the knees. What made this technique unique, Doc explained, was the combination of "intention" along with the innate intelligence of Leo's body. This sounded crazy to Leo, but Doc had never steered him wrong in the past. And since the new technique required so little—all he had to do was hold out his arm and keep an open mind—Leo decided to give it a try.

The doctor began by directing a number of questions to Leo's body, pressing down on Leo's extended arm with each one. Leo understood most of the questions, but a few of them made little sense. Doc reassured

Kathy O'Connor Burroughs, DC, began her career as a chiropractor in 1994 in Petaluma, California after graduating from Palmer College of Chiropractic in Davenport, Iowa. Her method of practice utilizes videofluoroscopy, to view the spine in motion, conventional X-rays, drop tables, and a computerized adjusting instrument that senses motion of the vertebra. She specializes in difficult cases, especially patients who have unsuccessfully tried conventional surgery. After a personal healing experience with the NeuroModulation Technique, she added this element to her practice. Her web site is www.dockathy.com. Photo by Stephanie Rausser.

him. The technique addressed the energy system in the body as well as the Autonomic Nervous System (ANS), and would engage a part of the body-mind that is not governed by speech. Leo did not need to understand the questions with his cognitive mind for the technique to work.

Thirty minutes later, the treatment was complete. That evening Leo experienced flu-like symptoms of fever and achiness. The next morning he awoke feeling fine. The pain in his knees had diminished noticeably. For the first time in years they felt pretty good. He decided to postpone surgery. Several more treatments addressing other ANS faults were completed over the course of the following month. At the end of the month, Leo noticed a definite improvement in his knees. They had improved by eighty-five percent. When he met with the knee surgeon, a fresh X-ray was taken. A full 1 mm of space could be seen between the bones where the cartilage had regenerated. Leo cancelled his surgery altogether.

Petaluma, California, September 2003: Both endometriosis and, later, fibroid tumors had troubled Sarah, a thirty-eight-year-old professor, for years. Her periods were painful, irregular and prolonged. Her stomach looked like that of a woman who was five months pregnant. The pain became so constant and intense that she began to talk with her gynecologist about having a hysterectomy. All the standard treatments—from hormone therapy to ablations—had been tried, and had failed. But the thought of having her reproductive organs removed was more than a little daunting. None of the options presented by traditional medicine appealed to Sarah and none held much promise that she would be better off.

> -§-
> Language—the spoken word, with precise terminology—along with intention and thought—is a key to healing.
> -§-

Not only would she forever lose the ability to bear a child, Sarah had heard horrible stories of women who never feel good again after a hysterectomy. They gain weight and can't lose it, suffer loss of memory and moodiness, and must take synthetic hormones for the rest of their lives. Books are written solely on post-hysterectomy complications. Sarah couldn't stop ruminating on all this. Her thoughts were driving her mad. She felt desperate, and searched and prayed for another way.

During a routine visit to her chiropractor, with whom Sarah had discussed the fibroid tumors in the past, Sarah described her worsening condition. While receiving an adjustment, Sarah revealed her deep fear, and grief at the thought of losing of her reproductive organs. Her chiropractor suggested a radical new treatment that works directly with the Autonomic Nervous System to correct bio-physical faults. In Sarah's case, the chiropractor instructed her ANS to recognize the fibroid tumors and correct all faults with the body's innate mechanisms for eradicating fibroids. This sounded weird to Sarah. She reflected, "Why shouldn't my body know how to repair itself? Cuts always heal. Colds are fought off." Sarah's chiropractor told her about another patient who had suffered extreme pain due to endometriosis. Two days after she received the new treatment, the woman began to shed old, dark menstrual tissue. Her normal cycle had not been due for another three weeks. The shedding continued for two days. During that time, the protrusion in her stomach went down a full two inches. Four months after the treatment, she was still symptom-free. Sarah made an appointment for the treatment.

When they began, Sarah's chiropractor asked her body a number of questions using the Applied Kinesiology technique, a widely used system for testing muscle response developed in the 1950s by Dr. George Goodheart, and scientifically validated using Galvanic Skin Response devices. Wherever muscle testing revealed weakness in Sarah's body, the chiropractor gave verbal instructions to Sarah's ANS to correct specific faults.

A day and a half later, Sarah began having intense cramps, similar to a miscarriage. She left a lecture early. Once home, she passed a fibroid. It was one-and-a-half inches wide and seven inches long. She then passed a second fibroid a quarter of the size. Her cramping stopped. The protrusion in her stomach quickly reduced by half. Two months later, her periods went from horrible to normal. She was so thrilled that she began telling anyone who would listen about her success.

Las Vegas, Nevada, March 2003: Thirty professionals from various disciplines—Chiropractors, Acupuncturists, Dentists and MDs—gathered at a NeuroModulation Technique (NMT) Training Seminar, to learn the technique that had helped Leo and Sarah.

A neurosurgeon named Jennifer was one participant. For twenty years, Jennifer had suffered anaphylactic reactions to bananas and avocados. She loved both foods, but if she ate either of them, her face and throat would swell up to the point where she couldn't breathe.

The instructor, Leslie Feinberg, D.C., asked Jennifer about incidents that had occurred in her life at the time the symptoms first appeared. Emotions affect bodily functioning. Every second of every day, the nervous system analyzes and catalogs information. An estimated 90% of the information it processes is thrown out or disregarded. But information regarded as important—especially information having to do with safety and survival—is tagged for future reference. In Jennifer's case, this function played a critical role in her allergic reaction.

-§-
Intention is often a more significant determinant of healing than treatment.
-§-

Twenty years earlier, Jennifer had been working at a tree farm. It was a very difficult time in her life. Her son had committed suicide a year before; it was the first the anniversary of his death. She was burdened with tremendous sadness and guilt. While trimming a Ficus tree one day, she found herself wishing she were dead. She felt her tears come, but continued to prune the tree. As she pulled a freshly cut limb from the tree, sap flew into her eye. Startled, she jumped back. Instantly, her eye began to swell. Shortly thereafter, she had difficulty breathing. Over the next several weeks, the same sequence of eye-swelling and breathing difficulty occurred several times right after a meal. The reactions intensified, and eventually, she was able to identify the offending foods: bananas and avocados. If she ate either, she had to be taken to the hospital.

Dr. Feinberg invited the professionals in the room to consider this proposition: Jennifer's nervous system had heard the message, "I want to die" and her body gave her the opportunity to do just that by generating an extreme reaction to the sap in her eye. Her nervous system tagged the information "sap-in-the-eye," connected it with thoughts of death, and later recognized a chemical similarity between sap, and bananas and avocados. Although getting Ficus sap in your eye is certainly unpleasant, there is nothing unpleasant—for most of us—about eating a banana or slicing up a nice ripe avocado. But to Jennifer's body-mind, bananas spelled "death threat."

When Dr. Feinberg concluded Jennifer's NMT treatment, he felt confident that her body had corrected all faults regarding allergies. He asked if she would like to test the treatment for effectiveness. She gave her enthusiastic consent. Jennifer kept her Benadryl close at hand, and the nearest hospital was located—just in case. Dr. Feinberg approached the test with caution. He began by having Jennifer rub a banana and then an avocado on the thin lining of her lip. No reaction. The following day, he muscle tested Jennifer again, and found her to be clear of any neurological faults regarding bananas and avocados. She ate a piece of banana. It tasted good to her. There was no reaction in her throat. Her breathing remained steady and normal. She ate a piece of avocado. The flavor and texture delighted her. No reaction. The next day, she ate a whole banana for breakfast. No problem. She had an avocado sandwich for lunch and felt just fine. To this day, she is free of her allergic reaction to bananas and avocados.

My professional interest in NMT began as the result of a personal experience of a similar, seemingly miraculous healing brought on by this method. In October 2001, while on vacation in Puerto Vallarta, Mexico, I noticed an itchy sensation on the inside of my wrists. It grew worse as days passed, until my wrists and palms itched constantly, keeping me awake half the night. By the end of the ten-day trip, I began to see little red spots creeping up my arms. Over the course of the next year-and-a-half, I tried various allergy treatments, consulted a dermatologist, and had all my hormone levels checked. I ordered tests to see if I had picked up a microscopic bug in Mexico. Nothing relieved the red spots and itching. The spots would fade, and then come back. The condition worsened, and I found myself with huge blotches of red, itchy hives covering my entire body nearly every day. The hives seemed completely random in their manifestation: anything, anytime, could bring on an attack of hives.

By December 2002, I was desperate. As I stood in the shower one morning, looking down at the water flowing over the ugly red blotches covering my arms and legs, I gave up trying to figure out the cause of the hives mentally. I was exhausted. Experience had shown me on countless occasions that my most difficult challenges are gifts from God that enable me to help others. So I prayed a very specific prayer: "Please show me what I need to learn from this soon and please, please, could the solution be simple and easy?"

A few days later, I heard about NMT. I had my first treatment in January 2003. Approximately sixty-five percent of my hives were gone within four hours! I knew I had stumbled into amazing new territory. A week went by; the hives did not get any worse, but they did not go away completely, either. The underlying cause of the hives was multi-faceted. A number of treatments were required to eradicate them completely.

NeuroModulation Technique takes us into the vast untapped potential and innate ability of the human body to heal itself. The basic theory is very simple. If you can discern from the nervous system what faults exist that result in disease and degeneration, and if you can instruct the nervous system to correct those faults, your body will simply heal itself. The human body is a miraculous self-healing system. Every human being has abundant evidence of the remarkable regenerative capacity of the body. We have all seen wounds heal, bruises fade, bones repair, infections clear, headaches lift, aches and pains somehow eventually resolve. The human body possesses remarkable resilience, and seems able to heal all parts of itself under the right circumstances. The question begging to be asked when in a healing crisis is, "What has my body forgotten that it has the capacity to do for itself?" The theory behind NMT suggests that what is needed is a conscious process by which we can communicate with the "other than conscious" part of us that silently runs the body. In this way, we remind the body to attend to something it has forgotten to do. In the same way that eyes may no longer see that treadmill in the corner of the bedroom waiting to be exercised on, or the pile of clothes laying in the corner waiting to be altered, certain clean-up and repair jobs in the body are not attended to for lack of attention. Until, that is, the light of awareness is shone in that corner. What directs that bright light is surprisingly simple: it is *clearly stated intent.*

Scientific studies around the world have amassed an amazing body of information on the power of intention. The fact that language — the spoken word, with precise terminology — along with intention and thought — is a key to healing is illuminated by Grazyna Fosar and Franz Bludorf in their book, *Vernetzte Intelligenz.*[1] Citing a number of studies by Russian scientists, geneticists and linguists, Fosar and Bludorf give credence to the concept that verbal mantras, self-talk, clairvoyance, spontaneous and remote acts of healing are ways the human body communicates with itself, and the world around it, in order to heal.

Only ten percent of the DNA in the human genome is used to build proteins and control physiology. This portion of DNA (codons) is what Western medicine has been studying in the hope of eradicating disease. The remaining ninety percent is considered "junk DNA." But the Russian researchers rejected this "junk" notion and found in their experiments that DNA is not only responsible for the construction of the body; it serves a communication function and a data storage function as well. They found that DNA follows the same rules as all human languages. In comparing the rules of syntax (the way words are put together to form phrases and sentences), semantics (the study of meaning in language forms) and basic rules of grammar, they found that the base pairs of our DNA follow a regular grammar and have set rules as is seen in language. Thus human language may be a reflection of the structure inherent in our DNA.

Even more astounding, when exploring the vibrational behavior of DNA, they found they could modulate certain frequency patterns onto a laser ray and with it, influence DNA frequency, and thus the genetic information itself. Since the basic structure of DNA base pairs and of language have the same structure, no decoding is necessary — one can simply use the words and sentences of human language to effect changes in the DNA.

Another glimpse of hard evidence that moves approaches like NMT out of the realm of hocus-pocus and into the realm of cutting-edge medical science can be seen in the work of Jacques Benveniste. In the 1970s, he and a team of other French scientists nourished a harvested guinea pig heart with chemicals to sustain it outside the animal's body. By delivering acetylcholine and histamine, he was able to increase blood flow in the coronary arteries, while with mepyramine and atropine, he could inhibit it. These chemicals are commonly known to do this. However, amazingly, Benveniste increased and decreased the blood flow using not the pharmacological chemicals themselves, but signature vibrations emitted from these chemicals. Using a transducer designed for this purpose, and a computer equipped with a sound card, he recorded low-frequency waves of the electromagnetic signals of the chemicals. His experiment showed that sounds emitted from each individual chemical are unique, that these sounds can be copied and repeated, and that their transmission effects a reaction in animal tissue similar to that of the chemicals themselves.[2]

Intention itself has been studied extensively. Helmut Schmidt developed the work of J. B. Rhine to show it is possible for a person to transmit information about card symbols to another person, or increase the odds of a certain number being rolled with a throw of the dice. While working for Boeing, Schmidt developed several machines designed to produce absolutely random outcomes. His goal was to see if a test subject's intention could produce a variation from the statistical average of fifty percent. His results showed that psychically talented individuals could reach a differential as high as fifty-four percent, a statistically significant result.[3]

At Princeton University, Robert Jahn teamed up with Brenda Dunne to determine whether we have the ability to change outcomes in our lives using our intent. With highly sophisticated machines designed to produce completely random results, these two scientists amassed substantial data over a period of twelve years. They found that nearly two-thirds of their subjects were successful overall in influencing the machines in the direction intended.[4] Their experiments showed the process to be universal and not limited to certain individuals or interactions. The "effect size" — a figure used by researchers to catalog the strength of the outcome of an experiment — of all these studies combined, is 0.2. This figure is larger than the effect size of many drugs deemed successful in medical trials.[5] Intention is often a more significant determinant of healing than treatment.

-§-
Each and every particle in this vast universe is intimately connected with—and influenced by—every other particle.
-§-

More startling concrete evidence of the ability of the human mind to effect changes in matter comes from the work by Dr. Masaru Emoto. Dr. Emoto, chief of the Hado Institute in Tokyo, has produced pictorial evidence of the ability of conscious intent to influence the physical properties of water crystallization. He took vials of water, then had people think and say specific thoughts directed toward the water vials. He then froze the water and photographed the water crystals. The samples of water with negative thoughts intended toward them showed fewer crystals, and malformed ugly crystals. The water samples with loving thoughts intended toward them developed a higher quantity of crystals, beautifully formed. He subsequently re-exposed negatively intended samples to people who intended positive thoughts to the water. Subsequent photographs showed that the water now revealed beautifully formed crystals.[6]

He also conducted an experiment in which large numbers of people gathered and spoke loving and healing words towards a polluted lake. The stagnant body of water was choked with weeds that produced noxious gases. The following summer, there was an almost complete absence of the weeds in the lake. There was also an increase of crystal formation in water samples photographed after the experiment was completed.

In her book, *The Field, The Quest for the Secret Force of the Universe,* Lynn McTaggart has beautifully summarized the studies conducted by Beneveniste, Popp and Schmidt, Jahn and Dunne, Targ and many more.[7] McTaggart's studies have led her to conclude that each and every particle in this vast universe is intimately connected with—and influenced by— every other particle. With this realization, we can conclude that all of our thoughts and actions do cause an effect—good or bad—on every person in this universe.

The bottom line of all these studies taken together points to the understanding that everything that exists in the universe is energy. In whatever form, internal or external to the body, energy is the only thing that exists. Every particle in the universe oscillates, quantifiably, with energy. We can now assert with confidence that every cell, molecule and atom is held together by energy. Physicists have found that the smallest particle they can isolate is further divisible. Literally, energy is all there is. Anything and every-thing we know to exist is, in essence, simple energy configured in a unique pattern. If all we are is energy, what is the best way to effect a change? With energy!

-§-

The new picture of our human future is...not full of drugs, surgeries and nursing homes.

-§-

The dawning discovery of the emerging paradigm of Energy Medicine is that energy from many, many sources can assist in our heal-ing process. By this I mean that energetic nudges that increase the ener-gy available for healing can be sourced both externally and internally. These energetic nudges can take many forms. Chinese medicine, for example, has a long and intricate history of treating illness manifestations with the strategic placement of delicate needles. The effectiveness of acupuncture is in no way diminished by the fact that its theoretical underpinnings lie in the energy realm.

The brains of meditators show measurable changes. Yogis are able to control bodily functions such as heart rate and blood pressure with inten-tion. But, what about the rest of us, who aren't trained in the skills required to shift energy in this way?

In normal folks, routine recurring bodily functions are controlled unconsciously by the quiet vigilance of the ANS, which is inaccessible to the conscious part of our mind. It has no power of speech. So how does it communicate with us?

It usually gets our attention in an indirect manner, through sensations or feelings. It produces a certain physical sensation that we know is hunger. We interpret other physical sensations as anger or sadness. Emotion and sensation are essentially the same.

NMT is a clear, concise methodology for establishing communication with the other-than-conscious side of ourselves. An energy transmission, in the form of a verbal script spoken by the practitioner, communicates information to the body on how to correct faults and, in turn, heal. These gentle energetic verbal nudges and intentions stimulate the body to acknowledge and correct faults, initiating the process of self-repair by drawing energy from many sources.

What this means for all of us in this world is that we can heal ourselves. We have the tools. We may need energetic nudges here and there, but the healing professions are discovering how to administer them. The new picture of our human future is all the brighter because of this, and it is not full of drugs, surgeries and nursing homes. The scientific world is showing us again what we always could do with our own minds and bodies but had forgotten. The exciting part of this is that our journey of discovery is just beginning.

-§-

Love, and the energy it brings, is the path to all healing.

-§-

We haven't yet begun to completely understand all the mechanisms of how the body heals and universe works, but we have a great start thanks to the hard work of scientists and doctors who are concretizing methods that mobilize our own healing capabilities.

The healing professions of the future will trend further and further away from current model of separateness of mind and body. There is an undeniable interconnectedness between the two and they are in turn connected to the entire universe. Increasingly, energy medicine is being used to take away the negative side effects of allopathic medicine. Eventually, healing will be entirely synchronistic with all functions of the body. There will be no need to fix the negative side effects of the cure.

All of our words, thoughts and actions affect each and every person, as well as the universe around us. We hurt each other with negative thoughts and heal each other with positive thoughts. Love, and the energy it brings, is the path to all healing.

PART FIVE

Ancient New
Approaches to Healing

BILL BENDA:

Unconditional Love of the People-Whisperers

A child with cerebral palsy struggles to take a step. An elderly man sits alone on a couch, staring blankly at a wall. Parents of an autistic child talk late into the night, fearful not only for the future of their child, but also for the entire family unit.

These stories, and hundreds of thousands like them, are repeated in countless incarnations in countless homes every day. It is not through lack of effort that those afflicted have not been cured. In fact, in most cases enormous energy and resources have been spent searching for solutions. Yet identifying the actual source of health and healing has always proven elusive to even the most dedicated researchers in the field of medical science.

Despite the daunting challenges faced by those with cerebral palsy, with senility, with autism, and with numerous other physical, psychological and emotional conditions, there is hope, a kind of hope that does not come from the laboratory bench or any other human technological achievement. It is a therapeutic approach that has been employed for centuries, although generally ignored by both conventional and alternative medical practitioners today.

What is most amazing is that this therapy often works where other methods fail. It is non-invasive, devoid of adverse side effects, and extraordinarily cost-efficient. And yet, when we visit our doctor with our stories of physical and emotional duress, this simple healing protocol is never recommended as an option, most likely because the doctor never

Bill Benda, MD, spent 20 years in academic and clinical emergency medicine before entering the world of complementary and alternative therapies. He is an editor, contributor, and medical advisory board member for numerous conventional and alternative medicine journals, and lectures extensively on a variety of topics in the integrative arena. As a research scientist at the University of Arizona, he is funded by the National Institutes of Health to investigate the effects of equine-assisted therapy in children with cerebral palsy, and is developing similar projects involving autistic children. Photos courtesy of Muscular Dystrophy Association.

heard of it either in medical school, residency, or in the countless journal articles that cross his or her desk each year.

The People-Whisperers

In the past decade we have been introduced to the concept of the "horse whisperer," a person who by training and intuition can communicate non-verbally with his or her equine counterpart, and thus experience inspiring and harmonious connection. What science has not yet grasped is that animals themselves are by nature "people-whisperers," and they have, whether innately or intentionally, the capacity both to restore and to sustain their human co-inhabitants of the planet.

The pleasure of emotional bonding with another species may at first appear self-evident to those who enjoy close association with their chosen pets. Over the past two decades, however, research studies have demonstrated that the benefits animals provide to *Homo sapiens* are far greater than simply pleasure or assistance with daily labor. As we will discuss in this chapter, animal companions and trained "animal therapists" provide outcomes that not only rival many modern medical advances, but also bestow help and comfort for chronic conditions that have yet to be satisfactorily addressed by our current technology-based paradigm.

-§-
What science has not yet grasped is that animals themselves are by nature "people whisperers," and they have the capacity both to restore and to sustain their human co-inhabitants of the planet.
-§-

One of the surprising facts about animal-assisted therapy is that certified centers and trained therapists have been providing such care for decades, functioning for the most part under the radar screen of our healthcare system. Institutions from schools to prisons to nursing homes have long employed dogs, rabbits, birds, and a variety of other species to help people of all ages and levels of disability. There are currently, for example, over 2,000 canine programs and over 650 equine therapy centers in the United States alone.

There are also countless four-legged therapists working incognito as everyday household pets. Indeed, between 1980 and 2001, the number of dogs and cats in the US grew from 98 million to 130 million, with no sign of slowing in sight. Without hesitation or complaint, Americans spend nearly three times as much money caring for their pets as the federal government spends on welfare. Sixty-three percent of pet owners say, "I love you" to their pets every day. Eighty-three percent refer to themselves as their pet's "mom" or "dad." Research shows that we use exactly the same facial expressions and vocal characteristics in speaking to a puppy as we do to a human infant. We agonize over naming our new pets, and hold birthday parties far more extravagant than we ever

would conceive for ourselves, never realizing that the addition and celebration of this particular family member is actually a major benefit to
our own health and well-being.

Health Benefits of Animal Companions

Cultural records throughout history, from the ancient Egyptians,
Greek and Romans on through educational offerings of the twentieth
century, describe animal-induced cures for physi-
cal and spiritual afflictions. In the past twenty
years, such anecdotal evidence has been examined
by the scientific methods of the twentieth century,
yielding significant findings. Although one can
attribute many of the physical benefits of protocols
like hippotherapy (physical therapy on horseback)
to sound physiological theory and reasoning,
improvements in emotional and psychosocial measurements have been more difficult to explain

-§-
Whether we are sick,
disabled, depressed,
cranky, grieving, or
afraid, our animal
companions accept
us just as we are, and
are usually delighted
to have unlimited
alone time with us.
-§-

objectively. If, however, we look beyond the rather rigid constraints of
the scientific method, we begin to intuitively understand a deeper
source of connection, and therefore healing, that can exist in relationship with members of another species.

Both the medical literature and our own experience reveal to us that
when we are sick, we often feel disconnected from even our closest friends
and find ourselves unable to function normally in everyday life. Long-
standing chronic illness or disability, with its social and cultural repercus-
sions, serves to intensify such perceptions of separation and isolation. Our
illness may also be reflected as concern, fear, and/or feelings of guilt in
our loved ones, resulting in a disruption of normal social behaviors that
can only add to overall stress levels.

By contrast, whether we are sick, disabled, depressed, cranky, grieving, or afraid, our animal companions accept us just as we are, and are
usually delighted to have unlimited alone time with us—thereby demonstrating we are still loved and needed by another. Although this concept
may appear to be simply a matter of temporal comfort during bouts of the
flu, those afflicted with disabilities that last months, years, or lifetimes
come to depend more and more upon the presence of such devotion and
companionship to sustain them both physically and emotionally.

The positive effects on human health from such relationships can be
and often are measured in scientific settings. Numerous research studies
have been quite definitive in demonstrating significant improvements in
physical and psychological well-being for a wide range of patients and illnesses. Economic indicators record less utilization of the healthcare sys-

tem by pet owners for minor or non-specific complaints. Physiologic measurements demonstrate that the presence of an animal companion results in lowering of blood pressure under stressful conditions, increased survival rates for patients after heart attacks, and improvements in strength, balance, mobility and language in children with disabilities such as cerebral palsy, spina bifida, traumatic brain injury, and muscular dystrophy. Psychiatric and psychosocial benefits include decreased anxiety and despair in psychiatric patients, increased socialization and decreased agitation in Alzheimer's patients, and increased verbalization and socialization as well as reduced aggressive behavior and self-mutilation in autistic children.

There are two demographics in our society, however, where a thorough review of the literature demonstrates the exceptional value of animal companions and animal-assisted therapy, and that is with children and the elderly. The aged in our society are at high risk for both physical and psychosocial illnesses, a growing dilemma given the graying of our baby boom generation. Having lost spouses to death, children to adulthood, and employment to retirement, the aging often lose interest in living, and Western culture does little to counteract this perspective. Here too, animals play a unique role, for luckily humans appear old, ugly, and sick only to themselves and other humans, and never to their animal companions.

-§-
Pets always have time for play, conversation, and acceptance, even when parents and siblings do not.
-§-

Despite the inevitable deprivations of aging, elders who are around animals or who have pets are less lonely, engage in increased physical activity and socialization, and sustain an overall higher quality of life. Geriatric studies have consistently documented improvements in mental outlook, socialization, and physical health as the result of a relationship with an engaging being that manages to fill in for a system of human support. Most significant, up to three quarters of seniors living alone report that their pet is their only friend, leaving us to imagine the cost should such companionship be lost.

If we contemplate the future of our own particular species, however, it becomes apparent that the true benefit of animal companions lies in their effect on our progeny. It is an unfortunate fact that children today have increasing social and environmental stress in their daily lives, permanently imprinting experiences that will dictate all future relationships and transactions during adulthood.

Animals have always been, and will always be, a constant presence and a consistent influence in a child's life. It is said that children who throw stones at birds and children who feed birds are both responding to an inherent tendency to focus attention on living beings. Which choice they make is a learned behavior, and the animal itself can be the source of learning and therefore affect present and future choices.

Pets always have time for play, conversation, and acceptance, even when parents and siblings do not. Animals provide security, value, acceptance, recognition, and a sense of value, all necessary for healthy personality development in the child. Relationships with non-human companions foster nurturing behavior and humane attitudes, increased socialization and emotional stability, and reduced feelings of isolation in both children and adolescents. It is especially significant to note that the more dysfunctional the family or social environment, the more pronounced the beneficial effects of animal friends.

Animals as Mystics

Animals have held mythical status in many cultures, often associated with fertility, power, the cycle of life, and good fortune. Renowned Swiss psychiatrist Carl Jung is primarily recognized for his work in identifying the *collective unconscious,* a transpersonal realm outside of our egocentric perspective of reality where all humans share common archetypal images and patterns of behavior. Ascribing animals a significant place in the process of soul development, Jung maintained that they appear in our dreams as guides, leading us through the difficulties of life's journey. Jung believed such creatures, unlike their human counterparts, to be symbols of true devotion; able to serve through their essential capacity to be exactly what God intended them to be. He theorized that how we relate in the physical realm to such divine emissaries is directly reflective of how we relate to our higher Self, and how we relate to our Self is a measure of our wholeness and health.

-§-
Unconditional love does not exist within the past or future, but only in the present.
-§-

Why are animals thought to hold such therapeutic power? I've come to believe that the answer lies in the often described but rarely experienced force we call *unconditional love.* Esoteric connotations aside, let us examine this concept a bit more objectively.

Fundamentally, loving is surrender, a willingness to become one with another without the egocentric personal boundaries that result in distance and separation. Perhaps this act of surrender opens the door to the realm of Jung's collective unconscious. Perhaps in such a communal space we experience the full, free potency of our heart and soul, allowing physical, psychological, emotional, and spiritual healing to take place.

Unconditional love does not exist within the past or future, but only in the present. One must live in the moment for unconditional love to manifest. Unfortunately, we humans, with our driven lifestyles and

hyper-intellectuality, are rarely capable of experiencing, much less expressing, unconditional love. Animals, however, have the capacity to live fully in the moment, and unless exposed to environmental stress to the point of acquiring human-based neuroses, they can indeed live nowhere else. The demonstration of selfless devotion inspiring the surrender of ego-driven needs is most readily witnessed in the canine/human relationship. This is quite likely why dogs, above all species, are sought both as pets and as therapeutic companions.

But *why* does the presence of an unconditionally-loving, living-in-the-moment animal being, inspire its human counterpart to transform? It is often pointed out in the psychology literature that deep emotional healing occurs within the context of relationships rather than in isolation. Viewing ourselves and our life dramas through our eyes only leads to a distorted concept both of who we are and how we relate to the outside world. To come to awareness of the truth, we need an open-hearted witness who holds the capacity of living fully in the truth of the present moment when we cannot.

-§-

An exceptional therapist has the capacity to be present, remain objective and demonstrate total acceptance while simultaneously opening his or her heart in unconditional love to the client.

-§-

An exceptional therapist has the capacity to be present, remain objective and demonstrate total acceptance while simultaneously opening his or her heart in unconditional love to the client; unfortunately such human practitioners are few and far between. There are, however, thousands of competent four-legged therapists all around us, and their services are given freely and without any expectations, but for one. Animals are incapable of lying. Animals require truth.

No living creature will engage *fully* with its human companion unless that human can manage to enter the same domain, the realm of the collective unconscious where all are connected in the One. It is in this space of egoless presence that we can witness our true self reflected back to us. And once we are capable of seeing and accepting who we truly are, we have the choice of making a profound and lasting shift, which is a prerequisite for emotional healing to take place.

If openness to another creates the space for healing to occur, what then is the actual source of such healing? Does it reside within the being reflecting love back to us? Or is that being simply a conduit for the healing power of a greater Source? Either case would contradict the basic premise of all spiritual and religious philosophies, which teach that we humans are but an earthly representation of the Universal, and that true understanding, and therefore the source of true healing, resides within us and not through another. The implication here is that unconditionally loving and accepting ourselves is the source of deep healing, and it may well be that the act of experiencing another being in touch with its own sense of presence and love opens the door for us to see and acknowledge those same qualities within ourselves.

This concept has deep roots within the field of psychotherapy. Jung tells us that a man's love for a woman and a woman's love for a man originate as projections of his *anima* or her *animus* – his female power or her male power. The healthier this inner projection, the healthier the love relationship between the two. It is not the other, but the healthy projection of our own capacity to love upon the other, that truly defines the relationship. In the same way, it may well be that the qualities of love and presence we ascribe to a non-human companion are indeed reflections of our own similar qualities that remain for the most part hidden from our consciousness.

-§-

It is not the other, but the healthy projection of our own capacity to love upon the other, that truly defines the relationship.

-§-

Some of the best examples I have seen of the power of the human/animal relationship occur in the numerous special camps for disabled children across the country, and especially at Whispering Hope Ranch in Payson, Arizona. This magical place was created with a vision to provide a rustic, natural setting for special needs children and their families, providing respite from the stresses of daily life not only to the special needs child, but to parents and siblings as well.

Although many such camps provide interaction with animals as part of their overall experience, Whispering Hope specifically addresses the benefits of the human-animal bond in a unique way. There are over 100 animal residents on property, including bunnies, burros, bovines, cats, chickens, deer, dogs, ducks, emus, geese, goats, horses, llamas, mules, peacocks, pigs, roosters, sheep and turkeys. What is most amazing is that each of the animals is in fact disabled as well, either from physical injury at birth or due to mistreatment, or psychological trauma secondary to abandonment or loss of their caregiver.

These emissaries happily greet all who approach, no matter whether the child has a scarred face, deformed limbs, or severe emotional dysfunction. When the child recognizes that, despite obvious physical challenges, the animal is still able to readily express love and acceptance, an emotional connection and bonding seems to occur far more quickly and deeply than even with normal animals. It is as if the child and the animal immediately and intuitively understand the other and the other's issues.

Why Science Ignores this Gift

It seems rational to argue that, if animals are capable of reflecting back to us our deepest and often subconscious emotional states, they themselves must be capable of feeling and expressing emotions. Or are we simply engaging in anthropomorphism, the transference of human

characteristics onto another species? Traditional science tells us that the latter is indeed the case, but our everyday experience of our pets comes into direct conflict with such "scientific reasoning." As well it might, for in this particular case science may well have a moral dilemma blinding its objective eye.

If the scientific establishment were to confirm the existence of an emotional life in laboratory animals subjected to pain, suffering, and imprisonment in the name of research, if it were to acknowledge that each day humans are the source of unending terror, rage, and despair, the entire academic system would be faced with a very real ethical predicament. The possibility of emotions in animals is therefore swept under the methodological rug, and the concept of animals as healers via reciprocating emotional bonding with humans remains unexplored territory in the highest echelons of medical science.

-§-
If animals are capable of reflecting back to us our deepest and often subconscious emotional states, they themselves must be capable of feeling and expressing emotions.
-§-

And yet, stories told by countless individuals, across the centuries and around the world, negate such blind rejection of the transformative potential existing within human/animal relationships.

A Story of Blind Love

Here is the story of an immediate interspecies connection between two individuals who have much in common. Jonothan is a delightful boy with an endearing sense of humor and a remarkably resilient spirit. Whenever possible, he loves to visit Whispering Hope Ranch, and in particular, one ranch resident with whom he has forged a special bond — one that only those who share a common life challenge can truly understand.

Jonothan was diagnosed in 1992 with a rare form of muscular dystrophy, which developed into Kearns-Sayre Syndrome, a rare and progressive form of the disease. Primary symptoms are blindness, external paralysis of the eye muscles, heart blockage, and skeletal muscle weakness. Only one-third of children with the disease survive to adulthood.

In 1997 Jonothan's symptoms worsened and he began to lose his vision. He can now only make out vague shapes and colors, although he retains his quick wit and sense of humor. On one of his first visits to Whispering Hope Ranch, Jonothan met Lucky Lady, a beautiful gray mare who had lost her vision at age three, after she fell backwards while being trained, damaging the visual cortex in the posterior part of her brain. Lucky is quick to offer her soft muzzle to children who want to stroke her face, and is remarkably responsive to the special children like Jonothan who come to "see" her.

Jonothan has formed an unusually deep bond with Lucky Lady and he lights up whenever he talks about her. "She is blind like me," he says. "I look at her and she looks at me and we stare into each other's eyes for the longest time. We understand each other because we both know what it is like to be different. Whenever I go to Whispering Hope, I get to talk to her again. We love each other."

Jonothan's physical condition is progressively deteriorating, but his mind and soul flourish with Lucky Lady's help. This scenario is indeed witnessed every day in countless children at the hundreds of animal-assisted therapy centers across the country. It is now up to us who bear witness to bring word of this healing work to those who care for these children. For if, as it is written, the kingdom of Heaven is open to those who do God's work, is most unlikely that this kingdom is reserved for one species only.

Jonothan and Lucky Lady

JEANNE ACHTERBERG:
The Healing Web of
Human Relationships

Healing work is soul work in the most meaningful, deepest sense. Beyond even the mission and purpose of service for the sick and the needy, we are also serving ourselves. The bonds we form are holy. While all of life is spiritual pathway, if and when we engage in our relationships with others with awakened consciousness about our effect on one another, allowing, if necessary, even our separate selves to bond and shatter, we are engaging in an authentic spiritual practice. The path is already there, winding through the riverbeds of our lives. Bringing the path and our actions to consciousness, we shift our inner reality. This will in turn shift the quality of health practices.

Below is a meditation, a composition derived from many sources; from quantum physicists, from the mystical tradition of the Kabbalah, from the Upanishads, from the Sufis, from electromagnetic field research, and from artists, poets, and mystics from every tradition.

Imagine, if you can, a universe where we are connected by an ineffable, invisible matrix. This matrix is a trellis upon which humanity weaves itself into an immense and dynamic tapestry. Each life, each soul, the essence of each being, is a point of light in the cloth. A light will fade at times, glow brilliantly here and then, and move in concert with the brightening and dimming of each other light point in the cloth. Like the web of a tireless spider, the warps and woofs gracefully dance and shape and reshape into multidimensional space. The cloth shrinks and it expands. It is a moving quilt, always in process. It folds upon itself and opens like a night-blooming flower in the path of the full moon. It's a crystalline, shimmering fabric, woven of countless filaments.

Jeanne Achterberg, Ph.D., is a scientist who has received international recognition for her pioneering research in medicine and psychology. She is currently a professor of psychology at Saybrook Graduate School. She co-chaired the mind/body interventions panel for the Office of Alternative Medicine at NIH, and has authored over 100 papers and five books. *Imagery in Healing* (Shambhala, 2002) is a classic, and *Woman as Healer* (Shambhala, 1991) is a ground-breaking survey from prehistoric times on. She is past president of the Association of Transpersonal Psychology, and Senior Editor for *Alternative Therapies* journal. Photo by Athi Mara Magadi.

The fabric of humanity is like a living skin. It repairs itself, degenerates, regenerates, develops scars, thins and thickens, and grows much more interesting with age. Think of the cloth as the consciousness of humankind grafting itself upon the source of its own divine origin. Connecting the glowing particles is a fluid and resonant force some might call energy. The matrix upon which it forms feels like love. Now, imagine a chorus of many voices, of sounds unique and resonant, shifting in tone and timbre. They cry out with pain and love and humility and passion and awe. Like tuning forks, they resonate dissonantly at first. Then one finds a way to make union with a single other, and then another, and a new pattern, a synchrony, a song comes forth out of the cacophony. Harmony. Celestial sound. The sounds of humanity are an orchestra, each voice essential, each note having purpose. When two lights — or two sounds — bond, energy is released, great quantities of light and sound, and the nature of both is changed forever. We merge together and with the Source from which we came.

-§-
Healing work is soul work in the most meaningful, deepest sense.
-§-

When we profoundly connect with another human being, we may not only polish our own souls and theirs, we may even release light and energy, according to these inspired words from the sages.

What about people who are in health crises? Why might the connections, the relationships, the bonds, themselves be healing? How might spiritual practice be a path to wholeness? Let me use an unlikely example, drawn from the filmmaker's art, and not from science or religion: the breathtaking scenes from the movie "Titanic." If you have seen it you know that, only in the most secondary instance, is it a story about a big ship sinking. First and foremost, it is a story about human love, healing, and soul work. The film expresses the deep human longing to be fully, totally loved — loved more dearly than life itself.

The scene that is most haunting is at the end. Jack and Rose, the young lovers, are holding onto one another in the frigid sea. Dead bodies in life jackets are bobbing around them. The screams of the hundreds who are drowning fill the black night. Neither Jack nor Rose is likely to survive. Jack tells her that she must promise to live: to live to have babies, to live to become an old woman. Fiction or not, I was reminded how often I've heard people who are very ill, or even dying, say that all they need is someone to hold on to them, to remind them that they are worthy and worth being loved, to give them hope. Not more medicine. Not more advice. Just someone to hold onto them. And maybe that's all we do anyway. We hold on to one anther in the dark ocean of crisis. There are people drowning around us, but there are also people singing around us and making music. That's what life is about. James Baldwin, the poet, wrote:

The moment we cease to hold each other,
The moment we lose faith with one another,

The sea engulfs us

And the light goes out.

We can look to many levels of information, beyond art and story, to describe how profound relationships are healing. We can find both metaphysical and physical sources. That relationships are healing is no longer in question from a research perspective. A brief excursion into the world of science yields many examples.

Researcher E. W. Bovard suggests that relationships act as stress buffers, and are mediated through the amygdala, stimulating the release of HGH, and inhibiting the brain's posterior hypothalamic zone, thus decreasing release of the adrenocorticotropic hormones: cortisone, catecholamines, and associated sympathetic autonomic activity[1]. To say that our relationships serve as buffers against stress is probably correct, if only partially so. To the extent that they do, we might look to the excellent work of Ronald Glaser and Janet Kiecolt-Glaser and their colleagues, who have shown that stressful situations can alter genetic expression and damage the DNA repair mechanism so that the damaged cells may repair improperly, and herald the onset of many diseases, including autoimmune and immune diseases such as cancer.[2][3] These same investigators studied marital relationship and immune function in 473 women. They found that the stronger and more supportive their relationships were perceived by the women, the higher their immune cell activity.

-§-

Often I've heard people who are very ill, or even dying, say that all they need is someone to hold on to them, to remind them that they are worth being loved.

-§-

Another researcher, J. P. Henry, has identified specific biological changes identified with social processes that may speed or impede healing. One of these changes is that, as a person moves from elation or security to dejection, there is a rise in adrenal corticosteroids[4]. As one moves from being a social success to an outcast, there is a fall in the plasma levels of gonadotrophins, which regulate both parenting and reproductive behavior. There is also significant evidence suggesting the emotional states associated with human relationships can either accelerate or inhibit tissue repair. Blood supply to a wound, critical to the healing process, is affected by our social circumstances and our emotions. Feeling loved, relaxed and happy reduces vasoconstricting catecholamines, and hope reduces growth-inhibiting corticosteroids.[5]

The astonishing thing about this line of research is that there is so much of it. Some studies are over twenty-five years old. Such work has been published in mainstream medical journals such as *Science, Lancet,* the *American Journal of Medicine* and the *American Journal of Epidemiology,* to mention a few. Ordinarily, scientists would drop everything else in order to study and facilitate any medical breakthroughs that have proven this robust, this enduring, this ubiquitous. This is not about medical treatment, not about psychotherapy. It is rather, about the most basic, primal, exalted events in our lives — our relationships. Every study reinforces the same point: We humans affect one another in exhilarating and terrible ways. We are made well through the bonds we form with others. Relationships are the essence of the healing process, especially when health is considered in its fullest sense of Hale (or wholeness) of the mind, body, and spirit. Common bonds. Uncommonly appreciated.

The Five Bonds of Healing Relationships

There are, no doubt, hundreds or thousands of types of bonds that one might identify as part and parcel of the network of support in healing relationships. Many types overlap. Some are as useless to one individual as they are life-saving for another.

Unfortunately, I have found that no matter how much I love someone (or they me), it is not possible to provide all levels of healing relationship oneself. It takes a community effort, one which is sadly unavailable to most people in our (or any) modern culture. It has five components; here are the qualities of the most important medicine in the possession of humankind.

1. The Transpersonal. These are the invisible connections some call prayer, energy, or more scientifically, "distant intentionality."[6] The evidence is that we influence one another's psyche and physiology, but not always in ways that we can predict or understand. When we focus our attention, even at a distance, on others, we are mutually joined and the physiology of both parties is changed. Research shows, among other things, that our thoughts can influence another's brain rhythms, blood cells, gross motor activity, and respiration.[7] Studies of prayer, itself, show positive results in survival of leukemic children, fewer complications post-myocardial infarct, increased self-esteem, reduced depression and anxiety, and improved recovery following hernia surgery — among many other healing effects.[8] I'm told that over fifty serious prayer studies are now underway around the US.

-§-

The emotional states associated with human relationships can either accelerate or inhibit tissue repair.

-§-

2. The Power of Presence and Touch. People in crisis need to be touched. They ask to be touched — we need to feel a physical presence on that life raft! One woman said to me, "When you are very sick and very old like I am, people are afraid to touch you. But I am still a sensual being. I can still feel. I would like to make love again. Just because you're sick doesn't mean you're dead." The burgeoning literature on massage, healing and therapeutic touch is supportive of the special role touch can have in health care practices. In a remarkable series of studies of people in comas by James Lynch, when a compassionate nurse or doctor stopped at the bedside and spoke to the patient or touched the person with a comforting hand, their electrocardiograms showed a slower rate.[9]

3. A Connection of Soul to Soul. What I mean by this is a relationship that is meaningful, beyond the physical self, and connects us beyond the egoic level of, "I am doctor, you are patient," or even, "I am man and you are woman." Beyond pathology. Beyond psychology. These relationships are medicine. They are the most difficult to describe, there certainly no research studies that I know of that measure them, but these soul-to-soul connections are probably the most important bonds of all. It is through them that we connect most intimately with another's humanity. Christopher Reeve, who played Superman in movies, sets a standard for us all in terms of courage, hope and humanity. During an interview on 20/20 with Barbara Walters, he talked about a time—not long after the spinal cord injury that left him a quadriplegic—when he had not yet turned the corner to embrace life. This beautiful man forgot his essential nature. He saw nothing worthy about himself to which life could cling. Then one of his children walked into his room and reminded him, "You are still my Daddy."

> -§-
> Every study reinforces the same point: We humans affect one another in exhilarating and terrible ways. We are made well through the bonds we form with others.
> -§-

Many healing professionals, working in the most difficult circumstances, with badly broken people, know that this practice demands deep, soul-to-soul connections. I spent several years working at the Burn Unit at Parkland Hospital. Every now and again I would hear a "thunk" and see one of my students passed out cold on the floor—a reaction to the terrible injuries of some patient. The student and I might later speak of the need to see through to the essence of that patient, to honor and respect that soul, and to communicate with that essential presence. Otherwise, the state of the physical body would steal our attention like a robber in the night, and we might forget who we are and they are—really. Soul-to-soul communication: It's hard. But we can do the best we can.

4. The Healing Web of Community. The importance of community and social support (variously defined) is the one level of relationship bonds in healing that has received the most interest, and has the longest history of solid, prospective research.[10] In a famous study that followed the health of nearly 7,000 residents of Alameda County for 17 years, the quality and extent of the social network of participants (how many people they felt close to, or could ask for help from) had the highest correlation with health and longevity out of 11 variables studied. Those variables included health-compromising habits such as smoking and alcohol use. A deficient social network was associated with death from all diagnoses, including heart disease, cancer, suicide and accidental death.[11] A study in Tecumseh Michigan replicated these findings in 1982.[12]

The second major community study that demonstrates the health-giving power of human relationships is the astonishing epidemiological findings of the residents of Rosetto, Pennsylvania, a small Italian-American community. The residents had half the rate of death from heart attacks as the US as a whole, including the neighboring communities. As a group, they were sedentary, overweight, and smoked a lot. The researchers believed that their relatively good health came from mutual social support in a village where cultural ties were strong, there was mutual support in crisis, and people felt a profound sense of belonging. Over the years, as the community lost its cultural identification and became more mobile and materialistic, whatever edge they had on healthy hearts was lost.[13]

The accumulation of empirical evidence shows that social relationships are a consequential predictor of mortality in human and even in animals, according to a review of over sixty studies published by James House and his colleagues in the prestigious journal *Science*, in 1988.[14] People who feel included in this "web of lights," as I call it, are at less risk for tuberculosis, accidents, psychiatric disorders, babies with low birth weight, complications from pregnancy, high blood pressure, cholesterol, arthritis, and death from many conditions including cardiovascular disease.[15] Higher levels of social support have also been associated with longer survival in acute leukemia, localized or regional breast cancer, mixed cancer disease sites, recovery from surgery, a reduced need for steroid therapy in asthmatics, reduced physiological symptomatology in those working in highly stressful environments, and on and on.[16] Social relationships—or the lack thereof—constitute a major risk factor for health, rivaling the effects of cigarette smoking on a variety of health conditions.[17] The relationship holds even after adjustment for biomedical risk factors. The relationship, even in controlled, prospective studies, appears to be robust and causal.

-§-
Our thoughts can influence another's brain rhythms, blood cells, gross motor activity, and respiration.
-§-

Support groups have been associated with classic findings in controlled studies of cancer and heart patients:

- The reduction of psychological distress, increased NK cell activity, increased NK cell phenotypes, and significantly increased life expectancy in melanoma patients.[18]

- Significantly increased life expectancy in women with metastatic breast cancer.[19]

- Decrease in number of recurrent myocardial infarcts.[20]

- Reversing the effects of heart disease.[21]

However, a sobering note was provided during the Society of Behavioral Medicine Meetings in New Orleans in 1997 when Vicki Hodgeson presented her study showing that cancer support groups may harm some women who claim their relationships suffered and they were more nervous as a result of the groups. Support groups aren't for everyone and adequate leadership is critical.

5. The Healing Force of Love. What's love got to do with it? One of the most astonishing results came from an Israeli study of 10,000 married men who participated in a five-year prospective study.[22] Many factors were measured, including medical and psychosocial factors. The best predictor of whether the men would develop angina pectoris was the question, "Does your wife show you her love?" The felt love of a wife apparently balanced out the risk, even in the presence of high risk factors.

The results of a remarkable natural experiment in post World War II in Germany was carried out by a British Nutritionist, Elsie Widdowson, and published in the *Lancet* in 1951.[23] She observed that children in two orphanages had very different growth rates, even though they received the same rations. At one, named Vogelnest, where children's growth was accelerated, the matron was kindly and beloved by the children. At the other, Bienenhaus, where the children did poorly, the matron, Fraulein Schwarz, was a strict disciplinarian. There was a small group who were Fraulein Schwarz's favorites and they were growing somewhat better. The kindly matron at Vogelnest left, and Fraulein Schwarz was sent there. At that time rations were increased in both places. But the Vogelnest children began to fall behind their Bienenhaus contemporaries in spite of better food, while the Bienenhaus children began to grow. This is one of many studies showing that children who are warmly cared for simply grow better.

-§-

They are the most difficult to describe, there certainly no research studies that I know of that measure them, but these soul-to-soul connections are probably the most important bonds of all.

-§-

What do people expect from their health care professionals? Above all they want compassion, sympathy and understanding. They also want information and to feel better. But they want information and better feeling delivered with compassion, sympathy and understanding. And when this happens, studies show a consistently beneficial effect—speed of recovery, less pain medication, and fewer postoperative complications.[24]

Many people, in the most dire of circumstances, keep themselves alive with love the memories of love. Viktor Frankl, the great German psychiatrist, was kept alive in the hideous and brutal conditions of a concentration camp by a vision of his wife. He writes, "Occasionally, I looked at the sky, where the stars were fading and the pink light of the morning was beginning to spread behind a dark bank of clouds. But my mind clung to my wife's image, imagining it with an uncanny acuteness. I heard her answering me, saw her smile, her frank and encouraging look. Real or not, her look was then more luminous than the sun which was beginning to rise… Had I known then that my wife was dead, I think that I would still have given myself, undisturbed by the knowledge, to my contemplation of her image, and that my mental conversation with her would have been just as vivid and just as satisfying. Set like a seal upon the heart, love is as strong as death."[25]

-§-
Many healing professionals, working in the most difficult circumstances, with badly broken people, know that this practice demands deep, soul-to-soul connections.
-§-

Spirituality is already embedded in the practice of healthcare. The essence of our spiritual work and the healing process is the bond we share in relationship with one another. The research is overwhelming: human bonds are medicine. Imagine the rise in the stock prices of any pharmaceutical company that could mimic even a modicum of the success rate of love and prayer and touch and community. And then imagine how medicine, any medicine, might be practiced if the bonds were common, commonly acknowledged, and commonly respected. Teilhard de Chardin, the great mystic, scientist, and Jesuit priest, tied these ideas together in some magnificent words: "Love is the free and imaginative outpouring of the spirit over all unexplored paths. It links those who love in bonds that unite but do not confound, causing them to discover in their mutual contact an exaltation capable, incomparably more than any arrogance of solitude, of arousing in the heart of their being all that they possess of uniqueness and creative power."

Teilhard also said, "Someday, after we have mastered the winds, the waves, the tides and gravity, we shall harness for God the energies of love. Then for the second time in the history of the world, we will have discovered fire."

JAMES DILLARD:

Pain as Our Greatest Teacher

Irv was just fifty-four years old. He had been a cop, and then had worked as a private investigator for about twenty-five years. He liked to go sailing in Sheepshead Bay, and did woodworking in his garage. When the heart attack hit, it felt like someone had slugged him in the chest with a 4x4 beam. He says he remembers just dropping like a leaf in the wind.

His wife and son held his hand at the bedside. The Columbia Presbyterian heart surgeon pursed his lips and looked down. "He's been in a coma for five days in spite of everything we've done. He's on the transplant list, but I don't think he'll make it long enough for us to find him a new heart." They cried and kissed him, and said goodbye.

It was five months later when Irv walked into my office. He was still a bit shaky, way overweight, and he looked pale. But he sat down, smiled, and said, "I shouldn't be here, Doc."

"How come?" I asked. He looked down at his hands. "Well, because I died five months ago..."

Or so it seemed to him. A heroic last-option quadruple bypass surgery saved his life—but just barely.

Irv had pretty bad diabetes for about fifteen years. That set him up for his severe heart attack, and a lot of other problems. It also left him with numb and painfully burning feet and hands. I couldn't do much about his diabetes; that was a job for another doctor, but as a pain doc I sure could help him with the burning damage to his nerves.

James Dillard, MD, has seen health care from many sides. Formally trained in three health professions—acupuncture, chiropractic and medicine—Dr. Dillard is an Assistant Clinical Professor at Columbia University College of Physicians and Surgeons. Dr. Dillard is the author of *Alternative Medicine for Dummies,* (IDG Books, 1998), and has written columns for the number one health website, OnHealth.com. In *The Chronic Pain Solution* (Bantam, 2003) he integrates the best of conventional and alternative medicine. He has been featured in *Newsweek* and *People,* and appeared on Oprah, NPR and The Today Show. Photo by Nancy Rica Schiff.

I adjusted his nerve medications, put him on a couple of new things, a couple of supplements, and then we just sat and talked for about 20 minutes. This was a man who had gone through a huge life crisis, and was actually still in crisis, still very wobbly. His struggle was something palpable in the room, like the shadow of death, still there. He talked about his family, his job, what had been important to him, his past sense of meaning and religious practice, and the future. Then he started to cry.

We talked for a while, then I looked down at my prescription pad and I began to write. As a Scottish Episcopalian who was not particularly religious, I had never written such a thing before in my career. I handed it to him and he looked down at the script. The prescription read, "Long conversations with your Rabbi, twice a week." He left the office with an odd smile on his face.

Over the subsequent six months, Irv got more involved with his synagogue. He took the opportunity to allow his terrifying brush with death to work a deep magic on his sense of himself and his day-to-day life. He finally found himself much less concerned with the small things. He still had significant symptoms, but the residual burning in his feet and hands did not bother him as much. He spent more time with his son. He complained much less and got out of the house much more.

He came back to me and told me he had started a program, through his temple, to provide services for older people in the community. His years as a private investigator had given him the ability to find many resources for his clients, and to protect them from fraud. He said that this was what he was meant to do, and that he could not have found it without going through his illness. He allowed the pain and suffering to become his greatest teacher. As he talked to me about his new calling, his face was bright and his hands were steady. The shadow of death was gone from the room.

Chronic pain is the third-largest health problem in the US. It disables more people than cancer and heart disease put together. One in four American families is affected by chronic pain. This tremendous public health problem has been largely ignored or poorly treated by academic and organized medicine, until recently. Now the Joint Commission for Accreditation of Hospitals Organization (JCAHO) has mandated the appropriate assessment and treatment of pain in all 14,000 American hospitals.

-§-

The prescription read, "Long conversations with your Rabbi, twice a week."

-§-

Pain must now be assessed as the fifth "vital sign" — along with temperature, heart rate, blood pressure and respiratory rate. This is a tremendous paradigm shift and advancement in how we treat (or have failed to treat) pain.

Pain is also the dominant reason why people use complementary and alternative medicine. Multiple surveys have shown that pain is the primary reason why people go to chiropractors, massage therapists, acupuncturists, Reiki practitioners, and Qi Gong masters, and is a major reason for taking supplements herbs and vitamins. In addition, there is an intense love-hate relationship that exists in our culture with pain medicines, from Advil to Oxycontin. Many of us love taking pills as a universal panacea for all that afflicts us, and others of us see these medicines as the work of the devil. The truth is undoubtedly neither of these polar opposites.

Most Americans see pain as something to be fought against and conquered, hence book titles like The *War on Pain* and *Fighting the Battle of Pain.* This is a typically Western aggressive approach. In fighting this war, one may suppress the foe—yet lose one's self in the process. One may miss the opportunity to learn something that could change one's life for the better, for things that are difficult can sometimes teach us so much.

Every day in my practice I am given the great opportunity—the difficult gift—of seeing people either accepting or rejecting this teacher. The Buddhists tell us that pain is the greatest teacher of all, because it does not kill us, yet it does not release us from a finite struggle with the fabric of the world. For every pain patient I see, for every last one, I know that pain holds a lesson for them, if they will only look for it and accept it.

Sometimes the lessons of pain are blatant and obvious: "I really do have to change my diet and lose the weight so my knees can stop hurting all the time," or, "I've got to get off of all this caffeine once and for all so I can get rid of this stupid crushing daily headache," or, "If I don't get a different job this jaw tension and resulting pain will never go away." Sometimes we face a very hard lesson about releasing ourselves from the fallacy that we control events. Sometimes the lesson is that we must find the strength to take control, where the opportunity for control clearly exists. For each pain patient the lesson is unique.

-§-
For every pain patient I see, for every last one, I know that pain holds a lesson for them, if they will only look for it and accept it.
-§-

Daniel had thrown his back out on the job. He and a co-worker had tried to move a heavy table just before a presentation for a new client. They had been able to move it, but by the time the presentation was over Daniel could hardly move. His boss let him hobble down to the local emergency room, where they x-rayed his back, and finally sent him home on Motrin, muscle relaxers, and painkillers. I saw him the following week and he hadn't improved much. Over the next eight weeks he had to skip work and do intensive physical rehabilitation. By the time he finally could work again, he had missed an opportunity to make a promotion that he had been counting on achieving that year. I clearly remember talking to him the following spring.

"I can't tell you what a blessing it was, doc." He said to me, with a big smile on his face. "What you mean, Daniel?" I queried, confused. "Well, you see, my daughter has just turned four. Those two months that I spent mostly at home, well, I got to know her, doc. It's like, we got to be friends for the first time. It's really changed my life. I sort of think that the pain came to teach me that there was something else so much more important than that promotion, so much more important. I'll still get the promotion, I think. But maybe I might never have gotten to know my daughter." For Daniel, his pain was a deep personal lesson that could not have been learned another way.

We doctors also have lessons to learn. As health care practitioners, sometimes we get into a rut. Sometimes we fall too much in love with what we think we know. Sometimes we fall too much in love with our own tools, and with the image of who and what we think we are as healers. The surgeon loves his own image with a scalpel, the acupuncturist with his needles, the Reiki master with his symbols, the herbalist with his formulas.

All too often we need to release our own ego from what we think we know and stand humbly before powers and curiosities that we may never understand. Sometimes we must allow people to choose ways of being with which we disagree. This is also a role of the healer. We have to encourage people to take care of themselves as much as they can, but we also have to let go, and let them make their own decisions, even if those decisions seem wrong to us.

A couple of years ago I was asked by an internist to see a patient of his who had just been admitted to the hospital. She was sixty-six years old, and was in the hospital because doctors thought she might have had a stroke. I had three other consultations to do that evening, so rather than sitting down to carefully read her chart first, I bundled it under my arm and went to her room.

I was totally unprepared for what I found. Lying on the bed was a 500 lb. woman. She was alert, talkative and pleasant, but she was too weak to lift her legs off the bed. She could only hold her arms up for just a moment. I sat with her for almost an hour to understand her story and then examined her. It is an hour that I will never forget.

Eight years before, she was a bit overweight, but she was holding down a job and getting around just fine. Then she broke her left ankle. It required surgery and pins in the bone to make it stable. She had tried physical therapy after the surgery, but she said it was just too painful. After a couple of months of hobbling around, she decided to put herself to bed. She had been there ever since. Her devoted but perhaps misguided husband had put plastic sheets on the bed and placed a small refrigerator on a stand right next to it, so she could eat whenever she wanted. She had paper towels and a lined waste can next to the bed. He would wash her when he got home at night, and change her sheets and clothes. It was remarkable that she was still alive. She had not left that bed for eight years.

I asked her what she did all day. She said she watched TV, mostly the home shopping channel. Sometimes she would buy something, but not too often. I asked her if she was happy. She said she was OK. I asked her, "If it were possible, would you like to walk again?" She said, "Not really." I asked her if she felt sad or depressed about life and she said, "Not really." I asked her if there was anything that I could do for her. She said, "Please help get me home."

I went out and put a detailed note in the chart. With her weight, weakness and atrophied joints, there was little choice but to send her home to the life she was used to. It turned out that she had indeed suffered a "mini stroke," so she probably would succumb to cerebral vascular disease (a big stroke) in a few years. It had taken eight paramedics to extract her from her house, and it would probably take eight to put her back into it. There was little else to be done.

Many people in the hospital were jumping up and down wanting to rescue this lady from herself. The surgeons wanted to cut open her joints to restore their range of motion. The cardiologist wanted to get her heart pumping faster. The neurologist wanted to get her brain firing better. The physical therapists wanted to get her into the rehab unit and do five hours of therapy on her every day. It would not have worked.

She wanted to go home, watch the home shopping network, and have her husband take care of her. Who were we to tell her that she was wrong? God? Did we get elected to that office? And if this had been a different sort of institution, she might have had people agitating for Pilates, acupuncture, yoga and spinal manipulation.

Practitioners often need to get past their own big egos, and let patients make informed decisions for themselves. We must not fall too much in love with what we think we know, and we must not fall in love with our tools. It's not about our tools; it's about you, the patient. And sometimes the other guy's tools are better for a particular patient than mine.

I wouldn't encourage you to go the way of my large patient. There were many other options for her earlier, but not by the time I saw her. Life is motion, and motion is life, but she chose the path of immobility. It was her choice to make.

Generally, we heal better when our bodies are in motion (except for bad sprains and fractures, of course). Our bodies evolved successfully over millennia of running, jumping and climbing. Each of us needs this motion to live. Without it, we get heavy, weak, depressed and ineffective in our lives. So don't settle for reasons to back off from your activities, to back off from your life. I know it's not easy, but it can make all the difference for the long run.

Our current culture is overrun with narcissism. We're preoccupied with presentation. This shows up as spin, as a focus on pre-adolescent beauty, in the sexualization of children, and in the triumph of style over substance. Critics don't even seem to be commenting or concerned about this trend anymore. Health practices have been deeply affected by this ubiquitous tendency. As health care practitioners, we can get caught up in it as well. I have seen large parts of what used to be called yoga go this way. It's a sad thing to watch.

If we are lucky, we all get the opportunity to get older and frailer. That thought and awareness can sharpen our values and our appreciation of each day, no matter what our age may be. I have patients who are facing terminal illness in their twenties. Their lives are not about presentation and posing.

Most people don't want to think about the potential for getting older and more frail, but there are critical decisions that we all must face as the years go by. We may be moving along through our normal, everyday lives, and then something goes wrong that leaves us just a little worse off than we were. Sometimes it's a subtle change that we don't see creeping up on us, and sometimes it's a specific condition or injury that sets us back.

-§-
Our current culture is overrun with narcissism. We're preoccupied with presentation. Health practices have been deeply affected by this ubiquitous tendency.
-§-

All of us go through this change sooner or later. Don't start getting depressed about it, because we've all known about its inevitability from the time we were very small children—it's not a secret. We need to talk about how to approach these physical setbacks, both as potential patients and as health care professionals. The roles are different, but our egos can get in the way in either situation. Here, too, is a great gift, full of potential lessons about humility and compassion, if we can only look for them.

The tremendous problem of pain in our culture, and the great interest in alternative medicine, creates an opportunity to use the many effective complementary therapies that are available mixed in judiciously with appropriate conventional pain medicine. Often I need to give patients strong combinations of conventional pain medicines and injection techniques just to control their pain well enough to get them into physical rehabilitation programs, to get them strengthened up and stretched out, and to get them a bit of hope that they can have their pain controlled and that they can get better.

Gradually I can teach them meditation techniques, breathing, visualization, and start them on acupuncture and massage therapy, manual therapies, self-care techniques and Reiki. I can get their diet cleaned up and start them on a few supplements that can quiet their inflammation and their jangled nervous systems. As they improve, the medication dosages come down. I've seen this progression happen hundreds of times. Of course, there are plenty of failures as well, and that's why I'm glad that there are other great practitioners out there. We all treat each other's failures, and that's OK too.

Every patient is an opportunity and somewhat of a curse. He or she is a difficult opportunity to find ways out of a unique tangle — anatomically, neurologically, medically, emotionally, spiritually, functionally — and to find sacred blessings and lessons. And each patient is a painful reminder of our limitations, both together and individually. The art of health care is painful; that emotional pain is something from which the healer cannot and should not entirely protect themselves, something to which they should not become inured. If it were not hard and painful, if it were all just fun and games, we would not need to be paid for our work.

-§-
The art of health care is painful; that emotional pain is something from which the healer cannot and should not entirely protect themselves.
-§-

For me, the heart of a healer is very humble and curious. For me, the heart of a healer looks always for the lessons — for my patients and also for myself. If I close myself to my own learning, if I think I know everything I need to know, and that I have everything required to teach others, it is then that I am lost.

DEAN ORNISH:
Love As Healer

Love and intimacy are at a root of what makes us sick and what makes us well, what causes sadness and what brings happiness, what makes us suffer and what leads to healing. If a new drug had the same impact, virtually every doctor in the country would be recommending it for their patients. It would be malpractice not to prescribe it — yet, with few exceptions, we doctors do not learn much about the healing power of love, intimacy, and transformation in our medical training. Rather, these ideas are often ignored or even denigrated.

It has become increasingly clear to even the most skeptical physicians why diet is important. Why exercise is important. Why stopping smoking is important. But love and intimacy? Opening your heart? And what is emotional and spiritual transformation?

I am a scientist. I believe in the value of science as a powerful means of gaining greater understanding of the world we live in. Science can help us sort out truth from fiction, hype from reality, what works from what doesn't work, for whom, and under what circumstances. Although I respect the ways and power of science, I also understand its limitations as well. What is most meaningful often cannot be measured. What is verifiable may not necessarily be what is most important. As the British scientist Denis Burkitt once wrote, "Not everything that counts can be counted."

We may not yet have the tools to measure what is most meaningful to people, but the value of those experiences is not diminished by our inabil-

Dean Ornish, MD, is one of America's best-known medical authorities. His ground-breaking experiments led to the development of diet- and exercise-based therapies for cardiac patients, and earned him international renown. He is the author of *Eat More, Weigh Less* (Harper, 1997), and several other books. He is the founder and president of the Preventive Medicine Research Institute in Sausalito, California. The material in this chapter is based on an interview in the *American Journal of Cardiology* (August 1st, 2002 issue) and in his best-seller *Love and Survival,* reprinted by permission of HarperCollins Publishers, ©1998 Dean Ornish.

ity to quantify them. We can listen, we can learn, and we can benefit greatly from those who have had these experiences. When we gather together to tell and listen to each other's stories, the sense of community and the recognition of shared experiences can be profoundly healing.

As recently as May 1997, an article in the *Journal of the American Medical Association* reviewed all of the known risk factors for coronary heart disease. While listing esoteric factors such as apolipoprotein E isoforms, cholesteryl ester transfer protein, and lecithin-cholesterol acyl transferase, it did not even mention emotional stress or other psychosocial factors, much less spiritual ones.[1]

How did we get to a point in medicine where interventions such as radioactive stents, coronary angioplasty, and bypass surgery are considered conventional, whereas eating vegetables, walking, meditating, and participating in support groups are considered radical?

I'm not against the use of statins, stents, bypass surgery, or anything that works in the short run as a way of temporizing, but we also have to deal with the underlying issues involved in being human. Doctors are missing the opportunity to be of greater service to people, and being reduced to technicians. Because of this, many patients are voting with their feet, and going to alternative practioners.

-§-
More money is spent out of pocket by patients today for alternative interventions than for conventional ones—even though there is little science to prove their efficacy—because alternative practitioners often fulfill patients' basic human needs.
-§-

Why? Because whatever the alternative modality—massage, acupuncture, chiropractic, therapeutic touch—what they all have in common is that they touch people. Practitioners spend time with their patients, and listen to them. Practitioners talk about these issues as part of their overall approach.

There is a fundamental basic human need for a sense of love, connection, community, and intimacy, and this is so often unfulfilled in a typical doctor-patient interaction. More money is spent out of pocket by patients today for alternative interventions than for conventional ones—even though there is little science to prove their efficacy—because alternative practitioners often fulfill patients' basic human needs. If conventional doctors don't address those needs, the medical profession is in danger because our patients are going to find alternative practitioners who do.

Healing and curing are not the same. Curing is when the physical disease gets measurably better. Healing is a process of becoming whole. Even the words "heal" and "whole" and "holy" come from the same root. Returning healing to medicine is like returning justice to law.

In my work with people who have heart disease, both healing and curing often occur. When the emotional heart and the spiritual heart begin to open, the physical heart often follows. But healing may occur even when curing is not possible. We can move closer to wholeness even when the physical illness does not improve.

The heart is a pump that needs to be addressed on a physical level, but our hearts are more than just pumps. A true physician is more than just a plumber, technician, or mechanic. We also have an emotional heart, a psychological heart, and a spiritual heart.

Our language reflects that understanding. We yearn for our sweethearts, not our sweetpumps. Poets and musicians and artists and writers and mystics throughout the ages have described those who have an open heart or a closed heart; a warm heart or a cold heart; a compassionate heart or an uncaring heart. Love heals. These are metaphors, a reflection of our deeper wisdom, not just figures of speech.

When I lecture at scientific meetings, hospitals, or medical schools, I always start by providing the scientific data as a way of establishing credibility. I show objective evidence from our randomized controlled trials that the progression of heart disease often can be reversed by changing lifestyle. Then I talk about what most interests me: the emotional, psychosocial, and spiritual dimensions of "opening your heart."

In the process of healing, you reach a place of wholeness and deep inner peace from which you can deal with illness with much less fear and suffering and much greater clarity and compassion. While curing is wonderful when it occurs, healing is often the most meaningful because it takes you to a place of greater freedom from suffering. When healing occurs, people often become more peaceful, centered, happy, and joyful.

That which seems the most "soft" approach to wellness—love, intimacy, and meaning—is, in reality, the most powerful. This part of my work is the least well understood and yet perhaps the most important. There is a deep spiritual hunger in our culture. There has been a radical shift in our society in the past fifty years, and we are only now beginning to appreciate the deep spiritual hunger that has emerged.

The real epidemic in our culture is not only physical heart disease, but also what I call emotional and spiritual heart disease—that is, the profound feelings of loneliness, isolation, alienation, and depression that are so prevalent in our culture with the breakdown of the social structures that used to provide us with a sense of connection and community. It is, to me, a root of the illness, cynicism, and violence in our society.

The healing power of love and relationships has been documented in an increasing number of well-designed scientific studies involving hundreds of thousands of people throughout the world. When you feel loved, nurtured, cared for, supported, and intimate, you are much more likely to be happier and healthier. You have a much lower risk of getting sick and, if you do, a much greater chance of surviving.

During the past twenty years of conducting research, I have become increasingly aware of the importance of love and intimacy and knew there were many studies documenting their power. Not until I systematically reviewed the scientific literature for this book did I realize just how extensive and rich is this field of study.

Studies Show: Intimacy Promotes Wellbeing

While some studies measure the number or structure of social relationships, I believe that it is your perception of the quality of those relationships—how you feel about them—that is most important.[2] As two distinguished researchers wrote recently, "Social support reflects loving and caring relationships in people's lives.... Simple ratings of feeling loved may be as effective, if not more effective, in assessing social support than more comprehensive instruments that quantify network size, structure, and function."[3]

At Yale, for example, scientists studied 119 men and 40 women who were undergoing coronary angiography, an X-ray movie that shows the degree of blockages in coronary arteries. Those who felt the most loved and supported had substantially less blockage in the arteries of their hearts.[4] The researchers found that feelings of being loved and emotionally supported were more important predictors of the severity of coronary artery blockages than was the number of relationships a person had. Equally important, this effect was independent of diet, smoking, exercise, cholesterol, family history (genetics), and other standard risk factors.

A study of 131 women in Sweden also found that the availability of deep emotional relationships was associated with less coronary artery blockage as measured by computer-analyzed coronary angiography. As in the Yale study, this finding remained true even when controlling for age, hypertension, smoking, diabetes, cholesterol, educational level, menopausal status, and other factors that might have influenced the extent of disease.[5]

Similarly, researchers from Case Western Reserve University in Cleveland studied almost ten thousand married men with no prior history of angina (chest pain). Men who had high levels of risk factors such as elevated cholesterol, high blood pressure, age, diabetes, and electrocardiogram abnormalities were over twenty times more likely to develop new angina during the next five years.

However, those who answered, "yes" to the simple question, "Does your wife show you her love?" had significantly less angina even when they had high levels of these risk factors. Men who had these risk factors but did not have a wife who showed her love had substantially increased angina—almost twice as much. The greater the cholesterol and blood pressure and the greater the anxiety and stress, the more important was the love of the spouse in buffering against these harmful effects.

As the researchers wrote, "The wife's love and support is an important balancing factor which apparently reduces the risk of angina pectoris even in the presence of high risk factors."[6] The researchers also found that those men who also had anxiety and family problems, especially conflicts with their wives and children, had even more chest pain.

In a related study, these researchers studied almost 8,500 men with no history or symptoms of duodenal ulcer. These men were given questionnaires before they developed ulcers, so their responses were not influenced by knowing they had this disease.

Over the next five years, 254 of these men developed ulcers. Those who had reported a low level of perceived love and support from their wives when they entered the study had over twice as many ulcers as the other men. Those men who answered, "My wife does not love me" had almost three times as many ulcers as those who said their wives showed their love and support. This factor was more strongly associated with ulcers than smoking, age, blood pressure, job stress, or other factors. Men who also had anxiety and family problems had more ulcers.[7]

> -§-
> It may be hard to believe that something as simple as talking with friends, feeling close to your parents, sharing feelings openly, or making yourself vulnerable to others can make such a powerful difference.
> -§-

When I reviewed the scientific literature, I was amazed to find what a powerful difference love and relationships make on the incidence of disease and premature death from virtually all causes. It may be hard to believe that something as simple as talking with friends, feeling close to your parents, sharing feelings openly, or making yourself vulnerable to others in order to enhance intimacy can make such a powerful difference in your health and well-being, but study after study indicates that they often do. It's easy to make fun of these ideas—talking about your feelings in a group, opening your heart to others, practicing yoga, meditation, or prayer to rediscover inner sources of peace, joy, and well-being—but look at what a powerful difference they can make in our survival!

In the Tecumseh Community Health Study, almost three thousand men and women were studied for nine to twelve years. After adjustments for age and a variety of risk factors for mortality, men reporting higher levels of social relationships and activities were significantly less likely to die during the follow-up period. Relationships included the number of friends, how close they felt to their relatives, group activities, and so on.

When these social relationships were broken or decreased, disease rates increased two to three times as much during the succeeding ten-to-twelve-year period, including heart disease, strokes, cancer, arthritis, and lung diseases.[8]

Thomas Oxman and his colleagues at the University of Texas Medical School examined the relationship of social support and religion to mortality in men and women six months after undergoing elective open-heart surgery (coronary bypass surgery, aortic valve replacement, or both). They asked two questions:

• Do you participate regularly in organized social groups (clubs, church, synagogue, civic activities, and so on)?

• Do you draw strength and comfort from your religious or spiritual faith (whatever religion or spiritual faith that might be)?

They found that those who lacked regular participation in organized social groups had a fourfold increased risk of dying six months after surgery, even after controlling for medical factors that might have influenced survival (such as severity of heart disease, age, previous cardiac surgery, and so on). Also, they found that those who did not draw strength and comfort from their religion were three times more likely to die six months after surgery.[9]

These results indicated that lack of group participation and absence of strength and comfort from religion had independent and additive effects. Those who neither had regular group participation nor drew strength and comfort from their religion were more than seven times more likely to die six months after surgery. Seven times! Even though I am unaware of any factor in medicine that causes a sevenfold difference in mortality only six months after open-heart surgery, how many surgeons even ask their patients these two questions in assessing the risk of cardiac surgery?

Love promotes survival. Both nurturing and being nurtured are life-affirming. Anything that takes you outside of yourself promotes healing—in profound ways that can be measured—independent of other known factors such as diet and exercise. There is a strong scientific basis documenting that these ideas matter—across all ages from infants to the most elderly, in all parts of the world, in all strata of life.

Creating Intimacy

Sharing feelings rather than attacking or criticizing makes it easier for others to listen; listening leads to empathy; empathy leads to compassion; compassion increases intimacy; intimacy is healing.

We ask everyone to resist the natural inclination to give advice on how to solve the problem (unless someone specifically asks for it) and, instead, to focus on feeling and expressing his or her own emotions and experiences. Remember: The problem we are trying to solve is a lack of intimacy, not the kid on drugs or the boss at work. The lack of intimacy can be solved even when the other problems cannot.

This process takes courage and practice. It is unfamiliar to many people precisely because the experience of intimacy is so rare and precious in our culture. Although many of our research participants were initially skeptical—and sometimes even hostile—to the group support process, most later said that they found the group support to be the most meaningful, helpful, and powerful part of their experience.

As we have seen, increasing scientific evidence documents the healing benefits of opening your heart. Many studies have shown that self-disclosure—that is, talking or even writing about your feelings to others—improves physical health, enhances immune function, reduces cardiovascular reactivity, decreases absentee rates, and may even prolong life.

-§-

The problem we are trying to solve is a lack of intimacy, not the kid on drugs or the boss at work.

-§-

Much of this important work has been conducted by James Pennebaker and his colleagues.[10,11] While disclosure of facts is helpful, disclosure of feelings is much more powerful.[12] The researchers also found that disclosure of traumatic or painful experiences had a more powerful benefit on health and healing than talking or writing about superficial events, even if in the short run the person felt worse. They found that the greater the degree of disclosure, the more benefits they measured. These benefits persisted over time. The benefits were particularly striking in those who talked about upsetting or traumatic experiences they had not previously discussed with others in detail.

What I try to do with patients, just as in my own life, is to help patients use the experience of suffering as a doorway to help transform their lives in ways that can make it richer and more meaningful. When most people think about my work, they think about diet, which is important, but to me it's the least interesting aspect of the work.

The experience of suffering comes in many forms, whether physical, or the deeper suffering which is harder to measure and yet ultimately more meaningful to people—their loneliness, depression, powerlessness, unhappiness, anxiety, fear, worry, sense of being cut off, sense of helplessness or hopeless, or a lack of meaning in their lives. All of these things I experienced to the nth degree when I was in college.

I've had patients say to me, "Having a heart attack was the best thing that ever happened to me." I would say, "That sounds crazy. What do you mean?" They'd respond, "Because that's what it took to get my attention—to begin making these changes I probably never would have done otherwise—that have made my life so much more rich, peaceful, joyful, and meaningful."

Part of the value of science is to help raise the level of awareness for people so that they don't have to suffer as much to gain insight. Awareness is the first step in healing. They don't have to wait until they get a heart attack to begin taking these ideas seriously and making them part of their lives.

Altruism Has Healing Power

Do you want to be Mother Teresa or Donald Trump? Do you choose to help only yourself or do you choose to help others?

Trick question. Fortunately, you don't have to choose.

When you help others, you also help yourself. Seen from that perspective, helping others—being unselfish—is the most "selfish" of all activities, for that is what helps to free us from our loneliness and isolation and suffering.

Compassion, altruism, and service—like confession, forgiveness, and redemption—are part of almost all religious and spiritual traditions as well as many secular ones. We are hardwired to help each other. This has helped us survive as a species for the past several hundred thousand years.

The Tecumseh Community Health Study found that activities involving regular volunteer work were among the most powerful predictors of reduced mortality rates. Those who volunteered to help others at least once a week were two and a half times less likely to die during the study as those who never volunteered. In other words, those who helped others lived longer themselves.[13]

Studies of volunteers have shown that not only do they tend to live longer, but also they often feel better, sometimes reporting a sudden burst of endorphins similar to a "runner's high" while helping others. This good feeling that comes from helping others is a subset of a larger context: Anything that helps us freely choose to transcend the boundaries of separateness is joyful. When you volunteer, you have a choice. When you are pressured or coerced to meet someone else's needs, the joy of helping and the health benefits are compromised or even counterproductive.

At its best, making love is an ecstatic experience when two lovers merge as one, opening their hearts to each other and melting the boundaries that separate them. After my first sexual experience as a teenager, however, I remember thinking, "Is that it? That's all?" There was a brief physiological release but hardly an ecstatic experience. Only much later in life, when I learned to make love with an open heart, did I begin to understand how joyful it could be. There is a growing interest in tantra and other approaches that help couples learn to combine sexuality and spirituality.

The ecstasy that comes from melting the boundaries between self and other is also part of most religious and spiritual traditions. While there are many pathways to experiencing God or the Self, praying with an open heart is one of the most powerful and joyful. Someone might choose to live a celibate life as a monk or a nun or a swami or a priest out of repression or fear of one's sexual impulses, but at its highest form they might renounce worldly relationships because the feelings of ecstasy and freedom that come from merging with God, with the Self, are so much more powerful even than merging with one's beloved mate.

On one level, we are separate from everyone and everything, the self with a small "s." You are your self, and I am my self. On another level, though, we are part of something larger that connects us all—the universal Self, by any other name: God, Buddha, Spirit, Allah, whatever.

Even to give a name is to limit it. When God was revealed to Moses, he asked, "When I tell the people that the God of their fathers has sent me, they will ask his name. What shall I tell them?" And God said, "I am what l am. Tell them l am has sent you."[14]

The vision of unity consciousness and oneness is found in virtually all cultures and all religions. God or the Self is described as omniscient, omnipresent, and omnipotent. As described in the Old Testament, "The Lord is One." If God is everywhere, omnipresent, One, then we are not separate from God.

What we experience as different names and forms is God or the Self in varying disguises, manifesting in different ways. All divisions are man-made. The word yoga is Sanskrit for "union." A central precept in Hinduism is "Thou art that.... The universe is nothing but Brahman."[15] According to Jesus, "The kingdom of God is within you."[16] Buddha taught, "You are all Buddhas. There is nothing that you need to achieve. Just open your eyes."[17] The Arabian prophet Muhammad, founder of Islam, wrote, "Wherever you turn is God's face.... Whoever knows himself knows God."[18] Albert Einstein, the greatest scientist of the twentieth century, wrote, "The true value of a human being can be found in the degree to which he has attained liberation from the [separate] self.[19] This experience is sometimes described as Oneness or at other times as complete emptiness, void; more precisely, as both. This paradox—everything and nothing—is at the heart of the transcendent experience, "an immediate, nondual insight that transcends conceptualization."[20] For it is our concepts of how we think things are that often keep us from seeing and experiencing how they really are.

CHAPTER TWENTY SIX

By analogy, Swami Satchidananda describes the one light in a movie projector manifesting as an entire universe of people, places, and dramas on the movie screen. When we can maintain this double vision—seeing the different names and forms while remembering it's just a movie and seeing the one light behind the many images—then we can more fully enjoy the movie without getting lost in it, without forgetting who we really are.

Although this experience of Oneness lies beyond the intellect, it can be directly experienced. Compassion naturally flows when the divisions that separate us from each other begin to fade.

Compassion helps to free us from anger. Anger itself is often a manifestation of the misperception that we are separate and only separate.

The Intimacy of Touch

What is the largest organ in your body? Your skin. We all know that a loving touch feels good, but did you know it can also affect your health and even your survival?

Intimacy is healing. Touching is intimate. Lack of human contact can lead to profound isolation and illness—and even death.

A number of studies are now showing the benefits of touch in newborns. At the Touch Research Institute in Miami, premature babies given three loving massages a day for ten days gained weight forty-seven percent faster and left the hospital six days sooner, saving $10,000 each.[21]

Despite this, we do not touch each other very much in the United States when compared with other parts of the world. Psychologist Sidney Jourard observed and recorded how many times couples in cafés casually touched each other in an hour. The highest rates were in Puerto Rico (180 times per hour) and Paris (110 times per hour). Guess how many times per hour couples touched each other in the United States? Twice! (In London, it was zero. They never touched.) He also found that French parents and children touched each other three times more frequently than did American parents and children.[22]

Again, awareness is the first step in healing. When we understand the healing power of touching, we can look for ways of increasing our contact with other people while respecting their boundaries. Give someone a pat on the back or a hug when they've done a good job—or even when they haven't. Get a massage or manicure or shampoo. Shake hands when you see a colleague. Hold hands with your beloved—and don't forget to kiss.

Therapeutic touch is a type of massage that also combines the intention of the person to help or heal while in a meditative state. It was pioneered by Dolores Krieger and is increasingly taught and used by nurses and other health practitioners. Therapeutic touch also can be practiced by simply placing your hands near someone rather than on them. The goal is to "rebalance energy" and to stimulate a person's own natural intrinsic healing responses. One of the leading practitioners and researchers of therapeutic touch is Janet Quinn, who described it this way: "Therapeutic touch, at its core, is the offering of unconditional love and compassion.... We're here for service. We're here to love other people.... The most fundamental longing of the human heart is for union with the Divine."[23]

Beyond your feelings and your body and your thoughts and your mind is the Self that witnesses all of this. While this Self is beyond the mind's capacity to experience it, you can feel this Self in your heart as love: "Love comes from God, and everyone who loves is begotten by God and knows God; those who don't love, don't know God; for God is love." (1 John 4:7)

When we realize that, this awareness creates tremendous freedom in making different choices. We can choose to live with an open heart, a love that can include everyone and everything. We are intimate with all things as all things. In that timeless moment, wherever we go, we find only our own kith and kin in a thousand and one disguises. We end where we started, with love and survival. Let's give the epilogue to the Sufi poet Rumi, who lived in the thirteenth century when he wrote:

> There is a community of the spirit.
> Join it, and feel the delight
> of walking in the noisy street,
> and being the noise...
> Why do you stay in prison
> when the door is so wide open?
> Move outside the tangle of fear-thinking.
> Live in silence.
> Flow down and down in always
> widening rings of being.

PART SIX

The Future of Medicine

GARY DANIEL:

Shamanism Plugs Into the Wall

The night air is still and the sky is delicately sprayed with pinpoints of light. Against the stark beauty of this blue-black backdrop you see rapid, random movement as though the stars have commenced an ecstatic dance. You listen carefully to a distant sound; its vibration and tone moves something in your chest that has long since been asleep. Filled with familiar feelings you cannot quite place in memory, your curiosity is piqued. As the rhythms get closer, you reach toward the mystical chant drumming in your inner ear. A huge fire flickers before your eyes, and you hear the steady ba-dum, ba-dum of a drum that evokes a subconscious memory of your mother's life-giving heartbeat keeping time with your own while you nestle in the womb. The infectious rhythm draws all your consciousness into its sound; you are so absorbed that all your problems seem to melt away. The experience refreshes your mind and renews your soul. In the secret place of the heart, you are reborn.

Healing rituals of this type have been conducted throughout human history in vastly different contexts, from ancient wizards, shamans, and witchdoctors, to modern rites of passage. The name such rites are given depends on the continent, culture and region of the world in which they are practiced. Shamanic healers throughout time have created dramatic healing events and profound results instantaneously, seemingly like magic. More often than not, they leave their patients better off than they found them. The mystical power of the shaman generates awe and wonder — some kind of major "Wow," when it occurs. That "Wow" factor is essential to the healing event.

Gary Daniel, Ph.D., has over 18 years of continuous work in the field of human performance and behavior modification. Dr. Daniel has created a simple proven process that can create, in most cases, immediate lasting changes in his clients. The system is call NIOS, the NeuroImaging Optimization System. It incorporates the powerful proven impact of NLP (neuro-linguistic programming), clinical hypnotics, biofeedback, vibra-acoustic articulation and laser technology. His clinic and spa, Allura du Jour, in Santa Rosa, California, combines traditional health and beauty treatments with advanced neurological technology. He's on the web at www.drgarydaniel.com.

CHAPTER TWENTY SEVEN

The Magical Healing Power of the Shaman

Where does the shaman get his or her magical healing power? What secret allows these individuals to bring about such an immediate and miraculous effect? These questions had the scientific community stumped for many years. Understanding the phenomenon of shamanic healing required an initial leap — the willingness to take shamanic healing seriously — and then a great deal of research. The key factor driving shamanic healing phenomena that all researchers had to confront boils down to one simple fact: *there really is a mind and body connection.* Shamanic healing taps the enormous unconscious power of the patient's belief in the shaman's authority, and ability to bring about *a true healing event.*

Consider the environment in which wizards of yesteryear practiced their craft. Shamans were removed from the general population, aloof. Rarely would a shaman be seen socializing or partying with the common people. They remained separate, even isolated, above the day-to-day reality of the tribe. The common person, for the most part, would only see the shaman when he or she performed his or her unique role within the group, conducting healing rituals again and again. That detachment gave the shaman the upper hand. In some cultures, few were allowed to see the shaman's face. The shaman remained masked or painted, and was often costumed in extraordinary ways, generating, in the perception of ordinary mortals, an aura of magical power.

Research has uncovered three key elements of the shamanic healing ritual. Together, these three elements have a profound effect on participants. The successful wizard of the past used an entrainment system to capture and optimize the conscious thoughts of the subject and hold those thoughts in a specific state to effect a desired change. The three key elements are the vital tools with which the shaman works his healing magic. They are: sound, touch, and light. These three elements *combined* allow the shaman to, in effect, enchant the mind. In modern-day scientific parlance, we know this enchantment occurs when the brainwaves shift into a theta state. Once the mind has ceased its ordinary pattern of thinking in the alpha and beta states, new thoughts — in the form of healing suggestions congruent with a person's belief system — can be easily embedded. These new patterns of thinking are what does the healing, often creating profound recovery and change, and often doing so immediately.

-§-
The successful wizard of the past used an entrainment system to capture and optimize the conscious thoughts of the subject.
-§-

Let us break this down a little further to see how the enchantment occurs. The dramatic effect of fire creates a rhythmic flickering in the eyes, even if they are closed. The flickering light effects retinal stimulation through the eye, causing a pattern of random stimulation in the optic nerve. Once the optic nerve is stimulated, the conscious mind will attempt to make sense of the random pattering and will quickly become overloaded. The effect of this overload is that a large portion of conscious awareness is captured. This, in turn, renders the subconscious mind more accessible, and thus more receptive to healing treatments and suggestions.

The shaman also introduces sound — beating drums, clapping sticks together, striking rocks against each other, stamping his or her feet on the ground, and chanting. Shamans often use music from ancient instruments — a drone or a didgeridoo — or their own voices. Using sound in this ritual manner has a similar effect on the auditory nerve as fire has on the optic nerve. Sound accomplishes two major tasks in the healing process. First, it overloads the auditory nerve, resulting in overload of the conscious mind, opening the unconscious mind to healing suggestions. The second task it accomplishes is tactile stimulation, through the vibrations of the sounds.

-§-

Once the conscious mind is in an overloaded state, the subconscious is wide open—ripe and ready to receive the new reality of healing.

-§-

Kinesthetic overloading of the body's tactile sense results. This allows the final sensory door to swing open, flooding the mind to the point of complete conscious overload.

The phenomenon is somewhat similar to an experience common to first time skydivers. Whether static line or piggyback freefall, first-timers are forewarned about "sensory overload" and instructed to expect the mind to blank out when they take that first step out of the airplane. This occurs when our main sensory input channels get too much new information all at once. The conscious mind temporarily shuts down. This tendency of the mind works to the shaman's advantage when he or she orchestrates a healing event.

Once the conscious mind is in an overloaded state, the subconscious is wide open—ripe and ready to receive the new reality of healing. If a person in this state believes that the shaman's power can heal him or her, the mind is in the perfect state to accomplish just that. The healing power of the shaman lies in the ability to create a specialized environment, one that allows the patient to actualize his or her belief in the power of a shamanic intervention to reverse or revise an unwanted condition.

Ancient Wisdom Meets High Technology

Imagine, now, in the present day, walking into a beautiful vintage building. Inside, the place is adorned with all the regalia of a small palace, and yet the environment is cozy and warm, like a favorite scene from a childhood storybook. Walking into the lobby immediately relaxes your body and mind. All your troubles are dwarfed by the sense that you have entered a very special realm designed by masterful hands for your pleasure and comfort. Sitting in the foyer and drinking a cup of green tea, you feel a deep sense of inner peace.

A smartly attired, poised man comes out to greet you. You are invited into an inner room that looks like something out of a science fiction movie. Your host directs you to a reclining chair reminiscent of the seat astronauts sit in while blasting into space. Mesmerized by all you see, your attention goes to a huge console with many lights and buttons and a computer above the control panel with a variety of green lines and numbers playing across its screen. The dimly-lit room looks much like a private viewing room, yet you feel as though you have just been placed into a welcoming adult-sized cradle. You feel totally relaxed, and you know you have made the right decision to come here. Your host displays total confidence in what he is doing as he instructs you to sit back, breathe deeply and enjoy the ride. As you close your eyes, you hear ocean waves crashing on the shore. It sounds like the beach is across the street, although you are twenty miles from the Pacific shoreline. Your host sits at the control panel and speaks to you about the behavioral changes you would like to make in your eating patterns and exercise habits. Further discussion branches out to a number of vital areas in your life. The enrichment you desire and progress you intend to make is reviewed, step by step.

-§-
I have simply harnessed these channels with modern technology to optimize mental functioning in much the same way shamans use fire, drums and chanting.
-§-

As the session continues, the lights dim and your chair leans back into a zero gravity position. The ocean sound gets louder and more intense, yet the crashing waves are most comforting. Your host, behind the control panel, asks you to close your eyes and keep them closed until invited to open them again. He pushes some buttons and an interesting light pattern begins to dance across your face. You realize the light is coming from the two laser projectors you saw mounted on the ceiling, but you simply lie back and enjoy the patterns as they play across your eyelids. As the session builds, you hear music emanating from the chair. Your host sits behind the console, monitoring your brainwaves and body stress, making system adjustments to optimize the process. The music is not like any you might hear on the radio, but the orchestrated and intermixed frequencies and tones create a perfect state of relaxation.

As the session progresses, you hear a series of affirmations, suggestions, and subtle directives that precisely describe the growth and development to which you aspire. The lasers are sequenced with your brain waves; you feel as though you are floating in space. Your host watches the response of your brainwave pattern to the affirmations and suggestions.

He pulls your brainwaves into congruity — and suddenly your brain gets the message, "Okay, I can do this." After a time, the affirmations stop, the lasers go off, and the lights in the room come up as the sound of ocean waves returns to the distance. Instructed to open your eyes as the chair rises to an upright position, you take a deep and refreshing breath, thinking to yourself, "That's almost better than sex." Since you began this new form of self-indulgence, you have lost twenty pounds, and regained a good deal of youthful verve. On top of that, you have made a number of positive new steps in your career.

This may sound like a scene out of a science fiction novel or a Jetsons cartoon, but it is not. The vintage building I have described is Allura du Jour, where I have my office in downtown Santa Rosa, California. The NIOS (Neuro Imaging Optimization System) chair sits in a room that looks just as I described it. I use it every day to help people achieve their optimum health and lifestyle. Some of my clients think of me as a new millennium shaman, a witchdoctor plugged into a wall; many have compared me to the wizard behind the curtain in *The Wizard of Oz*. But the heart of this unique healing process is not the man sitting at the console, or all the lights and waves. At the heart of this specific healing event are peoples' primary learning channels, and we are not talking TV. The primary learning channels live within the body-mind complex of an individual in the form of visual, auditory, and kinesthetic pathways. I have simply harnessed these channels with modern tech-

-§-
The power of positive thinking is overrated, because if you have to pause and think about something, it is already too late.
-§-

nology to optimize mental functioning in much the same way shamans use fire, drums and chanting. The "theatre of the mind," as Orson Welles called it, becomes a vital generator for new behavior, for changes in attitude, and for advanced learning. Years of research, backed by my clinical experience, have showed me how to optimize the theatre of the human mind by harmonizing visual, auditory and kinesthetic learning channels in order to create healing events far more predictably and rapidly than through traditional psychotherapeutic practices. I literally plug the ancient shaman's wisdom into the wall.

Thinking Influences Healing

Henry Ford said, "whether you think you can or you think you can't, either way, you'll be right." What this highlights about our thinking process is profound. It frankly states the fact that what you think will happen is, in all likelihood, predictive of what will happen. This statement is fundamental to creating change in all of us. It suggests that what you think about, the mind interprets as your dominant direction and desire. It will focus on making it come true. Therefore, the fuel that propels healing is hidden in our thought patterns, which are shaped by our beliefs.

From every corner of the human development field, we hear about the power of positive thinking: change your beliefs and change your life; if you think you can do something, you can do it. The generality of these statements raise certain questions. Are there not limits placed on all of us in the form of physical structure or mental capability? Isn't it a bit unrealistic to suggest that a 5′ 2″ 100 lb. person can think their way to being the world heavyweight boxing champion? Even if the person has a great attitude and all the positive thinking tracks aligned, his or her package of natural gifts simply do not allow it. But that does not discount the innate potential of the mind addressed by Henry Ford.

I contend that the power of positive thinking is overrated, because if you have to pause and think about something, it is already too late. What we can do, however, is *learn* how best to manage our thoughts. It is important to keep this fact in mind: the bias in our thinking process naturally goes to the negative. This is a basic survival mechanism within the human body-mind. The brain is wired to scan and sort for what does not work in our surroundings. This ensures that our prime directive will be met; that prime directive is always survival. The directive stems from the most primitive—and therefore least amenable to conscious control—part of the brain. At the base of the brain sits the medulla oblongata. This brain stem, sometimes referred to as the reptilian portion of the triune brain, works around the clock to keeps us alive and safe. If we did not automatically go the negative as a default brain setting, we would not make it through one day without coming into harm's way. This natural bias in our thinking will always focus on the negative, fearful, or dangerous aspects of our reality first.

-§-
In practice, much psychotherapy excites and reinstalls the trauma at an even deeper level.
-§-

What is so magic and unique about being human is our ability to think and reason. This ability is built in, and gives us the capacity to generate healing and resolution. Although the mind initially zeros in on what is negative or threatening, we can also take note of the positive side of things and find balance. This is a function of choice. A full understanding of this highlights the urgent need to become centered when faced with stress or a threat in order to focus and find the balance between negative and positive thoughts. This is a skill that can be learned. Without it, negative thoughts become like a train running downhill, making it difficult to anchor the positive thoughts and attitudes that promote healing and balanced thought processes.

Challenging Outdated Psychological Practices

A number of misconceptions exist within standard psychological practice as it has developed over the century since Freud — in the absence of any neuroscience to back his theories — advanced the psychoanalytic approach. One such misconception lies in the assumption that in order to heal wounds of the past we need to talk about what happened, to ponder and revisit the trauma. We must do this over and over until we are healed, or at least have control over the initial traumatic event. The question I have always felt compelled to raise is this: Why would a traumatic event that held our attention for a matter of minutes take years of therapy to heal? Psychotherapists often spend years helping a client work through an incident that, when it happened in real time, only involved moments.

The illusion at play in a talk-it-through-to-resolution model has to do with the notion we can unlearn something. The truth is that *we cannot unlearn anything.* Learning is both accumulative and uni-directional. I have actually heard of therapists telling their clients to "Just let it go." I say: preposterous! A number of mental laws exist, and one we need to take into account is the *neurological law of negation.* This law simply states: *In order to not do something you must first think about doing it.*

Just for fun, do this simple exercise: Clear your mind for a moment. Then, don't think of a banana. How did you do? Did you think about the banana? Did you not think about it? Did you notice that the moment you attempted to not think about it you had to think about it in order to not think about it? This self-defeating loop sets the mind up to do exactly what we don't want it to do. Many therapeutic approaches work in this same way, creating more of the exact problem a person is trying to resolve. In practice, much psychotherapy excites and reinstalls the trauma at an even deeper level. Once we realize the futility of trying to resolve trauma by going over and over it in the mind, we can put our attention on learning how to think differently.

-§-
Healing can happen in minutes when we shift how we look, hear, and think about things.
-§-

Healing is largely a matter of learning. When we seek healing, we are really asking to learn how to change the beliefs that support unwanted symptoms or behaviors. The cure lies in rethinking, learning and developing new skills and resources, giving us power over old ways of being that do not work. This is a function of belief and choice. The ancient shaman's ability to heal tapped into the richness of our human neurological depths to create new resources and therefore, wellness. With newly developed resources come new experiences and new beliefs, more powerful and life-enhancing than the old ones, which effectively render the old beliefs outdated, obsolete, and impotent. The old beliefs simply do not make sense anymore and eventually fall away, atrophy, and relinquish their power to influence consciousness.

After hearing a talk I gave on this subject last year, Clara called me for a phone consultation. At 285 lbs., she had all but given up on losing weight. She had tried and failed at all the major weight loss programs, including hypnotherapy. Understandably skeptical, she asked, "Can what you offer possibly be different?" At thirty-five years of age, she had never married and, as a business owner, was beginning to see the negative effect of her weight problem in her professional life. As we began our work together, she presented me with all the normal com-

-§-
If a person is not *really ready* to change, I will not accept him or her as a client.
-§-

plaints and resistance. Using the NIOS system in conjunction with advanced Neuro-Linguistic Programming techniques I have developed over the past ten years, I was able to help her curb her compulsive behavior. As a practitioner, it is my job to finesse a client into a state of mind that will support their goals without alerting their conscious mind to what is going on. I slip suggestions into the subconscious and alter the underlying belief structure, making it congruent with the client's goals. Once this is accomplished, behavior change occurs with amazing ease. Since we began our work together, Clara has lost sixty pounds without dieting.

Another misconception we would do well to challenge is the notion that *change is hard and can take years.* In truth, healing can happen in minutes when we shift how we look, hear, and think about things. As mentioned before, it is unrealistic to tell a person to "just let go" of their disease, trauma, or fear. I view symptoms from a negative experience as nothing more than the body's way of giving feedback and information. For example, phobic responses are nothing more than well-learned patterns built on a set of beliefs that have proven themselves effective in keeping a person safe from harm. Most phobias are not built on actual experience. They are built on thoughts about an experience, or a feared experience. What generates the phobic response is a set of negative beliefs about the phobic target. These beliefs are created by suggestions, fears, and referred experiences the person has come in contact with over time. The phobia is set to action when these suggestions accumulate, register as a threat, and are perceived as a serious danger in a person's mind. Once this happens, the individual will begin to experience symptoms that create neurological responses in the mind to divert the body from the perceived danger. Again, keep in mind that most people with phobias have never had a bad experience with the thing they fear. Phobias stem from perceived or suggested fear, not real-time experience. A phobia is really a thinking dilemma.

Understanding this makes it easy to see how change can happen fast. If a person can learn to become afraid and phobic *without any actual experience,* just by having thoughts about the experience, it stands to reason he can also learn to become phobia-free by using *the thought of the experience of staying safe in the face of perceived danger.* In both cases, the change occurs through mental processing, using the visual, auditory, and kinesthetic learning channels of the mind to write beliefs and patterns to heal the fear or install the fear.

Arbella, a fifty-year-old executive, came to me with a tremendous fear of snakes, frogs and spiders. She would almost pass out if she saw even the picture of a snake. She had tried drugs, desensitization, and psychological counseling, but these only deepened the problem and made it worse. Arbella began to also fear flying, which was a practical problem, since her career required travel. We eliminated her phobias in three sessions and she has had no problem since. Treating a phobia by trying to make sense of it does not work. With the NIOS system, we saturate and neurologically sensitize a person, then re-imprint them to alter the thinking pattern. Arbella recently phoned to update me on the miraculous changes that came about in many areas of her life from the work we did erasing her phobic reactions.

-§-

Most people with phobias have never had a bad experience with the thing they fear.

-§-

The power of change, whether dealing with phobias, emotional scars, or medical issues, lies in changing our beliefs and the way we think. Emerson said, "Change your thoughts and you change your world." If a person is ready and wants to make a change, seeming miraculous healing can occur. The important question here becomes, "What makes a person ready?" Quite often, "ready" equates with desperate, and what will leverage a person's ability to heal are matters of life and death.

The best example is something I see every week as a medical hypnotist. On a regular basis, I get special calls in emergency situations. Recently, I stood at the bedside of a forty-year-old man, a father of two, who had just been in a car accident and needed immediate surgery to reconstruct his pelvis. When the emergency anesthesiologist found him intolerant to all the knock-out drugs due to the fact he was already on a number of other medications, I was called in. A normal course of anesthesia could have put him into anaphalactic shock. Without the help of hypnosis, surgery would have been difficult if not impossible. Talk about "ready." This gave me exactly the leverage I needed to gain access to the hidden potential of this man's mind. I talked him into a theta brainwave state and gave him a set of precise instructions. Surgery was conducted under local anesthetic.

Less dramatic circumstances occur all the time. In the course of normal life, we all experience desperation thresholds when circumstantial pressure grows and we become ready and willing to change. In my healing practice, this evaluation is critical. If a person is not *really ready* to change, I will not accept him or her as a client. Therein lies the difference between the work I do and "traditional" therapy. Most of my clients get results in three to five sessions, and this is one strategy I use to guarantee change. Another crucial strategy has to do with clarifying goals. Statements like, "I want to feel better" or "I want more out of life" do not structure a person's thinking clearly enough to guide the process of change.

Creating a highly charged emotional environment is crucial to neuropsychology and the work of shifting neural patterns. I insist my clients be sensory specific as to what they want to be when they experience reaching their goals. Getting very detailed and specific about what they want to see, to feel and to hear, and generating those experiences in the imaginal realm provides the emotional charge needed to imprint and anchor a new, positive neural pattern over the old, negative one.

Let's Make it Happen Fast—And Make It Last

Applying the wisdom of the ages, and mixing in high technology bioacoustics, lasers and music, the new millennium shaman removes much of psychological guesswork. We can create optimal comfort for a client, develop an optimum learning environment, and optimize the innate potential of the mind more than ever before. By creating a stimulated emotional environment in which our suggestions will fire off a synaptic impression that will last, we can overpower outdated neurological pathways. Old beliefs can be recognized and recalibrated to present-day knowledge. The updated belief creates a healing path that makes sense to the mind and body at a subconscious level. When we tune the mental environment, and emotional attachment becomes transferred to target behavior, changes occur from that moment on. The future is on track. The track has been set by clearly defined goals, both emotional and philosophical. All of this occurs through the power of the mind, with a little help from technology to make the ride easier, faster and more pleasant.

-§-
Creating a highly charged emotional environment is crucial to neuropsychology and the work of shifting neural patterns.
-§-

The New Shaman—More User-Friendly Than Ever

When we plug into the wall, we replace fire, drums and magical potions with science and technology. The lasers are the fire; the computerized acoustic feedback is the drum, and self-defined goals are the magic potions my clients use to change their lives. By over-exciting the visual, auditory and tactile mental imaging with the NIOS system, new mental imaging takes root, creating new patterns at a significantly deeper level than ordinary hypnotic suggestion.

In our rapidly changing world of instant gratification and text messaging, we want results fast. Not so long ago, I had to take my car to a service station and leave it for a day to get the oil changed and the tires rotated. Today, this happens in the time it takes to buy a latte or a greeting card in the lobby of the local Quick Stop Oil Change.

The message from my clients is just as clear: They expect to make personal changes a short-term process. Forward-thinking practitioners of human development know the importance of getting results, getting them fast, and making them last. As a practitioner of hypnosis, NLP (Neuro Linguistic Programming), and Biofeedback, I realized that I had to find a way to do this—or go the way of the dinosaur. With the NIOS system, I discovered a way to marry the technology of sound, light, music, vibration, metaphor and isomorphism to create an integrated system. Technology helps me raise the bar, and achieve a level of success I could not reach using NLP and hypnosis alone. The next wave of our human potential is hitting the beach in the form of a "Healing Event" in the theatre of the mind. As more and more practitioners discover the amazing power of this new plugged-in process, old-style therapy may go the way of the dinosaur as well. *Light, Sound, Vibration and New Millennium Healing* is coming soon to a therapist near you!

ERIC ROBINS:

Future Cures: Cheap, Fast, Radical, Effective

Michelle, a bright, perky, twenty-one-year-old woman, arrived in my office complaining of severe bladder pain. She had to urinate frequently and urgently. I did a complete medical workup but could find nothing out of the ordinary — by the standards of my profession there was nothing wrong with Michelle. Yet it was clear to me that Michelle's pain was real, and her physical symptoms were real. After I had finished looking in her bladder with a cystoscope and found everything to be normal, I ventured, "Sometimes women with your symptoms have a history of sexual abuse or molestation. Is this possible with you?" In the corner of her eye, the slightest of tears welled up. It turned out that Michelle had been sexually penetrated by an uncle almost daily from the age of three, until she was ten years old.

I asked Michelle to think back upon these memories and find a part of her body where they were strongest. She said she could feel them acutely in her lower abdomen and pelvis. I asked her to rate them on a scale of one to ten, with one being the mildest and ten being the most intense. Michelle rated her feelings at ten out of a possible ten.

I then spent forty-five minutes working with Michelle, using some of the simple yet powerful techniques I describe below. I then asked her to rate her level of discomfort. It was a one — complete peace. I urged her to cast around in her body for the remnants of any of the disturbed feelings she had previously felt. She could not find them, no matter how hard she tried. The emotionally charged memories had been so thoroughly released that a physical shift had occurred in her body. Her bladder con-

Eric B. Robins, MD, is a board-certified urologist in practice in the Los Angeles area. He has an undergraduate degree in biology from the University of Texas at Austin. He attended medical school at Baylor College of Medicine, and completed a six-year urology residency at the University of Southern California. He has had a long-standing interest in the effect of emotions on health, and is a certified clinical hypnotherapist. He has also received training and certification in neurolinguistic programming and energy psychology, and is co-author of *Your Hands Can Heal You* (Free Press, 2003). He lives with his wife Linda and son Jonah.

dition disappeared. In the three years since that office visit, it has never once returned.

How are such apparently miraculous healings possible?

Many years ago, treating patients was much more difficult for me. I am a urologist in the Los Angeles area. Urology is a surgical subspecialty, which means that I spend much of my time in the operating room. Despite this fact, urologists still see a significant percentage of chronic and functional problems in the office. Patients with functional problems have real complaints and symptoms, yet physical exams, lab work and x-rays reveal no anatomic or "physical" findings. I've always believed that what these patients are feeling is real and genuine, and that the problems are not "just in their heads" as many physicians are prone to think.

Chronic problems are those conditions that patients have over long periods of time. To me, a chronic problem means that the body cannot heal itself. Taken together, chronic and functional problems make up about seventy percent of the cases that walk into a primary care doctor's office. Often, patients with these conditions get angry when I tell them that I cannot find the "cause" of their problem. After many years of urology practice, I found myself getting frustrated; I could dispense medications to treat the symptoms yet not be addressing the underlying cause.

When I first began to look for better ways to understand and treat chronic and functional problems, I had to look outside of the standard allopathic medical model. The reason I had to do this is because allopathic medicine is based on the belief that the body needs medications or surgery to heal. If you are interested in ways to get the body to heal itself, you've stepped beyond the realm of allopathic medicine. As I studied several different types of alternative healing, I saw a common thread. Whether found in acupuncture or acupressure or homeopathy or energy healing, the common belief is that *the body tends to heal itself, and there is a healing energy that flows through the body that allows this to happen.* If this energy gets blocked — producing either a congestion of dirty, stagnant energy, or a depletion of energy — this predisposes the body to disease. All these systems, with their various techniques, try to re-establish flow of energy.

-§-
These traumas might seem minor to an outsider looking in, but to the person who has experienced them they can have a big impact.
-§-

Early in my practice I noticed that I had a significant number of younger, sexually active women who would get recurrent urinary tract infections after intercourse. I rarely found an anatomic reason why this would be the case, despite doing a complete workup. I said to myself one day, "Many women are sexually active and are not getting urinary tract infections. So why do they recur in this sample of patients? It is almost as if the body's healing energy is not getting down to the pelvic area; if it were, their immune system would know what to do to prevent the infection from getting started." With this thought in mind, I began a study of the body's healing energy.

I was fortunate at the time to come across a healing system called "Pranic Healing." Master Stephen Co, one of the senior Pranic healing instructors in the world, was living and teaching in the Los Angeles area. I was able to spend a great deal of time studying the technique with him, as well as with the Grand Master of the system, Choa Kok Sui. Pranic healing is a powerful and effective *system* of energy healing. It incorporates all sorts of energy-related techniques, including feng shui, kundalini-based meditation, higher clairvoyance, sexual alchemy, and financial manifestation. Grand Master Choa has great ability to take complex esoteric topics and boil them down to their practical essence.

I began to use Pranic healing with my patients. It produced a number of recoveries like Michelle's, and gained the notice of other staff members at my medical center. Master Co and I subsequently wrote a book on self-healing entitled *Your Hands Can Heal You*. This book is a treasure of techniques that you can use to increase your vitality, your level of personal energy, and your health. As an example, one chapter teaches two simple yogic exercise routines that will literally double or triple a person's energy level. This is not like drinking a cup of coffee and getting a buzz for a couple of hours; the energy lasts the entire day. One of the biggest "complaints" that we get from folks who do these exercises is that their sex drive increases dramatically! The web site for Pranic healing is www.pranichealing.com, if you'd like to know more.

For the first couple of years that I was doing Pranic healing, I treated one to five patients a day in addition to my full-time urology schedule. When patients walked in the door, I used my hands to feel where the energy was out of balance in their bodies. I was able to sweep away the dirty, congested energy and subsequently pour some clean energy back.

Yet sometimes the treatment did not produce obvious results. Sometimes I would do a healing, fix the energetic defect and the patient would feel better. But they'd come back a week or two later. Their energy would be out of whack again, and their symptoms would have recurred. What factors were involved, I wondered, when people didn't heal as a result of the practice? Many of them were there because they hadn't been helped with a standard medical approach either, so they had run out of options. I began to wonder, *what might be causing the energetic defect to begin with?*

A principle of Pranic healing (and all other energy healing modalities) is that energetic changes precede physical changes. This means that before anything manifests physically, it is already present in the energy field. The work of Dr. Robert Becker elucidates this fact. Dr. Becker is an orthopedic surgeon who worked at New York University. He experimented with the use of electrical currents on bone healing. He did some interesting experiments on salamanders. If you sever the tail or the leg of a salamander it will regenerate a new one. Dr. Becker did an experiment in which he removed both the tail and the leg of a salamander. Then, when it began to regenerate a new tail, he scraped off some of the tail cells and moved them up to the area of the severed leg. The tail cells, whose DNA had already differentiated into tail cells, changed — and began to grow into normal leg cells. The same thing happened when he took regenerating leg cells and brought them down to the tail.

How did these cells know how to change so as to grow into the appropriate organ? Some researchers speculated that nearby nerves gave the signal, but further research showed these nerves to be silent. Becker's work suggests the presence of a larger energetic template that directed the cells to grow and differentiate into what was needed at a particular site. Similarly, when you cut your finger, just enough cells grow to fill in the wound. The body "knows" when to stop.

One day I was hit with an intuitive flash. I realized that the biggest factor that causes blockage of the body's healing energy is emotional issues, particularly how these are stored in — and processed by — the body. Stress and negative emotions aren't in the head; they are stored as tensions in the body. You don't need a double-blind university study to convince yourself of this. If you think about the last time you were angry or scared or depressed, notice where you felt those emotions inside.

Stress and negative emotions are frequently stored in the smooth muscles. The smooth muscles are those muscles that function automatically, without our conscious control. If people store tension in the smooth muscles of the blood vessels going to the head, we might call this a migraine headache. If they store tension in the smooth muscles of the air passages of the lungs we might call that asthma. If they store tension in the smooth muscle of the intestinal tract, they might have symptoms like nausea or bloating, or diarrhea alternating with constipation, or abdominal cramping. We might call that Irritable Bowel Syndrome or IBS. IBS is the second leading cause of missed work in the US, and accounts for some fifty percent of all visits to gastrointestinal specialists.

Emotions and Our Innate Healing Ability

Emotions stored in the body also affect our immune systems. Bernie Siegel discovered that exceptional patients viewed their cancers as representing or being the result of a psychological or spiritual conflict in their lives. Those patients who were able to look at their cancers in this way and then sought to make whatever changes were necessary did much better.

Dr. Paul Goodwin, a neural physicist at Alaska Pacific University, says that wherever stress and negative emotions are stored in the body, they create a blockage of the flow of the body's healing energy. This might explain why chronic conditions persist. For instance, the stomach sheds all its old cells and produces a new lining every seven days. So how can ulcers continue to exist for long periods of time? Why shouldn't all ulcers be healed within a week? They might be, unless the body's healing energy is not getting to that part of the stomach.

I categorize emotions and their effects on the body in one of two main ways. First, there are *distinct traumas* that occur to people in their lives. Some of these traumas might seem minor to an outsider looking in, but to the person who has experienced them they can have a big impact. Other times the traumas can be severe, including shocks like childhood abuse, rape, losing a parent or close friend, seeing or being involved in a serious accident, or war-time stress. These traumatic experiences are stored as memories inside our bodies at an unconscious level (some researchers say at a cellular level). Later on the unconscious mind will try to re-present these memories to our conscious minds so we can deal with them and resolve them. But because these memories are so painful, a part of us resists feeling or re-experiencing the memory. *In order to keep these memories from coming to conscious awareness, the body has to clamp down internally.* This internal clamping causes tension in the smooth muscles or skeletal muscles and is responsible for many of the functional diseases that people present with, ranging from hypertension to migraine headaches to chronic back pain to IBS.

> -§-
> Vast amounts of energy must be expended in order to keep painful emotions and memories held down in the body and outside of conscious awareness.
> -§-

Many times, the initial traumas are so deeply buried inside the body that they cannot be easily accessed by the conscious mind. When I was going through therapy it took me six months to get in touch with my deeper emotional pain and with the early memories that caused it. Before that time, anytime I got close to the pain I'd either fall asleep or "check out" and disassociate.

Vast amounts of energy must be expended in order to keep painful emotions and memories held down in the body and outside of conscious awareness. In my opinion this energy drain is one of the leading causes of chronic fatigue syndrome, fibromyalgia, and multiple chemical sensitivity disorder. These diseases are very real and the patients who have them are truly run down and depleted. The place to begin with these patients is by clearing any past emotional traumas so as to free up more energy for physical healing.

A second way to categorize emotions and their effect on the body is to *assess how early events shaped the way that we handle or process emotions.* One of the main functions of the unconscious mind is to keep us safe in our family while growing up. Often when we are young, events happen in our family that cause us to develop beliefs such as, "It's not okay to show our anger or anxiety." Showing these might upset our caretakers which would compromise our survival.

Harry, one of my clients, had chronic throat problems. Whenever a powerful emotion came up (either positive or negative) his throat would clamp down and get tight. He had three to four episodes of laryngitis a year during which he'd lose his voice. I did a session of hypnosis with him. We regressed the tight feeling in his throat, traveling all the way back in time to the first event he could recall. Harry was about six months old. He was crying inconsolably in the middle of the night and his father came to pick him up and comfort him. But his crying persisted, and after about thirty minutes his sleep-deprived father got frustrated and put Harry back somewhat abruptly in his crib with a mild jar (perhaps letting him drop two inches down into the crib).

-§-
It is not our negative emotions that cause the problem—but rather our resistance to feeling these emotions.
-§-

As a result of this seemingly minor event, Harry's unconscious mind developed several beliefs, one of which was, "It is not okay to express strong emotions like anger or fear." As I had Harry relive several repetitions of the event, I had him get in touch with and express his anger toward his father. Next, I had him look at the event from a more adult perspective during which he could understand that his father hadn't meant him harm, and certainly didn't mean to instill a belief that engendered lifelong emotional stifling. He proceeded to have a real breakthrough at the unconscious body level in his beliefs about expressing his feelings. That was more than eighteen months ago, and Harry has had no more problems with either laryngitis or sore throats.

This is more than academic theory. A model of how people abnormally process their emotions, and how to shift them, is responsible for the highest cure rate in the world among patients with chronic musculoskeletal pain. It has been well documented in the books *Healing Back Pain,* and *The Mind-Body Prescription* by Dr. John Sarno. Interestingly, it is not our negative emotions that cause the problem—but rather our resistance to feeling these emotions. My friend and internationally known psychologist Gay Hendricks once said, "All emotions are gentle and short-lived, unless we resist feeling them."

In Dr. Sarno's academic experience, his patients have about an eighty-eight percent rate of curing their severe musculoskeletal pain. An additional ten percent of his patients are much improved. Many of his patients had been in pain for twenty to thirty years prior to seeing him. Many had already undergone surgery or epidural injections into their spinal columns.

The way that he gets this amazing cure rate is by encouraging his patients, when they have pain, to ask themselves, "I wonder what I am angry or anxious about?" Once they get in touch with their anger or anxiety, the goal is not to push these emotions away or to act them out, but rather to allow themselves to feel them fully. Gay Hendricks (www.hendricks.com) describes this process of "putting nonjudgmental awareness on what you are feeling" as "presencing."

Rapid Healing Techniques

We are blessed to have been born at a time where there are very good techniques and modalities available to help us quickly resolve these emotional issues. There is a whole evolving field known as "Energy Psychology." The main belief behind this approach is that negative emotions are stored as disruptions in the body's energy system. If a person uses their fingers to hold or tap on certain energy points in the body while they are mentally focused on a traumatic memory or limiting belief or phobia, this clears the emotions out of the energy pathways, and the person experiences rapid and long-lasting relief.

At the outset of therapy I ask the client, "When you think of this problem, where do you feel it in your body?" Most folks feel emotions in their chest, solar plexus or throat, but others might feel it in their back, head or pelvis. I know that I am completely finished with the therapy if the person, when thinking about the original issue, can no longer feel the emotional pain in the body anymore. When this happens it means that the problem is cleared out at the unconscious level. The result is usually permanent. For me, this is the gold standard for whether a psychological intervention works.

Two of the most effective energy therapies are Emotional Freedom Technique (EFT), and Tapas Acupressure Technique (TAT). I have used both extensively in my clinic—with phenomenally good results. I have personally used EFT to completely resolve a number of cases of Post Traumatic Stress Disorder (PTSD) for which there is generally no cure within the standard psychological paradigm. EFT can be applied very quickly in the clinical setting to relieve stress, and about thirty to forty percent of the time can be used to improve physical pain. Dr. Joseph Mercola is a well-known physician with a huge practice in the Chicago area and one of the busiest "alternative healing" web sites on the Internet. His main emphasis is on finding natural ways for people to heal themselves, especially through diet and exercise. He, like many enlightened doctors, has seen the clear connection between stress and illness and espouses the regular use of EFT for many of his patients. With Michelle, the young woman with severe bladder pain with whom I started this story, I used TAT. If you are interested in checking out these modalities, the websites are www.emofree.com (EFT) and www.unstressforsuccess.com (TAT).

Sometimes painful traumas are very deeply repressed and people are not consciously aware of their presence—they can't remember them. In this case it is helpful to make the assumption that *the presence of the disease presupposes the existence of repressed emotional issues or traumas.* So how do we access that repressed material?

Hypnosis can be tremendously effective. About ninety-five percent of hypnotists use a "progressive relaxation" technique that draws the client into a light trance, where they are receptive to direct suggestions. This type of hypnosis can be effective. However, with deep-seated issues or serious illnesses, I have found that a deeper level of trance, followed by regression back to the original root cause of the problem, is necessary.

Pushing Above Our Upper Limits

There is one last level to consider in healing. This is what Gay Hendricks refers to as the "upper limits" problem. We all have an unconscious limit to how much positive energy we can handle coming at us from the world. If the energy begins to exceed this level, we will usually unconsciously sabotage ourselves so as to bring the energy back down again.

Almost everyone I've ever shared this with can relate to the upper limits problem. Right before a romantic three-day weekend, a fight breaks out between you and your partner. One of the children gets sick before a family trip. You obtain a much-needed vacation from work, and on the first day away from the office, you fall ill with the flu, and spend your vacation in bed.

For some people, having physical heath and vitality, financial success, relationship intimacy, or a full social schedule all represent too much positive energy, and this calls for an unconscious sabotage. Agnes, a nurse I work with, grew up in a poor section of East Los Angeles, an area known for crime and gangs. She is smart, pretty, and friendly, but cannot seem to form a relationship with any man who doesn't have a criminal record or history of incarceration. I have often thought about why Agnes isn't able to get into a stable relationship with a nice guy, perhaps a professional of some sort. After learning about the upper limits problem I could understand that being in a loving relationship with someone who has the ability for emotional intimacy and financial stability would represent too much positive energy for Agnes—it would make her feel uncomfortable. If you've ever heard the expression "water seeks its own level," what this means for my nurse friend is that she only feels chemistry for guys who will keep her energy level in her known comfort zone.

If we think of the upper limits problem in broader terms, we might say that everyone has a limit or *threshold* for how much "stuff" they can handle coming at them from their environment. A person raised in a dysfunctional environment tends to have a lower threshold than a person raised in a better home. Whenever we are pushed above our threshold we become stressed and anxious. We then try to deal with that stress through a variety of coping mechanisms learned during childhood. These include anger, depression, fear, substance abuse, overeating, plus others considered more healthy such as exercising, talking with friends, or isolation. Obviously it would be a great idea to be able to raise our own stress threshold rather than trying to alter our external circumstances all of the time (which is what is advocated by most stress reduction workshops). Just imagine if you could raise your stress threshold so much that no matter what was happening at home or at work, and no matter how hectic life became, it couldn't make you anxious. Now the technology has arrived to be able to do just that.

A couple of decades ago, researchers decided to evaluate advanced yogis. We're talking about people who have meditated six hours a day for fifteen years and who were amazingly relaxed, expansive, brilliant, and at peace in the most trying of circumstances. The researchers hooked these yogis up to EEG machines to find out what was going on with their brain waves during meditation. They made two distinct findings.

First, they found that these yogis were able to maintain conscious awareness while they slowed their brain waves from normal (waking) beta waves, down to alpha, then theta, and all the way down to delta patterns — theta is normally found only in REM sleep and delta is usually found only in deep, dreamless sleep. Second, they found that these yogis could think using their whole brain, as opposed to most of us, who are predominantly either right-brained or left-brained.

At about that same time research was going on involving bi-aural beat technology. Bi-aural beat technology demonstrated that, if someone is wearing stereo headphones and two different frequencies are played, one in each ear (for example 400 hertz in the left ear, and 410 hertz in the right), that whatever the difference is between the two (in this case ten hertz), the brain waves will be entrained to go to that frequency. So in simplistic terms what I'm saying is that by using stereo headphones, sound wave technology can be used to slow the brain waves down to the alpha or theta or delta range.

What is interesting about bringing someone's brain waves down to delta and then keeping them there for a while is that delta waves, although they are slow, contain tremendous amounts of energy. The waveforms are large. If you hold someone in delta for a while, you are forcing the brain to handle a lot more energy than it is used to. This forces the brain to develop new neural pathways to handle the increase in energy. It's like taking someone who doesn't exercise and having a drill sergeant show up at their door every day to make them run two miles: they *have* to develop more muscular strength in their legs and better pulmonary and cardiovascular ability to be able to handle the exercise.

In order to handle the increased energy of being held in delta, the two sides of the brain are forced to improve their cross-hemispheric communication. This releases endorphins, so participants oftentimes feel euphoric after a session. As cross-hemispheric communication is increased, people begin to naturally think with both sides of their brain. A few months after I had started listening to this technology my wife and I got into a disagreement. I was looking at the problem from my usual logical perspective and my wife was being (in my opinion) overly emotional. Then suddenly I found myself seeing things from her perspective; I could see the problem from a whole-brain perspective and could understand exactly where she was coming from. Nothing remained to argue about.

-§-
We are blessed today with simple, inexpensive, accessible techniques that have the potential to revolutionize our sense of wellness, shift the patterns that trap us in chronic disease, and dramatically raise our thresholds of happiness.
-§-

The best source of this bi-aural technology that I've found is a company called Centerpointe Research Institute (www.centerpointe.com). They produced a product called "The Holosync Solution" that will create the changes that I've delineated above. The Holosync tapes contain the bi-aural tones embedded underneath the soothing sounds of rainfall and crystal gongs. Since I've been listening to this technology my life has improved unimaginably as have the lives of several dozen of my friends and colleagues who are also listening. When patients come in wanting to relieve stress and anxiety, or when they ask for a very fast and effective way to get all the benefits of deep meditation I refer them to Holosync.

After using this technology for a relatively short period of time I observed that my own stress threshold markedly increased. I noticed that my busiest days at work, the ones that used to leave me tense, exhausted, and short-tempered, now had little effect. I also noticed that it was easier for me to share time with my family at home or on vacations; the increased energy generated by the fun and intimacy didn't push me over my threshold. I refer to this technology as "getting even with your past," since it is often a challenging childhood that lowers the threshold to begin with.

Another benefit of this technology is development of a "witness perspective." This means that you can develop the ability to step outside of yourself and witness your thoughts and emotions rather than being caught up in them. One of the main principles in *The Power of Now* by Eckhart Tolle is to be present in the now and to watch or observe your thoughts and emotional reactions to things. This process is extremely valuable although it can be difficult to do unless one has developed a witness perspective. In *The Dark Side of the Lightchasers,* author Debbie Ford talks about embracing our shadow and about coming to terms with and accepting all of the negative and disowned parts of ourselves in order to be whole again. Ford's explanations and processes are great and can be much faster and more easily implemented if one has developed a witness perspective.

We are blessed today with simple, inexpensive, accessible techniques that have the potential to revolutionize our sense of wellness, shift the patterns that trap us in chronic disease, and dramatically raise our thresholds of happiness. I challenge you to experiment with these methods and see what results they produce in your own life. And as you have the courage to travel healing journey, I salute the divinity within you and trust God's blessings with you always.

ANDREW VIDICH:

Theocentric Medicine

Mullah Nasruddin was a self-employed businessman who traveled back and forth between Saudi Arabia and Egypt. A border guard had the job of inspecting all traders as they entered or left Egypt to make sure they were not carrying any contraband. Every time that Nasruddin crossed the border, seven days a week, 365 days a year, he would be accompanied by a donkey carrying a saddlebag on his back. Each time he was inspected by the border officer, who never found anything suspicious. This continued for four years. Then, Mullah Nasruddin retired—a wealthy man. Soon after that, the guard retired too.

One day Nasruddin was sitting in a coffee shop in downtown Cairo sipping coffee. The former border guard walked by, noticed him, and was overwhelmed with curiosity. He introduced himself and said, "Mullah, I have retired myself and have no interest in persecuting you. I just want to know how you evaded my diligent searches. What were you smuggling?"

The Mullah paused for a moment, then said, "Donkeys."

Sometimes the most obvious facts in our lives are the very things we fail to see. These are the facts that we might call fundamental or self-evident truths that we miss because they are too close to us. Like the border guard, Western medicine is missing something fundamental. What is this missing ingredient? It is *consciousness* or *awareness.*

There is a direct relationship between spirituality and our health. Our spiritual consciousness and the life principle conditions our body. I call this approach *theocentric medicine.* Since meditation and prayer are two of

Andrew Vidich, Ph.D., holds a doctorate in religion with a specialization in the transformational methods within different religious traditions. He has authored several books on modern mysticism and healing, among them *Love Is a Secret: The Mystic Quest for Divine Love* (Aslan, 1990). Dr. Vidich offers seminars and workshops in the field of meditation, healing and personal transformation. He is the founding member of the Interfaith Council of New York. His consulting firm, Learning Excellence, teaches contemplative practice, stress reduction and conflict management in educational and corporate environments. Dr. Vidich is a disciple of Sant Rajinder Singh.

the most important disciplines by which we can develop spiritually, their connection to our understanding of healing is critical.

Three decades ago, when I began my meditation practice, I was often viewed as out of the mainstream, or belonging to a foreign Eastern cult. Today, with over two hundred studies done on the practice of meditation or the connection between spirituality and health, the tables have turned almost 180 degrees.[1] Wherever I go people are practicing meditation as a means to improve their health and overall well-being.

As a result of these numerous studies, we know that meditation and prayer are positive and successful forms of treatment for a variety of ailments including heart disease, stroke, chronic pain, stress reduction, hypertension, anxiety, depression, and even cancer. In the field of occupational stress management, meditation is considered the single most effective technique in reducing stress at work.[2] In a world struggling to find more effective ways to deal with pain, suffering and disease the possibilities inherent in the practice of meditation cannot be overlooked any longer. It is time to consider meditation as an effective *healing science* within the context of Western medicine.

-§-

We have become spiritual amputees, in need of an infusion of consciousness.

-§-

Why has this transition been so difficult to make? It implies a radical paradigm shift in the way we understand healing. Today the healing professions accept without argument that the human being has two aspects, a body and a mind. We recognize that these two systems are connected and interrelated and their proper functioning creates both psychological and physical health. We have a significant body of research that has explored the impact of the mind on the body, and vice versa. What we forget is that only forty years ago, the notion that the mind could affect the body was radical new territory. Today most health practitioners accept this without question.

Today another shift is taking place before our very eyes. This view holds that there is a third component to the human being, which we call *consciousness*. It is this consciousness (the life principle), which animates and enlivens the previous two components and which is responsible for the healthy functioning of the entire system. This new paradigm holds that human beings are made up of three components: body, mind, and consciousness, and their relative importance lies in this same ascending order.

The old model of the human being made famous by the 17th century philosopher Renee Descartes said, "I think therefore I am." The new paradigm says that this is radically wrong. We are more than thinking entities. The new model says, "I am conscious therefore I am." Awareness is different than thinking. We are conscious entities. From this perspective, all dis-ease results from the *breaking away of our individual self-awareness from the greater consciousness whole.* We have become spiritual amputees, in need of an infusion of consciousness. How is this accomplished? *Through the inversion of the attention within itself,* or meditation.

Meditation refers to a variety of practices within many different religious and spiritual traditions. In the Christian tradition, it has been referred to as *prayer with attention, centering prayer* and *unceasing prayer.* The Islamic Sufi Tradition calls it *dhikr* or *mushahada.* The Buddhists have referred to it as silent meditation, *vipassana,* and *dzogchen.* In Hinduism it's called *dhyana,* and in Judaism as the practice of *hitbodedhut.*

Meditation can be defined as an inversion of the attention through the process of concentration on our own essential Self. When attention is freed from both the body and bodily functions and the mind is freed from its various processes including, memory, discrimination, perception and ego,[3] the Self comes to know itself as pure consciousness. From birth until this present moment, our attention has been directed outward through the five organs of sense perception and we have forgotten our true nature. We suffer from the ultimate identity crisis. *We do not know who we are.* By shifting the attention inward, consciousness becomes liberated and discovers its innate self-luminous, self-energizing and self-revitalizing essence.

The health of the body and mind both depend upon the health of one's consciousness. And the total health of our consciousness depends upon not only the practice of meditation and prayer, but also our faith, spiritual beliefs, religious fellowship, thinking patterns and the way we interact with others.[4]

In studying meditation as a whole, we see certain universal elements that form the basis of almost all meditation practices. Each of these individual components can play a significant role in the journey toward individual healing and wholeness. The first is Right Practice.

Right Practice

The term *right practice* implies that we must begin our investigation within the human body. The point of concentration is not outside us but on the Self or *consciousness within* us. In effect, we are the subject of our own investigation. The human body is the laboratory where we begin. Our search begins with a shift from external observable phenomena, to internal, subjective (but also observable) phenomena viewed through internal subtle senses.

Another Nasruddin story relates the time when the Mullah lost his keys. He spent many hours searching all over his front and back yards, without success. Finally, his wife came out of the house to help him. She inquired, "Well dear, where do you last remember seeing your keys?" He replied, "In the basement." Baffled, she asked, "Why then are you looking for them out here on the front lawn?" Her husband replied forcefully, "There is more light outside!"

This Sufi teaching points to the futility of seeking spiritual truth in objective phenomena. After all, where is the scientific evidence that science alone can provide answers to all of life's questions? The search for health as well as spirituality begins within us.

Withdrawal of Sensory Awareness

The second element of meditation is called *pratyahara* in the Hindu tradition and literally translates as the withdrawal of the sense perception from the objects of the world. To illustrate this process more clearly we divide the functioning of the human body into two types of systems. The first system has been identified in Western medicine as the involuntary, sympathetic and parasympathetic nervous systems. These systems are responsible for the basic autonomic or involuntary functions including elimination, procreation, digestion, respiration, circulation, and the growing of hair and nails.

-§-
The mind is not conscious, but a vehicle through which our awareness works.
-§-

The second system is the sensory system. This system is responsible for the functioning of our five organs of perception, sight, hearing, taste, touch and smell. In contrast to the involuntary system, we have significant control over these sense organs. When we exercise control over our attention, we can, to a large degree, direct how we use them. Thomas Edison was once working on solving a difficult math problem in his study. A marching band went by his study window. Later, a friend came by and asked him if he had enjoyed the marching band. He said, "What band? I did not hear anything."

It is our attention, or consciousness, which enlivens our sense organs. At present our attention is diffused throughout the body at a microscopic and cellular level and pulled by the various sense organs to various sense objects. In the meditative state, it is withdrawn and concentrated at a single point within the body known as the *seat of the soul* or *consciousness* or *third eye*. In effect, the meditator ceases to be influenced by outer stimuli.

To assist the aspirant in accomplishing the withdrawal process, most meditation traditions provide a variety of preliminary practices or transitional exercises. These help transfer our mental awareness from the world into new spiritual dimensions. Some of these exercises are physical, others mental. Physical practices include hatha yoga, sacred dance, chanting, use of music and sound, visual aids including yantras, Tefilin, or prayer carpets. Mental preliminary exercises include reciting and reading of scripture, ceremonial prayer, and a variety of internal rites and rituals.

Both kinds of practices assist in separating our consciousness from our mind and its various processes. These include a) memory or recollection of past events, b) cognition, or awareness of what we perceive, c) discrimination, or our reasoning faculty, and d) ego or our sense of who we are based on our thoughts, words, and deeds. By taking our attention off the mind, it ceases to function. In effect, *the mind is not conscious, but a vehicle through which our awareness works.*

Meditation has been shown to decrease heart rate, decrease the rate of breathing, increase alpha waves in the brain, lessen pain, enhance creativity, improve memory, and bring the body into balance in many other ways.[5] Meditation techniques de-habituate the mind from conditioned and reactive patterns by realigning it along new and more healthy pathways of awareness.

Ethical Conduct and the Nature of the Mind

The third component of the meditation practice is traditionally known as moral or ethical conduct. In Judaism, this would include the Ten Commandments of Moses, in Christianity the ten Beatitudes of Jesus Christ, in Buddhism the Eightfold Path, in Hinduism the yamas and niyamas, in Islam, *Sharia* or *Adab* (good manners). What all these various ethical codes imply is that we cannot achieve higher states of consciousness unless we first become better human beings. As my Master, Sant Kirpal Singh, once said, "an ethical life is a stepping stone to spirituality."

Continual negative thinking, or what Joan Borysenko calls the "dirty tricks department of the mind" can become embedded or leave effects on the body causing disease and sickness. These include negative personal beliefs, social beliefs ("shoulds"), insistence on being right, rationalizing, disillusionment and despair.[6] The purpose behind living an ethical life is, in a sense, to heal the heart of its wounds and destructive habits. If the heart is not made whole it cannot withstand the luminosity of its own inner nature. In order for gold to be useable, it must be purified of all foreign elements. Until the heart is completely purified it cannot ascend spiritually. Rumi said, "We have to forsake one thousand half loves in order to bring one whole heart home." The soul is a conscious entity and therefore attachment to anything other than consciousness only brings suffering and disease in the end. Tarthang Tulku, a Buddhist teacher, tells us that when "positive or joyous feelings and attitudes pass through each

> -§-
>
> Meditation techniques de-habituate the mind from conditioned and reactive patterns by realigning it along new and more healthy pathways of awareness.
>
> -§-

organ and circulate throughout our whole system our physical and chemical energies are transformed and balanced." A recent study done by Wenneberg, Schneider, Walton and MacLean showed that the expression of anger was correlated to increased platelet aggregation (blood coagulation). Platelet aggregation promotes blood clotting, a major cause of coronary heart disease. Hostility contributes to heart failure.[7]

Akbar was a wise Mogul King in India. Chief among his advisers was a minister named Birbal. One day Birbal was instructing Akbar on the power of thought. He told the Emperor that thought was more powerful than even words or deeds. Akbar remained skeptical and wanted some visible proof. Birbal instructed the King to stand on a nearby hill, watch for the first person to walk over the hilltop and, "As this man approaches I want you to think of hurting him in the most violent way. Then we will ask him what he has been thinking." As the man approached Akbar began to think evil thoughts of the man. When he arrived Akbar greeted him and said, "Listen, you will be forgiven for whatever you say, but please answer my question completely honestly. When you saw my face what were you thinking?"

-§-
"Victory over the mind is victory over the world."
—Guru Nanak
-§-

"Forgive me great King, but when I saw your face I wanted to beat you up."

Birbal turned to Akbar and said, "Never underestimate the power of thought."

Each of us thinks hundreds of thoughts daily—many of them negative. These thought forms affect everyone, whether we are aware of it or not. It is for this reason that all the great wisdom traditions agree that if we seek true healing and true health we must exercise conscious control over our minds. From the perspective of this healing model, it is only when we can see ourselves honestly, accurately, and openly, that we can respond compassionately and appropriately. Fritz Perls, the founder of Gestalt therapy, once remarked, "Awareness per se—by and of itself—can be curative."[8] When we understand this, we become ever mindful of our thought content. The great Indian spiritual teacher Guru Nanak summed up the essence of this reality when he said, "Victory over the mind is victory over the world."

Concentration, Subliminal Repetition, and the Use of Mantra

The fourth component of the meditation journey is the use of a *mantra* (repetition of sacred names) as a means to develop deeper states of concentration. In the Hindu and Buddhist tradition, it is known as *mantra,* in the Sufi tradition as *Dhikr* and in the Christian traditions as a *litany.* The role and purpose of a mantra is to assist the aspirant in stilling his or her mind through the constant repetition of various names of God or sound vibrations. By constantly repeating the words either mentally or aloud, the mind becomes engaged and is unable to create new thoughts. Since the mind, as we have seen, is always in a state of agitation mystics use its innate tendency toward continuous thinking to the aspirant's own advantage.

One day a Hindu saint named Tukuram was discoursing on the power of a mantra. He said, "Mantra is the means to know ourselves, mantra can take us to God. Mantra is all powerful, mantra is the Highest Self." A skeptic confronted the swami: "Sir, with all due respect, what is the proof of what you say? After all, how can a few simple words take one to God? You say mantra can do this, mantra can do that, but this is all nonsense."

Tukuram replied, "You know you are nothing but a filthy scoundrel, a dirty rotten good-for-nothing thief. You are a heap of garbage, bringing disgrace and ignorance wherever you go." The skeptic exploded, "Who are you to call me these names? You don't even know me. You call yourself a saint—but what kind of a saint abuses, and condemns others?"

With perfect equanimity Tukuram replied, "My dear friend, if a few words of anger can cause such a violent reaction in you in a matter of minutes, imagine what the thought of God might do if you were to repeat it ceaselessly throughout the day."

Through the use of a mantra we can begin to consciously control our thoughts, and direct our thinking in more positive and uplifting ways. The real work of the practice is to remain *fully conscious* throughout the day. A recent study by John Kabat-Zinn and Dr. Richard Davidson discovered that meditators have healthier immune systems. The more conscious we become the healthier we are.

Contemplation

Contemplation has been defined as a stage in the meditation journey in which, as a result of continued concentration, there grows a continuous flow of perception, called dhyan. In the practice of *dhyan,* the attention is fixed on the *seat of consciousness, third eye* or *Anja* chakra, located between the two eyebrows and behind the eyes. When contemplation reaches its zenith, the aspirant develops one-pointed and unswerving concentration on the object of concentration to such an extent that she loses herself in the higher luminous reality. In essence, the seer becomes a Self-conscious entity.

At this stage, the mind comes under the conscious control of the aspirant and he experiences profound new states of bliss, halcyon calm and certainty of knowledge. Mental maladies like fear, doubt, agitation, depression, anger, and self-assertiveness disappear and gradually give rise to fearlessness, confidence, firmness, and evenness of temper.

An Eastern teaching story concerns a young farm boy whose efforts to meditate were unsuccessful. His mother sent him to a great master, who asked him what he loved most in the world. The boy replied, "The cow I milk each day." The master said, "Meditate on her, then," and sent him away to a cell, along with other acolytes. When the other boys emerged for dinner, this boy did not come out. The master knocked on his door, and again called for him to come out. The boy said, "I can't! My horns are stuck!"

-§-
The notion that my identity begins and ends with my physical body, and your identity begins and ends with your physical body, is a belief, which has no basis in higher states of awareness.
-§-

The more we become attuned to the greater consciousness, the more the apparent boundaries disappear. The notion that my identity begins and ends with my physical body, and your identity begins and ends with your physical body, is a belief, which has no basis in higher states of awareness. Gary Zukav says, "There is no here or there. We live in a non local universe"[9] The great Vedic masters expressed this view as the universal vision of the "All in the One and One in the All." Sant Darshan Singh once said, "The secret to successful meditation is one pointed concentration which is a byproduct of love."

Samadhi, Fana, or Union

Union with the divine is the last phase of the meditation journey. Most of what we know about these advanced states comes from various scriptures and oral traditions which describe the gradual development of *dhyan* until it culminates in *samadhi*. Sant Kirpal Singh said that samadhi occurs when "the contemplator or meditator loses all thought of himself and the mind becomes *dhya-rupa* the very form of his thought. In this state the aspirant is not conscious of any external object save of consciousness itself, a state of all bliss and/or perfect happiness."[10]

These advanced levels of expanded or cosmic consciousness lead to healing of body, mind, and spirit. They are also capable of transmitting profound healing energies to others at the physical, mental, and spiritual levels. The effects of this we might call *healing through radiation*. How do we explain them? The answer given by great adepts is that *consciousness itself is curative*. When an aspirant reaches the higher states of awareness she becomes a conduit for the divine storehouse of all health, energy and wisdom.

In the early 1950s the Chinese entered Tibet and destroyed thousands of monasteries and killed hundreds of thousands of monks and laypeople.

There was one Chinese warrior who was known for his skillful use of his sword. During the ravaging of one monastery, he had killed hundreds without mercy. As he approached, his victims fled down the hallways, but rarely escaped. Finally, he entered a large room where an elderly monk was seated in the half-lotus position, unmoved by the horrendous killings going on all around him. The arrogant Chinese warrior approached him and asked, "Don't you know who I am? I could sever your head in a single second with a flick of my wrist."

The old monk remained unmoved. He replied, "Don't you know who I am? I can sit here without fear, without loathing, and without blinking an eye, while you strike my head off." At that moment, the Chinese warrior recognized a divine power and unconditional love coming from this simple Tibetan monk. He realized he was in the presence of greatness. He bowed down and prostrated himself. He placed his head at the monk's feet and said, "Please show me heaven and hell." The monk replied, "Hell, my friend, was when you came in here filled with arrogance, pride and revenge. Heaven was when you realized the spark of divinity within another soul, and your own pride and ego—and from humility understood for the first time that you too are a spark of this great consciousness."

> -§-
> It is only by reconnecting to our essential nature as consciousness that true health of the body, mind, and spirit can be realized.
> -§-

The ultimate healing occurs when we are united with our source. Disease of the body or mind exists only in the context of spiritual fragmentation and isolation. It is only by reconnecting to our essential nature as consciousness that true health of the body, mind, and spirit can be realized.

Robert Dozor:

Integrative Clinic Meets Real World

As many as half the people in the US and other Western societies employ health or healing practices that are outside the scope of "regular medicine." I knew before I went to medical school that there was more—much more—to healing than I would be taught for my MD. Modern medicine is completely positivist, holding that scientific truth can only be gleaned by rigorous observation of nature, through mathematics and statistics. Integrative medicine respects this mode of knowing, but also ventures without apology into interpretation and meaning.

Conventional biomedicine brilliantly addresses acute and catastrophic illness, and strives for the finest in health care—yet fails to address the roots of illness and suffering. Biomedicine casts a deep shadow, and in this shadow, ancient healing wisdom has languished. It is time to remember the whole picture. The synthesis of these ways of knowing creates is an expanded vision of healing possibilities. Full health is never achieved by technological means alone. The fruit of wholeness is healing, a dimension of experience more health-promoting than medical technology. Integrative medicine is the search for wholeness and healing in the context of biomedicine. Researcher David Reilly puts it this way: "In recent decades orthodox medicine's successful focus on specific disease interventions has meant relative neglect of self healing and holism. [Yet] to ignore whole person factors is unscientific and less successful."

I practice medicine at the Integrative Medical Clinic of Santa Rosa (IMCSR). Much of what I do is what I was trained as a family doctor to do,

Robert Dozor, MD, was born in Philadelphia, and earned his baccalaureate with honors from the University of Chicago. He did his residency in Family Practice at the University of California at San Francisco (UCSF), where he was named Assistant Clinical Professor of Family and Community Medicine in 1986. He co-founded one of the earliest medical ethics committees in the United States in 1984, and was the original editor of the proceedings of the American Balint Society. Dr. Dozor and his wife—Ellen Barnett, MD, Ph.D.—have three children, and opened the Integrative Medical Clinic of Santa Rosa, California (www.imcsr.com) in 2001. Photo by RCI.

yet most of my patients also partake of "new medicine," things that they didn't teach me about in Medical school—Herbs, Chinese Medicine, Somatics, Nutrition, Meditation and much more. My practice setting includes: Chiropractic, Acupuncture, Naturopathy, Psychotherapy, Biofeedback, Massage, Feldenkrais, Hanna Somatics, and an herbal/nutritional formulary.

Personal experiences both in my own being and in moments of healing shared with patients inspired doubts about the foundational paradigm of biomedicine—the body as machine. One day, when I was a family practice resident, I was putting my infant son in the back seat of my car, and suffered an extremely painful back spasm. It turned out to be garden-variety lumbago, and it was "treated" the well-worn conventional way. Over the following few years the lumbago recurred, and I came to view myself as having a "bad back." I knew in my bones that there had to be a better way of treatment. So I began experimenting with unconventional remedies: acupuncture, chiropractic, massage, somatics and Qi Gung. Today my back is usually pain-free and I've reclaimed my athleticism. My once "bad back" has been healed. This is one of countless direct experiences of healing that pass below the radar of clinical trials—yet the patient certainly knows that healing has occurred.

-§-
"I think,
Therefore I am"
- Rene Descartes

-§-
"Don't believe every-
thing you think."
— A bumper sticker

--§-
"And in the end
The love you take
Is equal to the love
you make"
-John Lennon & Paul
McCartney

-§-

Traditionalists, Moderns and Post-Moderns

During my twenty years of family practice I have blindly groped the proverbial elephant of health and healing. Family Doctors are favored with a unique perspective to perceive the whole of it.

The majority of Westerners have evolved culturally from a "traditionalist"—basically Judeo-Christian—worldview, to the "modernist" worldview—that science and technology are steadily lifting the human condition from the shackles of superstition and ignorance. "Health" in this process morphs from being a gift of God (as a reward for avoiding sin) to an accomplishment of science and industry. In America, the spiritual value of industriousness allows one to earn the grace of health. God help the uninsured!

Healthcare is the biggest industry in the United States, dwarfing the scale of the health enterprise of any other country. The immensity of the health enterprise reflects the value that Moderns have for health, but the distribution of resources within this enterprise reflects darker and more conflicted values. For example, huge amounts of money are spent vainly and painfully trying to keep dying people alive during the very last days of their lives. There is very little money for preventative medicine, yet plenty to treat chronic illness. Lifestyle drugs are booming. There is darkness in the huge profitability of the pharmaceutical industry.

A smaller group of Americans are in the process of culturally evolving from Moderns to Post-Moderns, who see science and technology as both fundamental to our lives, but also as a threat to the environment and society that needs taming. "Health" in this paradigm is transformed from an accomplishment of science and industry into a holistic vision of the oneness of Spirit, Mind, Body, Society and Environment. No one can be truly well if others or the planet itself are suffering. Rather than pious industriousness, the driving spirit of healing is enlightenment and compassion. The post-modern health clinic may look like a spiritual retreat center.

-§-
Conventional bio-medicine brilliantly addresses acute and catastrophic illness—yet fails to address the roots of illness and suffering.
-§-

The sheer economic momentum of the massive health care industry, which three decades ago overtook the defense industry as the largest sector, seems out of control. Yet healthcare as it is now implemented is not sustainable. The demographic wave of aging chronically ill adults is already in sight, threatening to capsize the system when it hits. And despite spending three times as many dollars per capita as Europeans, Americans have a shorter life span, poorer health and less satisfaction with our health care system. We know we're in crisis, and we correctly perceive a threat to our way of life and health.

Ironically, despite this massive and doomed orgy of spending, integrative healing practices have almost no place in the official system. They are truly preventative, and as such they save money that would be spent if patients became sick. Yet to health insurance companies, integrative healing practices appear to be simply another expense. Why should an insurer pay out for care for someone who isn't sick, when they're already struggling to afford those who are? Moderns and Post-Moderns don't understand each other yet.

The Integrative Psychosomatic Network

The burgeoning basic science of Psycho-neuro-immunology (PNI) represents a scientific discipline that utilizes a holistic paradigm. One of the foremost of today's researchers, Candace Pert, says, "Since the 1980's, psychoneuroimmunology [has produced] findings that dismantle previously erected barriers between biological subsystems, bringing mental and emotional processes into the healing equation. Research on neuropeptides as informational substances continues to substantiate and elaborate the construct of an integrative psychosomatic network."

Neuropeptides, called neurotransmitters in the brain, are the substrate of consciousness. They interact with other kinds of cells—immune cells, gut cells, heart cells, maybe all cells. Their function is to coordinate. Neuropeptides can be viewed as "informational substances." Candace Pert says, "Information can be viewed as a unifying concept that spans many levels of organization in living systems, including emotional, energetic, biochemical, molecular and genetic levels." Neuropeptides get around the body in complex patterns—sometimes flowing in blood vessels, sometimes triggering other cells to secrete other neuropeptides or other biological effectors, such as cytokines or hormones. All this can be accurately called "information flow."

-§-
The post-modern health clinic may look like a spiritual retreat center.
-§-

The concept of an integrative psychosomatic network may prove as momentous to the next century as Darwin's monumental system of natural selection was to the last. It's the scientific foundation for the concept of "biological energy," which is central to all complementary and alternative healing systems. The "flow of informational molecules," is correlates with terms from alternative medicine such as bioenergy, qi, prana, healing force, kundalini and life-energy.

I find it a constant struggle to practice healing of the integrative psychosomatic network within the context of the illness-driven health care financing system. On the one hand, there are some insurance companies who cover integrative services such as mindfulness meditation, healing imagery, biofeedback, self-hypnosis, and progressive relaxation training, but almost always with caveats, limitations and daily struggles with the authorization process. Conventional physicians tolerate these complementary modalities, because Herbert Benson and others have demonstrated the wide-ranging health-promoting effects of "the relaxation response" for anxiety, migraine, irritable bowel syndrome, insomnia and chronic pain.

I have lectured about these modalities to physicians. Responses have ranged from mild interest to boredom. Responses to the more ambitious possibilities of mind-body medicine—such as treating heart disease, cancer and AIDS with meditation and visualization —are summarized by a comment I received on a feedback form: "He's gone off the deep end!"

Practicing Integrative Medicine in a Reductionist World

Integrative medicine has resisted the reduction of human life and health to the reactions of microbes and molecules. For example, the germ theory of disease—that infectious diseases are fundamentally caused by germs—is now appreciated as simplistic. According to common belief, the archetypal triumph of modern scientific medicine has been the conquest of infectious disease by antibiotics and vaccines. The myth is that germs cause disease, and antibiotics kill germs. The fact that infectious diseases—such as tuberculosis, influenza and measles—were already dwindling before any antibiotics or vaccines were available—is ignored. The disappearance of these virulent diseases was more a result of septic systems and clean water, electric lights and modern heating systems, leading to cleaner household air, and abundant refrigerated food. These technologies reduced exposure to pathogens and, through enhanced nutrition, immune competence.

Antibiotics and other chemicals are conceived as "magic bullets," targeting only the source of disease and leaving the rest of the body untouched, but such linear health models are simplistic and ultimately inadequate. Even conventional medicine is on a campaign to reign in the vast overuse of antibiotics. If our society had a social education plan to teach health, rather than selling pharmaceuticals, I believe our levels of wellness would take a dramatic upswing.

-§-
To health insurance companies, integrative healing practices appear to be simply another expense.
-§-

Abundant evidence demonstrates that emotions and mental states affect our immune cells. As Candace Pert puts it: "The cellular agents of healing—immune cells—produce the same chemical messengers we conceive as regulating mood and emotions. Because these cells also receive input from neuropeptides, there can be no doubt regarding bi-directional communication between brain and body." The mind and the body are one. Healers must pay as much attention to a person's psyche and social situation as to their chemistry.

Why is such an eminently reasonable statement viewed as radical by most of my profession? Physicians dismiss the placebo effect, the discovery that when patients believe they are being given treatment, many get well—as a whimsical curiosity, and a confounding variable. Yet it demonstrates the healing power of belief; disparaging references to placebos provoked Herbert Benson to propose abandonment of the term, in favor of "remembered wellness."

It is clear that modern scientific medicine has developed valuable cures, banishing smallpox and polio, treating diabetes, rescuing acute coronary cases, mitigating a few of the many types of cancer, and treating people suffering from physical injuries. Nonetheless, modern medicine has contributed relatively little to overall vitality and longevity. Americans, who have access to the most developed technology in the world, live neither longer nor healthier lives than Chinese, who don't. Cancer has been on the rise for a century; Alzheimer's dementia and other degenerative diseases are epidemic. Violence, a social plague, is pandemic. Scientific medicine will undoubtedly progress further, but the limits of its effectiveness and affordability appear evident, imminent, and inevitable.

There is good reason to expect that ancient medicine has valuable knowledge for us. Clearly, several thousand years of observation and practice have produced successful treatments. Tibetan medicine, for example, appears to have its own admirable successes. In his book Health through Balance, Yeshe Donden observes: "From my own experience I have found Tibetan medicine to be effective in certain cases of cancer... [and] to be extremely effective [for] hepatitis, certain types of mental disorders, ulcers, paralysis, gallstones, kidney stones, and arthritis." Western medicine does not have completely satisfying treatments for some of these conditions, and only marginally effective treatment or expensive and painful treatment for others. Rationally, we could be healthier by using both types of medicine with regard only to what works, but conceptual prejudices among the public and the medical profession often impair pragmatism.

-§-
The concept of an integrative psychosomatic network may prove as momentous to the next century as Darwin's monumental system of natural selection was to the last.
-§-

There is no paradigm for these two disparate medical systems to work together. Some people will seek Ayurvedic (either Tibetan or Indian), Chinese, or some other "alternative" medicine either for ideological or practical reasons, but there is a dense barrier of obscurity between the various practitioners, who rarely talk to each other, and seldom know or understand each other. For biological medicine to talk to Ayurveda requires a substantial effort of translation.

What is the role of "Complementary & Alternative Medicine" (CAM) in pragmatically bridging holistic approaches and mainstream medical literature? The work of Dean Ornish may be the most prominent example. He demonstrated that a program of a low-fat diet, meditation, support groups and exercise could reverse coronary artery disease—and quickly. Americans widely engage in many other alternative medical practices. Prayer is increasingly recognized as a valid healing exercise. Many studies demonstrate that meditation is healing. There is growth in the intellectual basis of integrative medicine, even though the facilities to practice it in the real world are still in their infancy.

Having a holistic worldview doesn't easily or automatically transform the practice of medicine. Virtually everything about conventional medicine works in the service of reductionism. Every day I refer patients to a CAM modality, such as acupuncture. To do this, I have to assign diagnosis codes and procedure codes that make sense to health insurance carriers—and that are virtually irrelevant to Chinese medicine. I have to write circuitous reports and schmooze claims adjusters as I seek to cram round pegs into square holes. I have to endure the often snide and occasionally offensive comments of medical specialists when I refer patients to acupuncture, and I completely hide the fact that a lot of my Chinese medicine colleague's treatments will be herbal. I usually dare not explain what I am really thinking, and demand authorization of treatment based on orthodox bases such as the National Institutes of Health's blessing of acupuncture.

This joke is wearing thin. Chinese medicine diagnoses are not congruent with the International Classification of Disease (ICD)-9 (or 10 for that matter!). Acupuncture procedure codes in the standard procedure book (CPT) are the American Medical Association's (AMA) idea of what Chinese medicine is. There is bold work being done developing an appropriate integrative medicine coding system, but the AMA writes the code books that insurance companies and government recognize!

The fact that there have been some clinical studies using Chinese medicine for conditions defined by the conventional diagnosis scheme is integrative, but cannot really bring us to healing and wholeness. Are all the world's medicines going to be reduced to new procedures in Western medicine? It's been fun to host a mediation class, and prescribe herbs and nutrition, but I still find myself stuck practicing reductionism. It's been enlightening to discover that PNI is congruent with Ayurveda, but if we don't do the hard work of thinking holistically, then reductionism will prevail—at the expense of our health.

-§-
Healers must pay as much attention to a person's psyche and social situation as to their chemistry.
-§-

Scientific Foundations of Integrative Medicine

The placebo effect as well as acupuncture has been connected with the endogenous opioid (neuropeptide) system. The psychosomatic network corresponds to the "psychic channels and chakras," or acupuncture's meridians and points. Suddenly we've come full circle, with the dawning awareness that ancient medical systems like Ayurveda and Chinese medicine may have been "real" sciences! Their discipline was elaborate observation, description and experimentation with patterns of informational molecules.

Perhaps the most effective complementary modality is exercise. Dr. Terrie Wetle, Deputy Director of the National Institute on Aging, testified to a Senate committee that, "Americans would pay almost any price for a pill that contained all the benefits associated with exercise: increased life expectancy, improved mental health, and decreased disability. Scientific research has shown repeatedly that exercise can benefit both the body and mind."

David Spiegel, a researcher at Stanford University, has shown that adding a support group to chemotherapy for Stage IV breast cancer patients not only helped these woman be "less anxious and depressed... and cope more effectively," but he also found that "they lived twice as long as those who were not in the groups—an average of 18 months longer." Breast cancer patients in support groups can re-write their personal script, and inform their bodies with greater resilience. Other studies demonstrate that social factors are more powerful in reducing deaths from infectious disease than the availability of antimicrobial chemicals.

Meditation is the pinnacle of psychosomatic interventions. It has shown wide-ranging benefits in such diverse conditions as: cardiovascular disease, chronic pain, gastrointestinal distress, high blood pressure, headaches, anxiety and panic, cancer, sleep disturbance, job and family stress, HIV/AIDS, type A behavior, fatigue and skin disorders. When introducing meditation to my patients, I begin with the relationship between mind and the detrimental effects of chronic stress, which impairs neuroendocrine and immune system functions. Meditation—all by itself—may offer more to the health of a modern American than all the pharmaceutical remedies put together.

-§-
Meditation—all by itself—may offer more to the health of a modern American than all the pharmaceutical remedies put together.
-§-

The NIH issued an assessment of acupuncture, endorsing it for: "adult post-operative and chemotherapy nausea and vomiting, and postoperative dental pain." Moreover, NIH stated that acupuncture offered substantial benefit for: "addiction, stroke rehabilitation, headache, menstrual cramps, tennis elbow, fibromyalgia, myofascial pain, osteoarthritis, low back pain, carpal tunnel syndrome, and asthma." The statement concluded that: "There is sufficient evidence of acupuncture's value to expand its use into conventional medicine and to encourage further studies of its physiology and clinical value." Chiropractic is now the consensus "best practice" for back and neck pain.

Supplements and herbs can be highly effective at promoting health and fighting disease. Diet, exercise and mediation can unblock coronary arteries. And according to an independent insurance company study, insurers saved an average of $17,000 per patient when compared to conventional approaches like angioplasties and heart bypass operations. Health is cost-effective.

The Integrative Medical Clinic of Santa Rosa

I personally reached a point in the mid-nineties, where I was both blessed and burdened with a vision of practicing medicine in the way that was as "right" as I could envision it. From this vision I became a Co-founder, along with Pam Koppel, of the Integrative Medical Clinic of Santa Rosa (IMCSR).

The seeds of this move were planted decades before, when I studied both Physics and Philosophy at the University of Chicago. I was fascinated by both science and philosophy. For six years after graduating, I split my time between studying Buddhism with a Tibetan Lama named Tarthang Rinpoche, and programming computers in a cardio-pulmonary research laboratory. Then I enrolled in medical school at the University of California at San Francisco.

I endured dismissive comments from my teachers, who felt that my intention to become a family doctor was quixotic. Nonetheless, I became one, and practiced conventionally for twelve years. Four things contributed to my breaking out of my family practice routine: botanical medicine, Naturopathy, meditation, and integrative medicine.

First, I intensively studied Western herbal medicine. Finding medicine in plants that I could find or grow and prepare myself was transformative. Most drugs prescribed have their origin in plants. And walking in the hills and finding valuable plants is one of life's supreme pleasures. Botanical medicine led me to study the broader field of Naturopathic medicine. I started teaching Meditation classes in my medical office, and introduced elements of other methods where I saw openings. A post-modern doctor can embrace technology, but look for true healing anywhere he or she can find it.

-§-

A post-modern doctor can embrace technology, but look for true healing anywhere he or she can find it.

-§-

Putting together a healing center in which all these ideas can be turned into practice has been rewarding—and immensely difficult. We opened the doors of the IMCSR in August of 2001. The business has been in the red from the beginning. It started off losing some $80,000 per month, and after two years the losses have been whittled down to about $20,000 per month. That level of financial investment is not for the faint-hearted or under-funded.

There is a core group of two family physicians, two chiropractors, one acupuncturist, three somatic therapists, one Naturopathic physician, one biofeedback practitioner, one Qi Gung practitioner, three massage therapists, two herbalists, one nutritionist and two psychotherapists. Two years before opening the clinic, we started envisioning a highly functioning, highly spirited team. Governing ourselves as a team, clinically democratic but fitting into a management structure, was difficult to implement. Compromises had to be made, and a number of practitioners resigned from the clinic in the early stages as we wrestled with difficult practical issues that challenged our ideals.

For example, I had envisioned relatively long visits with patients: one hour for a new patient and thirty minutes for a follow-up. We discovered that this ideal was not sustainable given our reimbursement rates by insurance companies. We now usually have twenty-minute follow-up sessions with the MDs.

We made a large investment in electronic medical record (EMR) technology. I expected EMR to so enhance efficiency that it would leave us more time to care for our patients, but other practitioners resented the technological intrusion of computers into the consulting room. Overall, however, the EMR has proven to be a great tool for integrating different types of treatment, since all practitioners make their notes in the same patient record. The acupuncturist can see a glance what the MD's diagnosis is; the Feldenkrais practitioner can determine when the patient last saw the chiropractor. But early on, the benefits were not so obvious, while the computer monitors were.

Our office has large and beautiful common spaces, accommodating lectures (maximum so far 120 people), movement classes, a waiting room, meditation space and library. The IMCSR also has a retail herbal formulary and kitchen. We compensate for the square footage used by common areas by employing interchangeable practice rooms, and a flexible system to allocate practitioners to rooms. This means that a chiropractor might be in three different rooms over the course of a week, still able to access all key information through the EMR computer system. This led to conflicts, as we discovered that practitioners can be territorial, wanting rooms for their own exclusive use.

-§-
A number of practitioners resigned from the clinic in the early stages as we wrestled with difficult practical issues that challenged our ideals.
-§-

Ultimately, the question is: What is the experience of our patients at IMCSR?

Patients tell us often that it is completely unlike the usual outpatient care setting. I have been able to help people here at IMCSR that I was never able to help before; I can get a consultation quickly from other practitioners.

One of our greatest clinical successes is with patients suffering from back pain. Back pain is the most expensive health care problem in the United States, when lost workdays are taken into account. The availability of physicians' diagnostics, prescriptions and trigger point shots, allied with chiropractic adjustments, acupuncture, somatics, massage, and physical therapy is extremely effective, and a quantum leap from conventional medical approaches.

We have a pain program at IMCSR called the Pain Rehabilitation and Education Program (PREP), which serves injured workers. It is perhaps our best effort yet in manifesting a team integrative approach. This program runs for twelve weeks, three days a week, three hours a day. It involves most of our practitioners. Roughly half of the program occurs in group sessions, and the other half is individual sessions. The program is individualized for each patient.

Larry Bailey, for instance, is a 56-year-old Vietnam veteran who came to us with chronic shoulder, neck and upper back pain from an old injury. He complained of severe pain. He was despondent; five years of conventional medical treatment had produced no improvement.

He was "totally skeptical" of alternative therapies to begin with, and expressed his opinions in direct and colorful language: "You can stick that aromatherapy where the sun don't shine." But at his last checkup, ten months after completing the PREP pain rehabilitation program, he reported his pain to be moderately better. He manages flares of pain with somatic awareness and Qi Gung, and he carries an aromatherapy kit around with him.

Another clinical success of Integrative Medicine is the treatment of hepatitis C. The hepatitis C virus is the largest cause of fibrosis, progressing to cirrhosis, liver failure, cancer and liver transplants. Conventional medical treatment is effective for some patients — but is very toxic and difficult for the body to tolerate. Chinese medicine, on the other hand, offers treatments that appear to prevent the process of fibrosis and to enhance the tolerability of the treatments — as well as mitigate the symptoms of hepatitis. At IMCSR we use sound and rigorous criteria for selecting patients to be treated with Interferon and Ribovarin (definitely a minority) and offer everyone Chinese medicine. The integrative physician must be bilingual, thinking of molecules and qi in the same sentence.

-§-
The integrative physician must be bilingual, thinking of molecules and qi in the same sentence.
-§-

We've also enjoyed success with a vexing cluster of overlapping syndromes: Chronic Fatigue Immunodeficiency Syndrome (CFIDS), Fibromylagia, and Multiple Chemical Sensitivities. There are more patients with CFIDS in the US than have AIDS, and it is more disabling! There are no effective treatments for CFIDS in conventional medicine, although some symptoms can be mitigated a little. Through the combined application of Naturopathy, Somatics, Pharmaceuticals, Nutrition and Massage, we have taken patients who would be condemned to years of suffering under conventional medicine and often given them their lives back.

A few months ago, a forty-three-year-old woman called Marion Westbury came to see me. Fifteen months previously, she'd started having flu-like symptoms which turned out to be fibromyalgia. She suffered from severe pain that affected her entire body. She experienced incapacitating fatigue. Needless to say, she had become depressed. She had been treated by her Family Doctor and a Rheumatologist. They had prescribed physical therapy, thyroid medication, Prozac and narcotic analgesics (time release morphine). Mary said that this treatment regimen "helped some."

We gave her an intensive evaluation at our clinic. We had her make nutritional changes. We gave her a course of acupuncture, massage, neuromuscular reeducation and energy medicine. Seven months later she noted, "I am so much better, I can't believe it. My energy level has increased. The pain in my lower body has diminished. I sleep better. I've had no headaches lately. My bowel movements have become regular again. I love the energy work with my practitioner, and I couldn't live without neuromuscular massage. I've begun taking walks again. Just wanting to get out and do something is huge! I feel more normal than I have in two years."

-§-
The survival of our clinic is as dependent on our business savvy as our clinical acumen and caring hearts.
-§-

It is a constant struggle to remain true to my original intention of practicing medicine congruently with the vision of interconnected wholeness. Much of what I am required to do is running a business, and a very hard business at that. Difficulties collecting money from patients and insurance companies has accounted for most of our revenue shortfalls. We've had to get good at this skill, which has nothing to do with medicine. The survival of our clinic is as dependent on our business savvy as our clinical acumen and caring hearts.

Are we in the midst of a fundamental shift in modern healing practices—or is integrative medicine a side branch that may soon either wither or be pruned? A huge body of important clinical information, previously branded as superstition, has suddenly become available to medicine. Mind-body approaches—previously dismissed by the medical establishment as "soft science" if not "pseudo-science"—now offer a way to restore people to high levels of wellness, at a fraction of a cost of conventional health care. As the established health care system implodes—a victim of patient demands, expensive exotic technology, and an aging population—establishments like the Integrative Medical Clinic, marrying modern scientific health care with complementary and alternative methods, may offer a path that synergistically unleashes the full healing power of all available approaches.

The Heart of the Healer
Communing With the Spirit of Your Unborn Child   Dawson Church
FACING DEATH, FINDING LOVE   Dawson Church
IF YOU WANT TO BE Rich & Happy   DON'T GO TO SCHOOL
SOUL RETURN
Intuition Workout   NANCY ROSANOFF
PRACTICING RADICAL HONESTY
Your Body Believes Every Word You Say 2nd Ed.   LEVINE
LOVE IS A SECRET: The Mystic Quest for Divine Love   Andrew Vidich
HONEST TO GOD
Lovers for Life
by Cynder Hypnosis
Candida Control Cookbook   Gail Burton

Dawson Church:

The Future of Medicine

Medicine in America is in crisis. Many informed people will tell you so: doctors, hospitals, insurers, politicians, alternative medicine practitioners, and the makers of public policy. But they are almost all wrong. They are wrong about the nature of the crisis, wrong about the causes of the crisis, and wrong about the solutions to the crisis. The debate about "health care" is everywhere; in magazines, in presidential debates, on web forums and the electronic media. It fills thousands of minutes, lines and bytes, yet all this chatter manages to miss the most important problems and solutions.

Take the much-quoted figure that 43 million Americans (some twelve percent of the population) do not have health insurance.[1] Getting these uninsured people into the system has dominated public debate for two decades. It was to be the social centerpiece of President Clinton's first term, until it hit the opposition of entrenched interests and floundered. It was the primary concern of virtually all the Democratic presidential candidates for the 2004 election.[2] Yet it's entirely the wrong direction for public policy to go: the system into which politicians want to bring the uninsured manages the remarkable simultaneous feats of incompetence at keeping people well, and spending obscene amounts of money to accomplish this.

The costs are truly staggering. The US spends about three times as much as Great Britain per person on health care, and twice as much as Canada.[3] Both those countries have universal health care—every single person is covered. The US spends almost twice as much as Germany and France, and more than twice as much as Japan.[4] These are all comparable

Dawson Church has edited or authored over 200 books. He is a co-founder of Aslan Publishing, a former CEO of Atrium Publisher's Group, and former publisher of Celebrity Press. During a long publishing career he has worked with many best-selling authors, as well as developing the careers of unknowns. He is passionately committed to social causes, especially ending homelessness, and his work is driven by ideas and practices that make a difference. He is working on several new books on the latest discoveries in healing. He teaches publishing classes, and assists authors who are self-publishing through www.AuthorsPublishing.com.

post-industrial societies and economies; some, like France, have inefficient, fossilized or costly systems. If American costs were twenty percent higher than the average among rich industrialized countries we would have cause for concern. Costs that are more than double the average are a national disgrace. And that's for a system that does not cover everyone.

Solutions like capping payments to doctors in the Medicare program which provides care to the elderly, or moving patients into Health Maintenance Organizations, have at best slowed the growth of spending. They have not brought costs down. Medicare is currently predicted to go broke by the year 2019.[5] The unfunded liabilities of the system for the next seventy-five years have been calculated at a staggering $27.7 trillion.[6] Faced with this crisis, national leaders have recently not been content with merely ducking the issue. They've made it worse by piling on added benefits for seniors (who vote in large numbers), that today's children (who can't vote at all) will have to pay for — with interest.

-§-
If this bizarre amount of spending were producing a marvelously healthy population, there might be some defense for it. It doesn't.
-§-

If this bizarre amount of spending were producing a marvelously healthy population, there might be some defense for it. It doesn't. Infant mortality rates are higher, and life expectancy lower, than every single one of the countries mentioned above.[7] According to a recent, large-scale study of twelve different metropolitan areas from Newark, New Jersey, to Miami, Florida, Americans get substandard medical care more than half the time, leading to "thousands of needless deaths each year."[8]

Asking questions like, "How can we slow the growing cost of our medical system," and, "How can we bring the uninsured into the system," have brought us to grief. They are the wrong questions. As long as we keep on asking them, we will get the wrong answers. If we stick with our current disease-centered and money-centered paradigm, our health will keep declining, and we will pay even more. Good ideas are what is needed; when our thinking changes, our institutions change with it. Changing the institutions without changing the flawed thinking behind them results only in hastening their collapse, as was evident in the Medicare prescription drug benefit recently passed by Congress; it brought forward the date of Medicare's insolvency by eight years.[9]

What then are the right questions?

Let's start with, "How can we make the largest number of people as healthy as possible?" This question abandons our old way of thinking, about how to tinker incrementally with our broken system, and invites a fresh awareness. Our assumption shifts away from treating disease, and toward creating health. As we create health, there is less disease to treat.

What can we teach every high school student, and every retiree, that would maintain their bodies in the best possible condition for the longest possible time? There are four simple and obvious ones. They cost almost nothing. They require very little time and attention; much less attention certainly than being sick does. And if implemented, they would radically alter the health picture of our entire nation within thirty days.

Here's the base line that every American could be supported in achieving:

• A period of aerobic exercise, flexibility and strength training averaging just twenty minutes a day.

• A diet based on lean protein and complex carbohydrates.

• Supplements: At minimum, a capsule each day of multivitamins, antioxidants and fish oils.

• Proficiency in a stress-reduction technique such as meditation, prayer, or contemplation.

The health benefits of meditation alone are well-documented and numerous. Dr. Robert Dozor, co-founder of the Integrative Health Clinic of Santa Rosa, California, says in the previous chapter in this book, "Meditation—all by itself—may offer more to the health of a modern American than all the pharmaceutical remedies put together."[10] Meditation has been shown to lower blood pressure, improve resting heart rate, reduce the incidence of strokes, heart disease and cancer, diminish chronic pain, ameliorate anxiety and depression, and have a beneficial effect on many other diseases.[11] If meditation were a drug, it would be considered medical malpractice for a physician to fail to prescribe it. The results of studies of prayer are equally impressive. A study currently underway at Duke University Medical Center shows that cardiac patients who are prayed for have far fewer complications than those who are not. The preliminary results of this study are so promising that it has been expanded to nine other hospitals.[12]

-§-
Good ideas are what is needed; when our thinking changes, our institutions change with it.
-§-

The answers to our dilemmas are staring us in the face. Millions of ordinary Americans are bucking the national trend towards obesity and illness by using one or all of these simple remedies. They are daily countering the dysfunctionality of the disease- and money-centered paradigm. If a majority of Americans followed the simple four-part prescription above, which takes less than half an hour per day and costs less than $1 per day, much of the superstructure of our current system would become obsolete. The numbers of people requiring treatment would drop precipitously. As far fewer people utilized the system, costs would fall, creating a pool of funds to treat all those, including the uninsured, who require the ministrations of allopathic and alternative medicine.

Not only are such interventions cheap and effective. They are fast. Recent studies show that fish oil supplementation leads to marked improvements in mental acuity in thirty days or less. Fish oils have been shown to prevent cancer,[13] heart attacks, improve cardiovascular health,[14] and reduce the incidence of diabetes, autoimmune diseases, and inflammatory diseases.[15] The supplements in antioxidant and multivitamin tablets are absorbed by the body in minutes or hours. Some of the benefits of exercise and meditation occur immediately, others show up cumulatively in the form of stronger, more durable bodies, and a reservoir of inner peace from which people who pray and meditate can nourish themselves in times of stress. The sense of physical and spiritual well-being that people get from these simple lifestyle choices can improve their lives dramatically in a month. When we start to ask the simple question about how we support ourselves in optimal wellness, we are led by compelling data to the four simple lifestyle choices above. Science now points us inexorably toward the value of diet, exercise, meditation, and wellness-based therapies.

-§-
The landscape of consciousness will be radically different by the second and third decades of the twenty-first century.
-§-

Shifting the health habits of an entire civilization seems like a tall order. The system towers like a giant immobile bronze statue over the country, impervious to any change except one which strengthens it. The frozen system affects every individual. People wishing to attend a yoga class, join a gym, get a massage, visit an alternative healer, or otherwise nurture their wellness, must pay for it themselves. Dr. Dozor observes, "To health insurance companies, integrative healing practices appear to be simply another expense."[16] Dr. Dean Ornish ponders, in another chapter, "How did we get to a point in medicine where interventions such as radioactive stents, coronary angioplasty and bypass surgery are considered conventional, whereas eating vegetables, walking, meditating, and participating in support groups are considered radical?"[17]

Yet I predict that our definition of what is—and is not—conventional in medicine will shift, and shift quickly. Scholar Jean Houston, in her book *Jump Time*, points out that social evolution does not happen in a gradual upward curve.[18] It is marked by long plateaus, followed by rapid jumps. She identifies the Renaissance as one such jump. Within twenty-five years, all the assumptions of society had changed—assumptions about politics and governance, about money and economics, about gender roles, about religion and science, and about health, medicine and wellness. She believes that we are in the middle of another such jump, and that the landscape of consciousness will be radically different by the second and third decades of the twenty-first century. A just-published study from the federal Centers for Disease Control has found that over a third of Americans now use complementary and alternative medicine; that figure jumps to almost two thirds when prayer is included in the list. The dollar amount spent on alternative therapies now exceeds Americans' out-of-pocket payments for conventional medical care, according to Dean Ornish.[19]

The benefits of getting and staying healthy are so obvious that they are attracting social consciousness like a magnet. As I have surveyed the field of wellness for this book, and other anthologies, I have been struck by two things. One is that our crisis is not one of money, access, or technology. It is a crisis of consciousness. As we reformulate our national debate in order to ask the right questions, as we change our collective minds, better answers will emerge as night follows day. All our efforts to change "the system" won't have nearly the effect that a change of heart and mind will have on all our systems, both global social systems and personal physiological systems.

-§-

Science will be welcomed as the ally of holistic approaches, rather than merely a tool of drug companies and medical technology manufacturers.

-§-

As we as individuals begin to set aside time in our busy days for meditation, prayer and contemplation, we become aware of the immanent side of existence. We become attuned to the flow of energy through our bodies, and we become more sensitive to the subtle forces that shape our lives. As well as tackling our challenges by outer action, we awaken of the power of pure awareness. As inner peace and serenity become an integral part of our daily practice of life, we become aware of the infinite possibilities of the energy fields in which we have our being. We see how changes in energy can result in changes in outer form, and how changes in our awareness can affect our world. From a calm mind and a serene heart, we see new potentials for our lives, and make choices that unlock those potentials.

Health care will look very different after the present jump. Clinics will be places of spiritual and emotional soothing, rather than service stations for mechanical defects in bodies. Science will be welcomed as the ally of holistic approaches, rather than merely a tool of drug companies and medical technology manufacturers. Doctors and patients may routinely pray together, and pray for each other. Many different healing modalities may be combined, with the line between what we now call "conventional" care and "alternative" care blurring into the question: "What combination of approaches will help us to be most well?"

I observe a collective social consciousness in the process of rapid, radical and irreversible change, a change only thrown into sharp relief by counter-indications like the alarming increase in obesity. Public society and governance are still mired in the wrong questions, about bringing the uninsured into the system, and about limiting cost increases. But enough individuals are finding personal answers that, in aggregate, may topple the seemingly-immovable statue of conventional medical care within the next few years. Margaret Mead famously observed: "Never doubt that a small group of thoughtful, committed people can change the world. Indeed, it is the only thing that ever has." Every day that you exercise, eat a healthy diet, pray, and maintain a calm state of mind, you give that old fossilized edifice a little nudge. One day soon, the aggregate of those nudges may bring it crashing down into the sea of common sense, out of which a new health care consciousness is right now being born.

CH 5   Bailey, A., *Esoteric Healing.* 1999. (New York: Lucis Press).

Brennan, B., *Hands of Light. A Guide to Healing Through the Human Energy Field.* 1987. (New York: Bantam Books), p 41-54, 93-97, 201-235, 243-250.

Brennan, B., *Light Emerging. The Journey of Personal Healing Through the Human Energy Field:* 1993. (New York: Bantam Books), p. 3-12, 31-42.

Hunt, V., *Infinite Mind. Science of the Human Vibrations of Consciousness.* 1989,1996. (Malibu, California: Malibu Publishing), p. 9-26.

Lyons, A. S., In: A. Lyons and R. J. Petrucelli II (Eds.), *Medicine: An Illustrated History.* 1987 edition. (New York: Times Mirror Books), p. 31-33.

Merkle, V., Class Teachings on Healing, Techniques, Ancient Wisdom, Higher Self Essence. The Victoria Merkle Center of Energy Medicine. www.victoriamerkle.com.

Oschman, J. L., *Energy Medicine. The Scientific Basis.* 2000. (New York: Harcourt), p. 27-38.

Page, C. R., *Frontiers of Health. From Healing to Wholeness.* 1986. (Saffron Walden, England: C. W. Daniel), p 11.

CH 6   The male pronoun is used throughout the discussion of the trickster because the trickster is "usually male but occasionally female or disguised in female form" according to the *Columbia Encyclopedia,* 5th ed.

Reports on the evidence of trickster tracks—areas of confusion and chaos—in contemporary medicine appeared in the following sources: T. E. Strandberg, "Long-Term Mortality after 5-Year Multifactorial Primary Prevention of Cardiovascular Diseases in Middle-Aged Men," *Journal of the American Medical Association* 266, no. 9 (1991): 1225-29; Leonard A. Sagan, "Family Ties: The Real Reason People Are Living Longer," *Sciences* (March/April 1988), 21-29; "Exercise, Health Links Need Hard Proof, Say Researchers Studying Mechanisms," *Journal of the American Medical Association* 265, no. 22 (1991); 298; M. Young and T. J. Marrie, "Interobserver Variability in the Interpretation of Chest Roentgenograms of Patients with Possible Pneumonia," *Archives of Internal Medicine* 154 (1994); 2729-32; R. Monastersky, "Kidney Stones: Don't Curb the Calcium," *Science News* 143 (March 17, 1993): 196; H. C Mitchell, "the Periodice Health Examination: Genesis of a Myth," *Annals of Internal Medicine* 95 (1981) : 733-35; B. Bower, "Anxiety before Surgery May Prove Healthful," *Science News* 141 (June 20, 1992): 407; B. Bower, "Depressing News for Low-Cholesterol Men," *Science News* 142 (January 16, 1993): 37; R. S. Eliot, "Community and Heart Disease," *Journal of the American Medical Association* 272, no. 7 (1994): 566; B. Bower, "Blood Pressure Lower for Working Women," *Science News* 148 (July 1, 1995): 6; R. Voelker, "Born in the USA: Infant Health Paradox," *Journal of the American Medical Association* 272, no. 23 (1994): 1803-4; R. Jerome, "Whither Doctors? Whence New Drugs" *Sciences* (May/June 1994): 20-25; B. Starfield, "Is U.S. Health Really the Best in the World?" *Journal of the American Medical Association* 284, no. 4 (2000): 483-85.

For reports on the effect of prayer on humans and nonhumans, including bacteria, fungi, and mice, see R. C. Byrd, "Positive Therapeutic Effects of Intercessory Prayer in a Coronary Care Unity Population," *Southern Medical Journal* 81 (1998): 826-29; C. B. Nash, Psychokinetic Control of Bacterial Growth," *Journal of the American Society for Psychical Research* 51 (1982): 217-21; J. Barry, "General and Comparative Study of the Psychokinetic Effect on a Fungus Culture," *Journal of Parapsychology* 32 (1968): 237-43; William H. Tedder and Melissa L. Monty, "Exploration of Long Distance PK: A Conceptual Replication of the Influence on a Biological System," in *Research in Parapsychology* 190, ed. W. G. Roll et al., 90-93; Bernard R. Grad, "Some Biological Effects of Laying-on of Hands: A Review of Experiments with Animals and Plants," *Journal of the American Society for Psychical Research* 59 (1965): 95-127; Bernard R. Grad, R. J. Cadoret, and G. I. Paul, "The Influence of an Unorthodox Method of Treatment on Wound Healing in Mice," *International Journal of Parapsychology* 3 (1961): 4-24.

Jonas Salk's sojourn in Italy is recounted in "Dr. Jonas Salk, 1914-1995: A Tribute" AAF (American Architectural Foundation) News, *AIARCHITECT* (September 1995): 20.

Frank Barron's insights on the unharnessable aspect of the creative process appeared in Frank Barron, "The Psychology of Imagination," *Scientific American* (September 1958).

Myrin Borysenko's experience with the healer in Boston is recounted in Larry Dossey, *Meaning and Medicine,* 159-60.

Richard Smoley's description of the trickster appeared in Richard Smoley, "My Mind Plays Tricks on Me," *Gnosis* 19 (Spring 1991): 12.

The Winnebago trickster story was reported in S. M. Wilson, "Trickster Treats," *Natural History* (October 1991): 4-8.

Barre Toelken describes his fieldwork experience in "From Entertainment to Realisation in Navajo Fieldwork," in Bruce Jackson and Edward D. Ives, eds., *The World Observed: Reflections on the Fieldwork Process* (Urbana: University of Illinois Press, 1996).

The Ken Wilber quotation on being aware of our opposites is from Ken Wilber, *The Spectrum of Consciousness* (Wheaton: Theosophical Publishing House, 1977), 216.

CH 10 l.   Diana Russell, *The Secret Trauma: Incest in the Lives of Girls and Women* (New York: Basic Books, 1986), Introduction to the 1999 Edition: xvii.

2   U.S. Advisory Board on Child Abuse and Neglect (ABCAN), *Child Abuse and Neglect: Critical First Steps in Response to a National Emergency* (Washington, D.C.: DHHS, 1990), quoted in Judith Lewis Herman, *Father – Daughter Incest* (Cambridge Mass.: Harvard University Press, 1981, 2000), p. 222.

3   "UN Details Widespread Violence against Women," *Boston Globe,* Wednesday, July 23, 1997, p. A4, quoted in Judith Herman, *Father – Daughter Incest,* p. 220.

4   Diana E. H. Russell, *The Secret Trauma,* p. 9-11.

5   A. Jacobson and B. Richardson, "Assault Experiences of 100 Psychiatric Impatients: Evidence of the Need for Routine Inquiry," *American Journal of Psychiatry* (1987), 144:1426-1430; A. Jacobson, "Physical and Sexual Assault Histories among Psychiatric Outpatients," *American Journal of Psychiatry* (1989), 146:755-758; J. Briere and L. Y. Zaidi, "Sexual Abuse Histories and Sequelae in Female Psychiatric Emergency Room Patients," *American Journal of Psychiatry* (1989), 146:1602-1606, quoted in Judith Herman, *Father – Daughter Incest,* p. 224.

6   Vincent J. Felitti, "Long-Term Medical Consequences of Incest, Rape, and Molestation," *Southern Medical Journal* (1991), 84:328-331.

7   Russell, *The Secret Trauma,* p. 172-173.

8   Herman, *Father – Daughter Incest,* p.224.

9   D. Finkelhor, "Sexual Abuse in a National Survey of Adult Men and Women: Prevalence, Characteristics, and Risk Factors," *Child Abuse and Neglect,* 1990, 14:19-28.

CH 11 1   *Kahuna La'au Lapa'au: The Practice of Hawaiian Herbal Medicine* by June Gutmanis, (Aiea, Hawaii: Island Heritage, 1976), p.42.

2   E.S. Craighill Handy and Mary Kawena Pukui, *The Polynesian Family System in Ka-'u, Hawai'i,* (Rutland, Vermont: Charles E Tuttle, 1996), p94.

3   Ibid., p 94.

4   *Kahuna La'au Lapa'au: The Practice of Hawaiian Herbal Medicine* by June Gutmanis, (Aiea, Hawaii: Island Heritage, 1976), p.42.

5   Powell, Wayne Kealohi, *The Way of Aloha,* http://www.hawaiiheart.com/wayne.html

6   Michael Sky, *Sexual Peace,* (Santa Fe: Bear & Company, 1993), p.112.

CH 12 1   The research upon which this chapter is based was conducted for my book *The Beethoven Factor: The New Positive Psychology of Hardiness, Happiness, Healing, and Hope.* (Charlottesville, Virginia: Hampton Roads Publishing Company, 2003).

2   Languishing is now more prevalent than major clinical depression. Eight of ten adults between ages 25 and 74 are languishing. See Keyes, C. L. M. "Complete Mental Health: An Agenda for the 21st Century." In C.L. M. Keyes and J. Haidt (Editors). *Flourishing: Positive Psychology and the Life Well-Lived.* Washington, D. C.: American Psychological Association, 2003.

3   Ibid, p. 294.

4   Kabat-Zinn, Jon. *Full Catastrophe Living: Using the Wisdom of Your Body and Mind to Face Stress, Pain, and Illness.* (New York: Delta, 1990).

5   Ryff, C. D. and Singer, B. "Ironies of the Human Condition: Well-Being and Health on the Way to Mortality." In L. G. Aspinwall and Ur. Staudinger. (Editors) *A Psychology of Human Strengths: Fundamental Questions and Future Directions for a Positive Psychology.* (Washington, D. C. American Psychological Association, 2003), pp. 271 – 287.

6   Russell, B. *The Conquest of Happiness.* (New York: Liveright, 1958).

7   For example, Carol D. Ryff and Burton Singer write, "We do not invoke the necessity that one must know pain to find the essence of what is good in life; rather, we see research on resilience as a valuable realm of balance." In their work *"Flourishing Under Fire: Resilience as a Prototype of Challenged Thriving."* In C. L. M. Keyes and J. Haidt. (Editors). *Flourishing: Positive Psychology and the Life Well-Lived.* (Washington, D. C.: American Psychological Association, 2003), pp. 15 - 36.

8   Some of these characteristics of thrivors are described in Tedeschi, R. G. and Calhoun, L. G. *Trauma and Transformation: Growing in the Aftermath of Suffering.* (Thousand Oaks, Californian: Sage, 1995).

9   Tedeschi, R. G., Park, C. L., and Calhoun, L. G. (Editors) *Posttraumatic Growth: Positive Changes in the Aftermath of Crisis.* (Mahwah, New Jersey: Erlbaum, 1998).

10   Settersten. R. A. Lives in Time and Place. *The Problems and Promises of Developmental Science.* (Amityville, New York: Baywood, 1999).

11   Wethington E. "Turning Points as Opportunities for Psychological Growth." In C.L. M. Keyes and J. Hadit (Editors) *Flourishing: Positive Psychology and the Life Well-Lived.* (Washington, D.C.: American Psychological Association, 2003), pp. 37 – 53.

12   M. Solomon. *Late Beethoven: Music, Thought, Imagination* (Berkeley, California, 2003), pp. 228 and 245.

13   Ibid, p. i.

14   Ibid. p. 3

15   Ibid. p. 6.

16   Ibid. p. 7.

17   Carver, C. S. and Scheier, M. F. Three Human Strengths. In L. G. Aspinwall and U. M. Staudinger. (Editors) *A Psychology of Human Strengths: Fundamental Questions and Future Directions for a Positive Psychology* (Washington, D. C.: American Psychological Association, 2003), p. 89.

18   Ibid. p. 95.

19   Csikszentmihalyi, M. *Flow: The Psychology of Optimal Experience.* New York: Harper & Row, Publishers, 1990.

20   Antonovsky, A. *Health, Stress, and Coping: New Perspectives on Mental and Physical Well-Being.* San Francisco: Jossey-Bass Publishers, 1979.

21   Tenner, H. and Affleck, G. "Benefit-Finding and Benefit-Reminding." In *Handbook of Positive Psychology.* C. R. Snyder and S. J. Lopex (Editors). New York: Oxford University Press, 2002. pp. 584 – 597.

22   Seligman, M. E. P. *Learned Optimism.* New York: Knopf, 1991.

CH 22 1   Grazyna Fosar and Franz Bludorf, *Vernetzte Intelligenz* (Bongart-Meier, Germany: Omega Publishing, March 2001).

2   J. Benveniste, B. Arnoux and L. Hadji, "Highly dilute antigen increases coronary flow of isolated heart from immunized guinea-pigs", *FASEB Journal*, 1992; 6: A1610. Also presented at "*Experimental Biology – 98 (FASEB),*" San Francisco, 20 April 1998.

3   Lynne McTaggart (cited below), telephone interview with Helmut Schmidt, May 14, 2001.

4   R. G. Jahn et al., "Correlations of random binary sequences with prestated operator intention: a review of a 12-year program." *Journal of Scientific Exploration*, 1997; 11:350.

5   R. D. Nelson, "Effect size per hour: a natural unit for interpreting anomalous experiments," *PEAR Technical Note 94003*, September 1994.

6   Masaru Emoto, *Messages From Water*, (Japan: Hado Kyoiku Sha, June 1999).

7   Lynne McTaggart, *The Field: The Quest for the Secret Force of the Universe*, (New York: Harper Collins, 2002).

CH 24 1   Bovard, E. W. (1985). *Perspectives on behavioral medicine.* Volume 2. New York: Academic Press.

2   Kiecoll-Glaser. J. K., Stephens. R. E., Hepetz, P. D., et al. (1985) Distress and DNA repair in human lymphocytes. *Journal of Behavioral Medicine.* 8(4), 311-320.

3   Glaser, R., Lafuse, W. P., Bonneau, R. H. (1993) Stress-associated modulation of proto-oncogene's expression in human peripheral blood leukocytes. *Behavioral Neuroscience.* (107) 3, 525-529.

4   Henry, J. P. (1982) The relation of social to biological processes in disease. *Social Science and Medicine* 16. 369-380.

5   Melnechuk, T. (1989). Biological healing , its psychological modulation, and possible molecular mechanisms. Report presented to the Institute of Noetic Sciences and the Joan B. Kroc Foundation for Psychoneuroimmunology. Draft.

6   We created a special issue of the *Alternative Therapies* journal around this topic (November, 1997).

7   Braud, W. (1991) conscious interactions with remote biological systems. *Subtle Energies*, 2(1). 1-40.

8   For reviews see Benur. D. J. (1992) *Healing Research.* Deddington. England: Helix Editions. Hd. For a popular review, see Dossey, L. (1993). *Healing Words: The Power of Prayer and the Practice of Medicine.* San Francisco: HarperSanFrancisco.

9   Lynch, J. J. (1977) *The Broken Heart.* New York: Basic Books.

10   For a Review of these studies, see Green, J. & Shellenberger, R. (1996) The healing energy of love, *Alternative Therapies in Health and Medicine*, (2) 3, 46-57.

11   Berkman, L., & Breslow, L. (1983) *Health and Ways of Living: The Alameda County Study.* New York: Oxford University Press.

12   House, J., Robbins, C., & Metzner, B. (1982) The association of social relationships and activities with mortality: Prospective evidence from the Tecumseh study. *American Journal of Epidemiology.* 116. 123-140.

13   Brolin, J. & Solf, S. (1979) *The Roseto Story.* Norman, Okla.: Univ. of Oklahoma Press.

14   House. J. S., Landis, K. R. & Umberson, D. (1988) *Science.* (241) 4865, 540-545.

15   Ibid.

16   Green & Shellenberger, op. cit. provide a review of these studies.

17   House, et al. Op. cit.

18   Fawzy, F. L., Kemeny, M. E., Fawzy. N. W., et al. (1990) Structured psychiatric intervention for cancer patients. H. Changes over time in immunological measures. *Archives of General Psychiatry,* 47, 729-735.

19   Spiegel, D., Dlooni. J. R., Kraemer, H. C., & Gottheil, E. (1989) Effect of psychosocial treatment on survival of patients with metastatic breast cancer. *Lancet.* 338, 881-891.

20   Friedman, M., Thorssen, C., Gill, J., et al. (1986) Alteration of type A behaviour and its effect on cardiac recurrences in post myocardial infarction patients: Summary results of the recurrent coronary prevention project. *American Heart Journal.* 112, 653-675.

21   Ornish, D., Brown, S. E., Scherwitz, L. W., et al. (1990) Can lifestyle changes reverse coronary heart disease? *Lancet,* 336. 129-133.

22   Medalic, J., & Goldbourt, U. (1976) Angina pectoris among 10,000 men: Psychosocial and other risk factors. *American Journal of Medicine,* 60, 910-921.

23   Widdowson, E. (1951). Mental contentment and physical growth, Lancet 1, 1316-131.

24   Caplan, G. (1981) Mastery of stress: Psychosocial aspect. *American Journal of Psychiatry,* 138, 413-420.

25   Frankl, V. ibid.

CH 26 1   Joeg, J. M. "Evaluating coronary heart disease risk: tiles in the mosaic." *Journal of the American Medical Association,* 1997, 277:1387-90.

2   Greenwood, D. C., K. R. Muir, C. J. Packham, et al. "Coronary heart disease: a review of the role of psychosocial stress and social support." *Journal of Public Health Medicine,* 1996, 18:221-31.

3   Russek, L. G., and G. E. Schwartz, "Feelings of parental caring predict health status in midlife: a 35-year follow-up of the Harvard Mastery of Stress Study." *Journal of Behavioral Medicine,* 1997, 20:1-13.

4   Seeman, T. E., and S. L. Syme. "Social networks and coronary artery disease: a comparison of the structure and function of social relations as predictors of disease." *Psychosomatic Medicine,* 1987, 49(4):341-54.

5   Horsten, M., R. Kirkeeide, B. Svane, K. Schenck-Gustafsson, M. Blom, S. Wamala, and K. Orth-Gomér. Social support and coronary artery disease in women. Personal communication.

6   Medalie, J. H., and U. Goldbourt. "Angina pectoris among 10,000 men. II. Psychosocial and other risk factors as evidenced by a multivariate analysis of a five year incidence study." *American Journal of Medicine,* 1976, 60(6):910-21.

7   Medalie, J. H., K. C. Stange, S. J. Zyzanski, and U. Goldbourt. "The importance of biopsychosocial factors in the development of duodenal ulcer in a cohort of middle-aged men." *American Journal of Epidemiology,* 1992, 136(10):1280-87.

8   House, J. S., C. Robbins, and H. L. Metzner. "The association of social relationships and activities with mortality: prospective evidence from the Tecumseh Community Health Study." *American Journal of Epidemiology,* 1982, 116(1):123-40.

9   Oxman, T. E., D. H. Freeman, Jr., and E. D. Manheimer. "Lack of social participation or religious strength and comfort as risk factors for death after cardiac surgery in the elderly." *Psychosomatic Medicine,* 1995, 57:5-15.

10   Berry, D. S., and J. W. Pennebaker. "Nonverbal and verbal emotional expression and health." *Psychother. Psychosom.,* 1993, 59:11-19.

11   Pennebaker, J. W., C. F. Hughes, R. C. O'Heeron. "The psychophysiology of confession." *Journal of Personality and Social Psychology,* 1987, 52:781-93.

12   Francis, M. E., and J. W. Pennebaker. "Putting stress into words." *American Journal of Health Promotion,* 1992, 6:280-87.

13   House, J. S., K. R. Landis, and D. Umberson. "Social relationships and health." *Science,* 1988, 241:540-45.

14   Exodus 3:13

15   Satchidananda, S. *The Yoga Sutras of Patanjali.* (Buckingham, VA: Integral Yoga Publications, 1990).

16   Luke 17:21

17   Mitchell, S., ed. *The Enlightened Mind.* (New York: HarperCollins Publishers, 1991).

18   Ibid.

19   Ibid.

20   Shantideva. *The Way of the Bodhisattva.* (Boston: Shambhala Publishers, 1997).

21   Field, T. "Massage therapy for infants and children." *Journal of Developmental & Behavioral Pediatrics,* 1995, 16(2): 105-11.

22   Jourard, S. M. "An exploratory study of body-accessibility." *British Journal of Social & Clinical Psychology,* 1966, 5(3):221-31.

23   Quinn, J. "Therapeutic touch and a healing way." *Alternative Therapies in Health and Medicine,* 1996, 2(4) :69-75.

CH 29 1   Michael Murphy and Steven Donovan, *Contemporary Meditation Research; A Summary of the Field with A Bibliography of 926 entries.* (San Francisco, California: The Esalen Transformation Project, 1985).

2   Murphy R. Lawrence, "Stress Management in Work Settings; A Critical Review of the Health Effects." *American Journal of Health Promotion,* vol. ii, no. 2. Nov./Dec. 1996, p. 132.

3   Later in this article we can further define these mental processes in more lay terms. For now, they represent the full mental functions or operations of our mind.

4   Levin, Jeff, *God, Faith, and Healing,* (New York: John Wiley, 2001) p. 4.

5   Dr. Herbert Benson, *The Relaxation Response,* (New York: Avon, 1975).

6   Joan Borysenko, *Minding the body, Mending the Mind,* (New York: Bantam, 1987), pg.11.

7   Wenneberg, Schneider, Walton MacLean *Behaviour Medicine,* 1997 Winter; 22(4): (174-7).

8   Roger Walsh and Francis Vaughn, *Paths Beyond Ego: The Transpersonal Vision,* (New York: Tarcher/Putnam, 1993), p.51.

9   Zukav, Gary, *The Dancing Wu Li Masters; An Overview of the New Physics;* (New York: Bantam), p. 302.

10   Kirpal Singh, *The Crown of Life,* (Bowling Green, Virginia: Sawan Kirpal Publications, 1980), p. 74.

CH 31 1   Freudenheim, Milton (January 20, 2004). Broader health coverage may depend on less. *New York Times.*

2   Toner, Robin (January 14, 2004). Democrats See A New Urgency In Health Care. *New York Times.*

3   Myatt, Arthur (2001). Comparison of Health Care Systems—Europe, and the US. Michigan Universal Health Care Access Network (http://michuhcan.tripod.com/every_other0.htm)

4   ibid.

5   *The Economist* (March 27th, 2004). Crunch-time coming: Concern, but no action, on rising health-care costs for the elderly. 34.

6   ibid.

7   ibid, Myatt.

8   Kerr, E. A., McGlynn, E. A., et al (2004). Profiling the quality of care in twelve communities: results from the CQI study. *Health Affairs,* 23 (3), 247-256.

9   ibid, *The Economist.*

10   Dozor, Robert. (2004). Integrative health clinic meets real world: *The Heart of Healing* (Santa Rosa: Elite Books). 310.

11   Murphy, Michael, and Donovan, Steven. (1985). Contemporary meditation research: a summary of the field with a bibliography of 926 entries. (San Francisco: The Esalen Transformation Project).

12   Krucoff, Mitchell, and Crater, Suzanne (2004). MANTRA (Monitoring and Actualization of Noetic TRAinings) Project results, *American Heart Journal,* Nov 1st, 2004.

13   Reddy, B.S., Burrill, C. and Rigotty J. (1991). Effect of diets high in omega-3 and omega-6 fatty acids on initiation and postinitiation stages of colon carcinogenesis. *Cancer Research.* 51: 487-491.

14   Simopoulos A. P. (1997). Omega-3 fatty acids in the prevention-management of cardiovascular disease. *Canadian Journal of Physiological Pharmacology,* 75(3); 234-239. Also, Hu, Frank B., et al. (2002) Fish and omega-3 fatty acid intake and risk of coronary heart disease in women. *Journal of the American Medical Association,* Vol. 287, pp. 1815- 21.

15   Lou J, et al. (1996). Dietary (n-3) polyunsaturated fatty acids improve adipocyte insulin action and glucose metabolism in insulin-resistant rats: relation to membrane fatty acids. Journal of Nutrition, 126(8):1951-1058. Also, Borkman M, et al. (1989) Effects of fish oil supplementation on glucose and lipid metabolism in NIDDM. *Diabetes.* 38(10):1314-1319.

16   ibid, Dozor, 307.

17   Ornish, Dean (2004). Love as healer: *The Heart of Healing* (Santa Rosa: Elite Books). 256.

18   Houston, Jean (2000). *Jump Time: Shaping Your Future in a Time of Radical Change.* (New York: Tarcher/Putnam).

19   ibid, Ornish, 256.